*The Best*
AMERICAN
ESSAYS
1991

GUEST EDITORS OF
*The Best American Essays*

1986 Elizabeth Hardwick
1987 Gay Talese
1988 Annie Dillard
1989 Geoffrey Wolff
1990 Justin Kaplan
1991 Joyce Carol Oates

# *The Best* AMERICAN ESSAYS 1991

Edited and with an Introduction
by JOYCE CAROL OATES

ROBERT ATWAN,
Series Editor

TICKNOR & FIELDS · NEW YORK · 1991

ISSN 0888-3742
ISBN 0-89919-929-1
ISBN 0-89919-928-3 (PBK.)

Printed in the United States of America

HAD 10 9 8 7 6 5 4 3 2 1

"Random Reflections of a Second-Rate Mind" by Woody Allen. First published in *Tikkun*. Copyright © 1990 by Woody Allen. Reprinted by permission of the author.

"The Female Body" by Margaret Atwood. First published in *Michigan Quarterly Review*. Copyright © 1990 by Margaret Atwood. Reprinted by permission of the author.

"The Female Body" by John Updike. First published in *Michigan Quarterly Review* with the title "Venus and Others." Copyright © 1990 by John Updike. Reprinted by permission of the author.

"Silent Dancing" by Judith Ortiz Cofer. First published in *The Georgia Review*. Copyright © 1990 by Judith Ortiz Cofer. Reprinted by permission of the author.

"Running the Table" by Frank Conroy. First published in *GQ*. Copyright © 1990 by Frank Conroy. Reprinted by permission of the author.

"Life with Daughters: Watching the Miss America Pageant" by Gerald Early. First published in *The Kenyon Review*. Copyright © 1990 by Gerald Early. Reprinted by permission of the author.

"This Autumn Morning" by Gretel Ehrlich. First published in *Antaeus*. Copyright © 1990 by Gretel Ehrlich. Reprinted by permission of the author.

"Wounded Chevy at Wounded Knee" by Diana Hume George. First published in *The Missouri Review*. Copyright © 1990 by Diana Hume George. Reprinted by permission of the author.

"Counters and Cable Cars" by Stephen Jay Gould. First published in *Natural*

# Contents

Foreword by Robert Atwan    ix

Introduction by Joyce Carol Oates    xiii

WOODY ALLEN. *Random Reflections of a Second-Rate Mind*    1
*from Tikkun*

MARGARET ATWOOD. *The Female Body*    9
*from Michigan Quarterly Review*

JOHN UPDIKE. *The Female Body*    13
*from Michigan Quarterly Review*

JUDITH ORTIZ COFER. *Silent Dancing*    17
*from The Georgia Review*

FRANK CONROY. *Running the Table*    26
*from GQ*

GERALD EARLY. *Life with Daughters: Watching the Miss America Pageant*    33
*from The Kenyon Review*

GRETEL EHRLICH. *This Autumn Morning*    51
*from Antaeus*

DIANA HUME GEORGE. *Wounded Chevy at Wounded Knee*    63
*from The Missouri Review*

STEPHEN JAY GOULD. *Counters and Cable Cars*    78
*from Natural History*

ELIZABETH HARDWICK. *New York City: Crash Course*  87
from Granta

GARRETT HONGO. *Kubota*  97
from Ploughshares

NAOMI SHIHAB NYE. *Maintenance*  109
from The Georgia Review

RICHARD RODRIGUEZ. *Late Victorians*  119
from Harper's Magazine

DORIEN ROSS. *Seeking Home*  135
from Tikkun

MARK RUDMAN. *Mosaic on Walking*  138
from Boulevard

REG SANER. *The Ideal Particle and the Great Unconformity*  154
from The Georgia Review

AMY TAN. *Mother Tongue*  196
from The Threepenny Review

JANE TOMPKINS. *At the Buffalo Bill Museum — June 1988*  203
from The South Atlantic Quarterly

MARIANNA DE MARCO TORGOVNICK. *On Being White, Female,
and Born in Bensonhurst*  223
from Partisan Review

MARIO VARGAS LLOSA. *Questions of Conquest*  236
from Harper's Magazine

JOY WILLIAMS. *The Killing Game*  251
from Esquire

Biographical Notes  269

Notable Essays of 1990  273

# Foreword

IT'S BEEN over two hundred years since one of our first important essayists — an English-educated Frenchman who went by the name of J. Hector St. John de Crèvecoeur — asked, "What is an American?" His question reverberated through American literature, as many of our major writers proposed a wide variety of answers. Emerson tackles this central question, as do many others — Henry James, F. Scott Fitzgerald, Gertrude Stein, Saul Bellow, and especially James Baldwin, for whom the problem of American identity is a dominant issue.

Crèvecoeur's image of a "melting pot" no longer possesses the influence it once had for generations of Americans, but his picture of an ethnically and culturally diverse nation is of particular relevance today. This sixth edition of *The Best American Essays* shows how many talented contemporary writers are still attracted to the theme of America's diversity. For many of them the topic is closely tied to the personal essay, as they explore in autobiography and memoir the complicated interrelations of heritage, background, and individual identity. The essay, as Montaigne proved long ago, is the perfect vehicle for experiments in self-discovery.

This year's collection ranges over a wide territory of cultural realms and geographical regions, of voices and tones: the Puerto Rican barrio of Paterson, New Jersey (my own hometown); the uncompromising streets of New York City; the Pine Ridge Sioux Reservation in South Dakota; a San Francisco homosexual community; a Palestinian-American household in Texas; a Japanese-American family in Oahu, Hawaii; the Italian-American neighborhood of Bensonhurst; the Buffalo Bill Museum in Cody, Wyoming; a spot in the Grand Canyon appropriately known as the Great Unconformity. In this year's volume you will also find the sounds and accents of many languages, even — as the paired essays of Margaret Atwood and John Updike reveal — the subtle language of the female body. There are, as Amy Tan puts it, many "different Englishes."

The volume ranges, too, over an exciting diversity of essay forms. Here are reflections and meditations, philosophical fragments, personal narratives and anecdotes, cultural critiques and impassioned arguments — a few of these on what Woody Allen would call "touchy subjects." Today's essay assumes many shapes, though some of the genre's most venerable traditions are still visible despite new twists and turns. In calling his essay "Mosaic on Walking," Mark Rudman at once reminds readers of the long tradition of "walking" essays and gives that tradition a contemporary spin.

We "relish diversity," says Stephen Jay Gould, speaking as an evolutionary biologist in "Counters and Cable Cars," an essay that in many ways captures the spirit of this volume. Biologists, of course, have their own scientific definitions of diversity. Gould is writing, however, not about his usual subjects — biology, natural history, or paleontology — but about the special joys of a San Francisco breakfast counter and an early morning cable-car ride. "I therefore tend to revel most," Gould writes, "in the distinctive diversity of geographical regions when I contemplate the aesthetic pleasure of difference." For Gould, regional and cultural diversity seems to satisfy a fundamental human need — the need for authenticity.

The essays in this volume, though they represent — as Joyce Carol Oates notes in her introduction — a "diversity of voices," are united in their quest for authenticity, their demand for real feeling and genuine experience. The personal essay in our time, as both Joyce Carol Oates and Stephen Jay Gould recognize, stays alive because it dares to be unique and because it strenuously resists the encroachments of standardization, whether social, cultural, or academic. Essayists have a sharp eye for the local and for the wonderful variety of life that can be found in any authentic place. Take Julian's, for instance, the famous New York City pool hall where Frank Conroy learned not only how to play but to talk a good game. He learned there, too, another one of our many different "Englishes" — the kind you apply to a cue ball.

*The Best American Essays* features a selection of the year's outstanding essays, essays of literary achievement that show an awareness of craft and a forcefulness of thought. Roughly 300 essays are gathered from a wide variety of regional and national publications. These essays are then screened and turned over to a distinguished guest editor, who may add a few personal favorites to the list and who makes the final selections.

To qualify for selection, the essays must be works of respectable literary quality, intended as fully developed, independent essays (not excerpts or reviews) on subjects of general interest (not specialized scholarship), originally written in English (or translated by the author) for first appearance in an American periodical during the calendar year. (Readers may notice that the British magazine *Granta* is now on our list. With its U.S. editorial offices and its receptivity to American writers, *Granta* has become an important part of our literary scene.) Publications that want to make sure their contributors will be considered each year should include the series on their subscription list (Robert Atwan, *The Best American Essays*, P.O. Box 416, Maplewood, New Jersey 07040).

I'd like to thank two good friends, George Dardess and Peggy Rosenthal, for all the suggestions and support they've given me since I started the series in 1985. I'm grateful to Michael McSpedon for his help with all the paperwork that went into this year's edition. As always, I appreciate the assistance I receive annually from the fine public libraries in South Orange, Maplewood, and Millburn. And I'd like to thank Joyce Carol Oates, whose creative range is truly astonishing. A novelist, short story writer, poet, and essayist, she proves in this volume that the essay is not a distant relative of imaginative literature but a member of the immediate family.

# Introduction

Why does authenticity . . . exert such a hold upon us?
— Stephen Jay Gould

Be it life or death, we crave only reality.
— Henry David Thoreau

As A CHILD I seem to have made the distinction, without examining much evidence, that "reading" (as in "reading material") was of two types: for children, and for adults. Reading for children was simple-minded in its vocabulary, grammar, and content; it was always about unreal or improbable or unconditionally fantastic situations, like Disney films and cartoons, and comic books. It might be amusing, it might even be instructive, but it was not *real*. Reality was the province of adults, and, though I was surrounded by adults (I was an only child for five years, and those five years seem, in retrospect, to have shaped my life), it was not a province I could enter, or even envision, from the outside. To explore *reality*, I read books.

Or tried. Very hard. As if — but why did I imagine this? — my life depended upon it.

One definition of the "imaginative" personality is that it makes much of things. To some observers' eyes, too much. The motive for metaphor — the passionate motive for writing, thus recording, and supposedly making permanent what is ephemeral — remains a mystery. Most writers will say that they write in order to understand, but out of what impatience with things-as-they-are does the motive to understand spring? Writing is a form of sympathy, but there are other forms of sympathy, less circuitous and vulnerable to misinterpretation.

One of the earliest adult books I read, or tried to read, was a book from a shelf at school, an aged *Treasury of American Literature* that had probably been published before World War I. Mixed with writers long since forgotten (James Whitcomb Riley, Eugene Field, Helen Hunt Jackson) were our New England classics — though I was certainly too young, at nine or ten, to know that Hawthorne, Melville, Poe, et al. were "classics" or even to comprehend that they belonged to and spoke out of an America that no longer existed and had never existed for my family. I took it for granted that these writers were in the full possession of *reality*. That their *reality* was in no way contiguous with my own did not discredit it, nor even qualify it, but confirmed it: adult writing was a form of wisdom and power (the two, in my imagination, inextricably bound), difficult to understand, in fact frequently impossible to understand (what *was* "Ralph Waldo Emerson" saying?), but unassailable. These were no children's easy-reading fantasies but the real thing, voices of adult authenticity. Engrossed in tortuous, finely printed prose on yellowed, dog-eared pages (this too was a measure of authenticity — the very agedness, brittleness, of the book), I was capable of reading for long minutes at a time, retaining very little but utterly captivated by another's voice sounding in my ears. (What a rich fund of words for my "vocabulary list"! There would never be an end to the words I didn't know, thus never an end to the excitement of learning them. So, today, four decades later, my heart leaps when I encounter an unfamiliar word — something for the "vocabulary list.")

Our school in rural Niagara County, on the Tonawanda Creek near Millersport, New York, approximately twenty-five miles north of Buffalo, was an old wood-frame one-room schoolhouse in which eight quite disparate grades were taught, and taught very capably, by a heroic woman named Mrs. Dietz. For decades my memory of my first teacher was that of a child's-eye view of a giantess, or a deity: could Mrs. Dietz really have been as tall as I remembered? — so full-bodied, muscular, stoic? When, a few years ago, my parents unearthed an old photograph of Mrs. Dietz and some of her pupils, taken in the schoolhouse, circa 1948, I saw that, yes, Mrs. Dietz had been of above-average height and girth. But then she would have to have been, for not only was it this woman's task to lead eight grades, in turn, through their lessons every school day, but to keep discipline in the classroom, where certain of the overgrown farm boys, attending school only reluctantly, had to be kept from pummeling one another or bullying the girls and younger children; it was her responsibility too to keep the ancient wood-burning stove, the building's single source of heat, going on winter mornings when the temperature might hover at zero degrees Fahrenheit and the windows would be covered, inside, in frost and even rivulets of ice. Studying this old photograph, I feel an identification not with the ten-year-old girl who is, or was, myself, but with Mrs. Dietz — what a paragon of patience she must have been, how overworked and surely underpaid! I remember Mrs. Dietz's emphasis upon such time-honored pedagogical exercises as penmanship, memorization, sentence diagramming, spelling (you stand beside your desk and pronounce your word; then, enunciating carefully, you spell out your word; then you pronounce your word again; then sit down). I remember her deep seriousness, her zeal in her calling — her very *teacherliness*.

The *Treasury of American Literature* was one of probably fewer than a dozen books of its sort kept in a bookshelf for use during study time, a reward for having finished classwork early. I tackled it as I might tackle a tree difficult to climb. The poetry — which was called "verse" — I immediately discounted as both too hard and "not real"; even if you could make sense of rhyming lines, they were not, somehow, required to be truthful as prose was. I must have felt challenged by those lengthy, near-impenetrable paragraphs of prose so unlike the brief, simple paragraphs of our readers, the typeface itself small, fussy as lace. The writers, of course, were mere names, words. "Washington Irving," "Benjamin Franklin," "Nathaniel Hawthorne," "Herman Melville," "Ralph Waldo Emerson," "Henry David Thoreau," "Edgar Allan Poe," "Samuel Clemens," and numerous others: I did not think of these as actual men, human beings who might have lived and breathed like the adults of my world; the writing attributed to them *was* them, autonomous, self-generated, inviolable, and immortal. If I could not always make sense of what I read, I at least knew it was true.

The first "essay-voice" of my experience was Henry David

Thoreau. Admirers of the essay form invariably speak of Thoreau with reverence, for no one has stated the case for a first-person accounting of oneself so succinctly as Thoreau: *I should not talk so much about myself if there were anybody else whom I knew so well.* My early reading or attempted reading of Thoreau has long since been layered over by subsequent readings of *Walden,* "Civil Disobedience," and other works, but I must have been struck by this writer's vivid, direct, precise language, both "poetic" and colloquial, above all different from the abstract, preacherly, obdurate style of Emerson — a wonderful essayist, as adults know, but of limited appeal to a child.

It was the first-person voice, the (seemingly) unmediated voice, that struck me as *truth-telling.* The difference between the plain-speaking "I" of Henry David Thoreau and the plain-speaking "I" of Samuel Clemens is after all a subtle one. The difference between the "I" of Emerson and the "I" of Hawthorne and of Poe is a subtle one. I no longer remember what the earliest prose pieces by Clemens/Twain were that I read, but I'm sure I read them unquestioningly, as *real* — "The Story of the Old Ram" from *Roughing It,* for instance, or "The Notorious Jumping Frog of Calaveras County." I do remember struggling with Poe's "The Gold Bug," which seemed to me an authentic account of an exotic and rather tedious but not improbable adventure, and I still have to think twice to recall whether "The Imp of the Perverse" is an essay — as, so reasonably, it seems to set itself up to be — or one of the *Tales of the Grotesque.* Poe was a master of, among other things, the literary trompe l'oeil, in which speculative musings upon human psychology shift into fantastic narratives while retaining the same first-person voice. The artful blurring of boundaries between what we call "history" and what we call, simply, "story" has been a characteristic of literature, as of art generally, from the very beginning of our recorded human enterprise.

Why is it that the earliest, most "primitive" forms of art seem to have been fabulist, legendary, and surreal, populated not by mortal men but by gods, giants, and monsters? Why was realism so slow to evolve? It is as if, looking into a mirror, humankind wished to see not its own self-evident face but something very other — exotic, terrifying, comforting, idealistic, or delusional — but distinctly *other*. The seemingly direct, confessional, self-abrading manner of Montaigne strikes the ear as radical, even astounding, for its time and place. For even Rabelais, rubbing mankind's collective nose in the comical filth of the physical life, was an artist of the fabulist and the surreal.

Writers of earlier centuries — Defoe, Fielding, Swift, to name only a few — presented their wildly imaginative work as *history;* in our time, writers whose essential subjects are themselves — Proust, Joyce, Lawrence, Wolfe, Hemingway, and numberless of our contemporaries — present autobiographical work as *fiction.* Norman Mailer and Philip Roth have invented personae — "Mailer" and "Philip" — as characters in works of fiction; the unnamed narrator of Milan Kundera's *Book of Laughter and Forgetting* frequently interrupts his fictional narrative to explain his authorial strategies and to editorialize on history, totalitarianism, the motives for his writing. In such texts, the "I" of the narrative voice so reasonably melds with the "I" of the authorial voice that it is natural to assume, though we understand that we should not, that the two are often one.

In any case, it seemed only reasonable to me as a child, *and I wanted it to be so,* that writing by adults, for adults, was "real" and to be trusted. With another part of my imagination I was captivated by works of obvious, irresistible fantasy — Lewis Carroll's *Alice* books above all. But those hefty blocks of prose by "Emerson," "Thoreau," "Poe," those monuments to *hard reading* — their special value lay in their employment of the "I"-voice, conspicuously missing from elementary school readers. It was, and in some quarters still is, a seeming imprimatur of truth-telling.

> Talking much about oneself may be a way of hiding oneself.
> — Friedrich Nietzsche

How to define the essay as a genre, clear and distinct from all other genres?

Given that the title of this volume is *The Best American Essays 1991,* there should be some loci of defining (thus of exclusion), but, as a writer, I am strongly skeptical that there is, still more should be, a quintessential "essay" any more than there is, or should be, a quintessential "novel," "short story," "poem," "play" — what are these, despite the efforts of critics to taxonomize them, but experimental modes of writing, continuously shifting their borders, testing constraints? (Randall Jarrell once wittily said, in a parody of critical myopia, that the novel may be defined as a prose work of a certain length that has something wrong with it.) The essays selected for this volume might be described as prose works of certain lengths that have many more right things about them than wrong.

To my mind, the "essay" might be as brilliantly gemlike and condensed as the briefest of Pascal's *Pensées,* or the aphorism of Nietzsche's cited above. (Nietzsche believed that one should philosophize with a hammer. In his most characteristic practice, Nietzsche philosophized with a surgical scalpel.) Are not aphorisms and epigrams essays of a sort? — miniature, to be sure, but legitimately "essays"? (To "assay" — try, attempt, analyze, judge, "to prove up in an assay.") Indeed, set beside such fast-flying particles, the more conventional essays of a Carlyle or an Emerson lumber along like becalmed elephants.

Like rock strata, genres shift through time. Form and content always seem inevitable, yet the one is easily detached from the other, when purpose and intention alter. The earliest narratives were poems to be sung; the earliest essays were poems to be read — most famously Virgil's *Georgics.* Lucretius's *De Rerum Natura* — which, like everyone else, I knew as *On the Nature of Things,* or *The Nature of the Universe* — was poetry with a messianic purpose: the spreading of the gospel of Epicurus's fundamentally materialist, unsuperstitious teachings in a world in which capricious gods still ruled. And there were those arduous essays of the English Renaissance, Samuel Daniel's "Musophilus," Sir John Davies's "Nosce Teitsum," Michael Drayton's geographical-minded "Polyolbion" — instruction and edification in the form in which our ancestors believed sugar-coated the pill of didacticism, poetry. (As a graduate student in English literature, I read such works with impatience, even dismay — didn't poets understand that poetry is too wonderful a medium to be wasted on such efforts?) In our time, didacticism in the form of poetry is rare; rarer still, outright instruction, edification. One might argue that such long works as L. E. Sissman's *Dying: An Introduction* and John Updike's *Midpoint* are autobiographical essays in poetic form, to name two contemporary poems that idiosyncratically, and most effectively, subvert genre.

Yet, our efforts to define the elusive "essay" remain undiminished. In *Habitations of the Word*, William Gass, himself an essayist of bold and original notions, states that the genre is biblio-centric and -generated: "Born of books, nourished by books, a book for its body, the essay is more often than not a confluence of such little blocks and strips of text." This is true of some essays, perhaps, particularly certain English essays, but it is hardly true of most contemporary essays of interest; and hardly applicable to the *unpassive* mode of the essays in this volume, some of which possess a very nearly cinematic clarity and urgency.

With the aggressive modesty that makes an admirer wince, E. B. White perversely defined the essay, the very genre in which he excelled, as "second-rate" — to which my reply is, "There are no second-rate genres, only second-rate practitioners." Compare, for instance, Flannery O'Connor's essays in *Mystery and Manners* with the strongest of her short stories; Raymond Carver's essays, *Fires*, with the strongest of his. Compare the essays of Edward Hoagland and Peter Matthiessen with their best fiction, and essays by Annie Dillard, Oliver Sacks, Joan Didion, Francine du Plessix Gray, Richard Selzer, Elizabeth Hardwick, and other of our most acclaimed essayists (some of whom will be found in this volume) with the best work by any of our contemporaries. First-rate writers produce first-rate work, regardless of genre.

The critic and scholar William Howarth, who has written so lyrically, and informatively, on, among others, Thoreau, discusses in a recent essay ("Itinerant Passages: Recent American Essays," *Sewanee Review*, 1988) the "itinerancy" of the essay form; as if, along with transcribing a literal journey, the form constitutes a journey for both essayist and reader. Certainly this is true of many excellent essays (among them, in this volume, works as heterogeneous as those by Reg Saner, Mark Rudman, Stephen Jay Gould), but one can argue that the same is true for many — most? — works of fiction too. Sam Pickering appropriates the genre as congenial to relaxation, musing aloud, coming to no conclusions: "Instead of driving hard to make a point, the essay saunters. . . . Instead of reaching conclusions, the essay ruminates and wonders. . . . Instead of being serious, it is often light-

hearted" (from "Being Familiar," in *The Right Distance,* 1987).
G. Douglas Atkins pushes this idea even further, declaring that
essays *smile:* "Whether or not they make you smile in turn, essays
can make you feel good, comfortable, at ease. They're familiar
and personal. It's impossible to be with them and remain tight or
glum. . . . The smile that creases the face of the gardener-essayist
betokens love" (from "In Other Words: Gardening for Love —
The Work of the Essayist," in *Kenyon Review,* Winter 1991).

Most of the essays in this volume, chosen, in part, to represent
the diversity of voices that now constitute the American literary
community, have been written out of a sense of urgency, both
personal and cultural; there is no questioning their authenticity,
thus their power. Of course, there is humor here — in, among
others, Woody Allen's characteristically mordant little essay: how,
in anything by Woody Allen, could there *not* be humor? — and
there are moments of clarity, beauty, epiphany, transcendence;
but the dominant mode is urgency. As I am not drawn to art that
makes me feel good, comfortable, or at ease, so I am not drawn
to essays that "smile," except in a context of larger, more complex ambitions.

Indeed, anger, grief, pity, moral outrage, characterize a number of these essays which, for all their stylistic polish, read like
cries from the heart. Richard Rodriguez's elegiac (and controversial) "Late Victorians" has the emotional density of a novel in
miniature; Judith Ortiz Cofer's "Silent Dancing" transforms the
family memoir into a work of surpassing beauty, and irony: "The
only thing [Father's] money could not buy us was a place to live
away from the barrio — his greatest wish, Mother's greatest fear."
Garrett Hongo's "Kubota," a memoir of his dispossessed grandfather, is almost too painful to be borne, as is, in its very different
way, Dorien Ross's "Seeking Home," which begins with the tone
of a breezy column in a glossy career-woman's magazine, and ends
with a shocking revelation. Anger, bewilderment, and nostalgia
are held in dramatic suspension in Marianna De Marco Torgovnick's "On Being White, Female, and Born in Bensonhurst," another essay with the emotional gravity of a work of fiction. And
there are essays in which cultural criticism is transformed by personal experience from witnesses born outside the cultures in
question — Jane Tompkins's "At the Buffalo Bill Museum" (where

adult shame and "an image of the heart's desire" contend); Diana Hume George's "Wounded Chevy at Wounded Knee," a meditation upon the genocidal consequences of American policy toward Native Americans which is altogether different from the kind we are accustomed to reading or seeing on the screen. Gerald Early's provocative "Life with Daughters: Watching the Miss America Pageant," like most of his work, manages to be funny, and ironic, and self-effacing, and, not least, taunting: "It is impossible to escape that need to see the race uplifted, to thumb your nose at whites in a competition. . . . Perhaps this tainted desire . . . is the unity of feeling which is the only race pride blacks have ever had since they became Americans."

Stephen Jay Gould's "Counters and Cable Cars" is, among other things, a lyrical tribute to the "moral and aesthetic value of diversity." Amy Tan's "Mother Tongue" is a movingly personal, intimate analysis of language strategies, ways of defining the private/public/ethnic/"American" self. One of the most unusual essays is Naomi Shihab Nye's "Maintenance" — an abstract subject made memorable by a metaphor come to life; the most unabashedly nostalgic essay is Frank Conroy's "Running the Table": "Why the orderliness of pool, the Euclidean cleanness of it, so appealed to me." The most ambitious essay in terms of its historic scope and political implications is Mario Vargas Llosa's "Questions of Conquest." And then there is Joy Williams's "The Killing Game": blunt, eloquent, defiantly polemical, as confrontational as a beaker of blood in the face.

In the tradition of our richest nature essays, from Henry David Thoreau to Annie Dillard and Barry Lopez, Reg Saner's "The Ideal Particle and the Great Unconformity" and Gretel Erhlich's "This Autumn Morning" are meticulously observed, instructive, written with enormous care and ambition. Each is a monument in language to what Saner calls "the littlest causes, their long continuance." ("Nature" as subject and theme is probably the inspiration for most essays that are written; among these, in our era of ecological sensitivity, are the most consistently compelling.) The New York–inspired essays of Elizabeth Hardwick ("New York City: Crash Course") and Mark Rudman ("Mosaic on Walking") make a lively, informal pair — entirely different responses to an identical environment. The pairing of Margaret Atwood's "The

Female Body" (a prose-poem crackling with the author's characteristic dry-ice wit) and John Updike's graceful response to Atwood (and through Atwood to the mystery of female/male
mythologizing) should be explained: they were written by invi-
tation for the special issue of *Michigan Quarterly Review*, "The Female Body."

These excellent essays, as I've indicated, seem to me linked by
a common tone of urgency, even tension, however diverse their
voices. Most of them provide news, facts, information — I am
predisposed to the essay with knowledge to impart — but, unlike
journalism, which exists primarily to present facts, the essays
transcend their data, or transmute it into personal meaning. The
memorable essay, unlike the article, is not place- or time-bound;
it survives the occasion of its original composition. Indeed, in the
most brilliant essays, language is not merely the medium of communication, it *is* communication.

Editors of such yearly anthologies as this one customarily explain
their final choices in terms of "excellence" and "personal taste" —
it's to be hoped the two are not incompatible — but it should be
added, for the record, that editing any volume in which space is
at a premium forces choices upon the editor that might not otherwise be made. Ideally, I could have included twice the number
of essays I have included. But, after a year of sifting through
photocopies of essays sent to me by the indefatigably capable and
enthusiastic series editor, Robert Atwan, after decisions, indeci-
sions, revisions, insomnia, and a mounting sense of frustration
and loss at being required to leave out so much excellent work
(the memoirs alone! — of fathers, families, mentors, famous elders!), I resigned myself to the fact that exclusions would have to
be made, in many cases, on quite arbitrary grounds. (No more
than a single essay by a writer — obviously. No more than one,
or at the most two, essays on a single topic. No excerpts from
diaries or journals. No reportage or opinion pieces, however well
done. And no book reviews — even when the review is by Larry
McMurtry and the subject is "How the West Was Won or Lost.")
I was determined to include as many new and emerging writers
as possible; at the same time, I was determined not to omit an
important essay simply because its author happened to be well

known. I was determined to choose essays from a variety of magazines; at the same time, it seemed wrong to discriminate against *Harper's* and *The Georgia Review* simply because, of American magazines of our time, they happen to publish the most essays of quality, frequently several in a single issue.

As I neared the end of my editorship of this volume, a task that, for all its frustrations, I enjoyed very much, I began to consider how many theoretical volumes of approximately twenty essays I might assemble out of the approximately three hundred essays available to me, in various combinations. A physicist friend did the calculations — the number is $10^{31}$. That's to say, ten thousand billion billion billion possible *The Best American Essays 1991*.

In the light of such a daunting statistic, it seems a bold, even a brash, act to present the volume you hold in your hand as, in fact, *the* best. But so it is — or seems so to me. I hope the claim will prove a reasonable one.

JOYCE CAROL OATES

WOODY ALLEN

# Random Reflections
# of a Second-Rate Mind

FROM TIKKUN

DINING at a fashionable restaurant on New York's chic Upper East Side, I noticed a Holocaust survivor at the next table. A man of sixty or so was showing his companions a number tattooed on his arm while I overheard him say he had gotten it at Auschwitz. He was graying and distinguished-looking with a sad, handsome face, and behind his eyes there was the predictable haunted look. Clearly he had suffered and gleaned deep lessons from his anguish. I heard him describe how he had been beaten and had watched his fellow inmates being hanged and gassed, and how he had scrounged around in the camp garbage for anything — a discarded potato peel — to keep his corpse-thin body from giving in to disease. As I eavesdropped I wondered: if an angel had come to him then, when he was scheming desperately not to be among those chosen for annihilation, and told him that one day he'd be sitting on Second Avenue in Manhattan in a trendy Italian restaurant amongst lovely young women in designer jeans, and that he'd be wearing a fine suit and ordering lobster salad and baked salmon, would he have grabbed the angel around the throat and throttled him in a sudden fit of insanity?

Talk about cognitive dissonance! All I could see as I hunched over my pasta were truncheons raining blows on his head as second after second dragged on in unrelieved agony and terror. I saw him weak and freezing — sick, bewildered, thirsty, and in tears, an emaciated zombie in stripes. Yet now here he was, portly and jocular, sending back the wine and telling the waiter it seemed to him slightly too tannic. I knew without a doubt then and there that no philosopher ever to come along, no matter how profound, could even begin to understand the world.

Later that night I recalled that at the end of Elie Wiesel's fine book *Night,* he said that when his concentration camp was liberated he and others thought first and foremost of food. Then of their families and next of sleeping with women, but not of revenge. He made the point several times that the inmates didn't think of revenge. I find it odd that I, who was a small boy during World War II and who lived in America, unmindful of any of the horror Nazi victims were undergoing, and who never missed a good meal with meat and potatoes and sweet desserts, and who had a soft, safe, warm bed to sleep in at night, and whose memories of those years are only blissful and full of good times and good music — that I think of nothing but revenge.

Confessions of a hustler. At ten I hustled dreidel. I practiced endlessly spinning the little lead top and could make the letters come up in my favor more often than not. After that I mercilessly contrived to play dreidel with kids and took their money.

"Let's play for two cents," I'd say, my eyes waxing wide and innocent like a big-time pool shark's. Then I'd lose the first game deliberately. After, I'd move the stakes up. Four cents, maybe six, maybe a dime. Soon the other kid would find himself en route home, gutted and muttering. Dreidel hustling got me through the fifth grade. I often had visions of myself turning pro. I wondered if when I got older I could play my generation's equivalent of Legs Diamond or Dutch Schultz for a hundred thousand a game. I saw myself bathed in won money, sitting around a green felt table or getting off great trains, my best dreidel in a smart carrying case as I went from city to city looking for action, always cleaning up, always drinking bourbon, always taking care of my precious manicured spinning hand.

On the cover of this magazine, under the title, is printed the line "A Bimonthly Jewish Critique of Politics, Culture & Society." But why a Jewish critique? Or a gentile critique? Or any limiting perspective? Why not simply a magazine with articles written by human beings for other humans to read? Aren't there enough real demarcations without creating artificial ones? After all, there's no biological difference between a Jew and a gentile despite what my Uncle Max says. We're talking here about exclusive clubs that serve no good purpose; they exist only to form barriers, trade commercially on human misery, and provide additional differences amongst people so they can further rationalize their natural distrust and aggression.

After all, you know by ten years old there's nothing bloodier or more phony than the world's religious history. What could be more awful than, say, Protestant versus Catholic in Northern Ireland? Or the late Ayatollah? Or the expensive cost of tickets to my local synagogue so my parents can pray on the high holidays? (In the end they could only afford to be seated downstairs, not in the main room, and the service was piped in to them. The smart money sat ringside, of course.) Is there anything uglier than families that don't want their children to marry loved ones because they're of the wrong religion? Or professional clergy whose pitch is as follows: "There is a God. Take my word for it. And I pretty much know what He wants and how to get on with Him and I'll try to help you to get and remain in His good graces, because that way your life won't be so fraught with terror. Of course, it's going to cost you a little for my time and stationery . . ."

Incidentally, I'm well aware that one day I may have to fight because I'm a Jew, or even die because of it, and no amount of professed apathy to religion will save me. On the other hand, those who say they want to kill me because I'm Jewish would find other reasons if I were not Jewish. I mean, think if there were no Jews or Catholics, or if everyone was white or German or American, if the earth was one country, one color; then endless new, creative rationalizations would emerge to kill "other people" — the left-handed, those who prefer vanilla to strawberry, all baritones, any person who wears saddle shoes.

So what was my point before I digressed? Oh — do I really want to contribute to a magazine that subtly helps promulgate phony and harmful differences? (Here I must say that *Tikkun* appears to me as a generally wonderful journal — politically astute, insightful, and courageously correct on the Israeli-Palestinian issue.)

I experienced this type of ambivalence before when a group

wanted me to front and raise money for the establishment of a strong pro-Israel political action committee. I don't approve of PACs, but I've always been a big rooter for Israel. I agonized over the decision and in the end I did front the PAC and helped them raise money and get going. Then, after they were off and running, I quietly slipped out. This was the compromise I made which I've never regretted. Still, I'd be happier contributing to *Tikkun* if it had a different line, or no line, under the title. After all, what if other magazines felt the need to employ their own religious perspectives? You might have: *Field and Stream: A Catholic Critique of Fishing and Hunting.* This month: "Angling for Salmon as You Baptize."

I have always preferred women to men. This goes back to the Old Testament where the ladies have it all over their cowering, pious counterparts. Eve knew the consequences when she ate the apple. Adam would have been content to just follow orders and live on like a mindless sybarite. But Eve knew it was better to acquire knowledge even if it meant grasping her mortality with all its accompanying anxiety. I'm personally glad men and women run to cover up their nakedness. It makes undressing someone much more exciting. And with the necessity of people having to earn their livings by the sweat of their brows we have a much more interesting and creative world. Much more fascinating than the sterile Garden of Eden, which I always picture existing in the soft-focus glow of a beer commercial.

I also had a crush on Lot's wife. When she looked back at the destruction of Sodom and Gomorrah she knew she was disobeying God. But she did it anyway. And she knew what a cruel, vindictive character He was. So it must have been very important to her to look back. But why? To see what? Well, I think to see her lover. The man she was having an extramarital affair with. And wouldn't you if you were married to Lot? This self-righteous bore, this paragon of virtue in a corrupt, swinging city. Can you imagine life with this dullard? Living only to please God. Resisting all the temptations that made Sodom and Gomorrah pulsate with vitality. The one good man in the city. Indeed. Of course she was making it with someone else. But who? Some used-idol salesman? Who knows? But I like to think she felt passion for a human being while Lot felt it only for the deep, pontificating voice of the creator of the universe. So naturally she was crushed when they had to leave town in a hurry. And as God destroyed all the bars and broke up all the poker games and the sinners went up in smoke, and as Lot tiptoed for the border, holding the skirts of his robes high to avoid tripping, Mrs. Lot turned to see her beloved *cinque à sept* one more time and that's when unfortunately the Almighty, in his infinite forgiveness, turned her into a seasoning.

So that leaves Job's wife. My favorite woman in all of literature. Because when her cringing, put-upon husband asked the Lord "Why me?" and the Lord told him to shut up and mind his own business and that he shouldn't even dare ask, Job accepted it, but the Missus, already in the earth at that point, had previously scored with a quotable line of unusual dignity and one that Job would have been far too obsequious to come up with: "Curse God and die" was the way she put it. And I loved her for it because she was too much of her own person to let herself be shamelessly abused by some vain and sadistic Holy Spirit.

I was amazed at how many intellectuals took issue with me over a piece I wrote a while back for the *New York Times* saying I was against the practice of Israeli soldiers going door-to-door and randomly breaking the hands of Palestinians as a method of combating the *intifada*. I said also I was against the too-quick use of real bullets before other riot control methods were tried. I was for a more flexible attitude on negotiating land for peace. All things I felt to be not only more in keeping with Israel's high moral stature but also in its own best interest. I never doubted the correctness of my feelings and I expected all who read it to agree. Visions of a Nobel danced in my head and, in truth, I had even formulated the first part of my acceptance speech. Now, I have frequently been accused of being a self-hating Jew, and while it's true I am Jewish and I don't like myself very much, it's not because of my persuasion. The reasons lie in totally other areas — like the way I look when I get up in the morning, or that I can never read a road map. In retrospect, the fact that I did not win a peace prize but became an object of some derision was what I should have expected.

"How can you criticize a place you've never been to?" a cabbie asked me. I pointed out I'd never been many places whose politics I took issue with, like Cuba for instance. But this line of reasoning cut no ice.

"Who are you to speak up?" was a frequent question in my hate mail. I replied I was an American citizen and a human being, but neither of these affiliations carried enough weight with the outraged.

The most outlandish cut of all was from the Jewish Defense League, which voted me Pig of the Month. How they misunderstood me! If only they knew how close some of my inner rages have been to theirs. (In my movie *Manhattan*, for example, I suggested breaking up a Nazi rally not with anything the ACLU would approve, but with baseball bats.)

But it was the intellectuals, some of them close friends, who hated most of all that I had made my opinions public on such a touchy subject. And yet, despite all their evasions and circumlocutions, the central point seemed to me inescapable: Israel was not responding correctly to this new problem.

"The Arabs are guilty for the Middle East mess, the bloodshed, the terrorism, with no leader to even try to negotiate with," reasoned the typical thinker.

"True," I agreed with Socratic simplicity.

"Victims of the Holocaust deserve a homeland, a place to be free and safe."

"Absolutely." I was totally in accord.

"We can't afford disunity. Israel is in a precarious situation." Here I began to feel uneasy, because we can afford disunity.

"Do you want the soldiers going door-to-door and breaking hands?" I asked, cutting to the kernel of my complaint.

"Of course not."

"So?"

"I'd still rather you hadn't written that piece." Now I'd be fidgeting in my chair, waiting for a cogent rebuttal to the breaking-of-hands issue. "Besides," my opponent argued, "the *Times* prints only one side."

"But even the Israeli press —"

"You shouldn't have spoken out," he interrupted.

"Many Israelis agree," I said, "and moral issues apart, why hand the Arabs a needless propaganda victory?"

"Yes, yes, but still you shouldn't have said anything. I was disappointed in you." Much talk followed by both of us about the origins of Israel, the culpability of Arab terrorists, the fact there's no one in charge of the enemy to negotiate with, but in the end it always came down to them saying, "You shouldn't have spoken up," and me saying, "But do you think they should randomly break hands?" and them adding, "Certainly not — but I'd still feel better if you had just not written that piece."

My mother was the final straw. She cut me out of her will and then tried to kill herself just to hasten my realization that I was getting no inheritance.

At fifteen I received as a gift a pair of cuff links with a William Steig cartoon on them. A man with a spear through his body was pictured and the accompanying caption read, "People are no damn good." A generalization, an oversimplification, and yet it was the only way I ever could get my mind around the Holocaust. Even at fifteen I used to read Anne Frank's line about people being basically good and place it on a par with Will Rogers's pandering nonsense, "I never met a man I didn't like."

The questions for me were not: How could a civilized people, and especially the people of Goethe and Mozart, do what they did to another people? And how could the world remain silent? Remain silent and indeed close their doors to millions who could have, with relative simplicity, been plucked from the jaws of agonizing death? At fifteen I felt I knew the answers. If you went with the Anne Frank idea or the Will Rogers line, I reasoned as an adolescent, of course the Nazi horrors became unfathomable. But if you paid more attention to the line on the cuff links, no matter how unpleasant that caption was to swallow, things were not so mysterious.

After all, I had read about all those supposedly wonderful neighbors throughout Europe who lived beside Jews lovingly and amiably. They shared laughter and fun and the same experiences I shared with my community and friends. And I read, also, how they turned their backs on the Jews instantly when it became the fashion and even looted their homes when they were left empty by sudden departure to the camps. This mystery that had confounded all my relatives since World War II was not such a puzzle if I understood that inside every heart lived the worm of self-preservation, of fear, greed, and an animal will to power. And the way I saw it, it was nondiscriminating. It abided in gentile or Jew, black, white, Arab, European, or American. It was part of who we all were, and that the Holocaust could occur was not at all so strange. History had been filled with unending examples of equal bestiality, differing only cosmetically.

The real mystery that got me through my teen years was that every once in a while one found an act of astonishing decency and sacrifice. One heard of people who risked their lives and their family's lives to save lives of people they didn't even know. But these were the rare exceptions, and in the end there were not enough humane acts to keep six million from being murdered.

I still own those cuff links. They're in a shoe box along with a lot of memorabilia from my teens. Recently I took them out and looked at them and all these thoughts returned to me. Perhaps I'm not quite as sure of all I was sure of at fifteen, but the waffling may come from just being middle-aged and not as virile. Certainly little has occurred since then to show me much different.

MARGARET ATWOOD

# The Female Body

FROM MICHIGAN QUARTERLY REVIEW

> . . . entirely devoted to the subject of "The Female Body." Know-
> ing how well you have written on this topic . . . this capacious
> topic . . .
> — letter from *Michigan Quarterly Review*

1.

I AGREE, it's a hot topic. But only one? Look around, there's a
wide range. Take my own, for instance.

I get up in the morning. My topic feels like hell. I sprinkle it with
water, brush parts of it, rub it with towels, powder it, add lubri-
cant. I dump in the fuel and away goes my topic, my topical topic,
my controversial topic, my capacious topic, my limping topic, my
nearsighted topic, my topic with back problems, my badly behaved topic, my vulgar topic, my outrageous topic, my aging topic,
my topic that is out of the question and anyway still can't spell, in
its oversized coat and worn winter boots, scuttling along the sidewalk as if it were flesh and blood, hunting for what's out there,
an avocado, an alderman, an adjective, hungry as ever.

2.

The basic Female Body comes with the following accessories:
garter belt, panti-girdle, crinoline, camisole, bustle, brassiere,
stomacher, chemise, virgin zone, spike heels, nose ring, veil,
kid gloves, fishnet stockings, fichu, bandeau, Merry Widow,

weepers, chokers, barrettes, bangles, beads, lorgnette, feather boa, basic black, compact, Lycra stretch one-piece with modesty panel, designer peignoir, flannel nightie, lace teddy, bed, head.

3.
The Female Body is made of transparent plastic and lights up when you plug it in. You press a button to illuminate the different systems. The circulatory system is red, for the heart and arteries, purple for the veins; the respiratory system is blue; the lymphatic system is yellow; the digestive system is green, with liver and kidneys in aqua. The nerves are done in orange and the brain is pink. The skeleton, as you might expect, is white.

The reproductive system is optional, and can be removed. It comes with or without a miniature embryo. Parental judgment can thereby be exercised. We do not wish to frighten or offend.

4.
He said, I won't have one of those things in the house. It gives a young girl a false notion of beauty, not to mention anatomy. If a real woman was built like that she'd fall on her face.

She said, If we don't let her have one like all the other girls she'll feel singled out. It'll become an issue. She'll long for one and she'll long to turn into one. Repression breeds sublimation. You know that.

He said, It's not just the pointy plastic tits, it's the wardrobes. The wardrobes and that stupid male doll, what's his name, the one with the underwear glued on.

She said, Better to get it over with when she's young. He said, All right, but don't let me see it.

She came whizzing down the stairs, thrown like a dart. She was stark naked. Her hair had been chopped off, her head was turned back to front, she was missing some toes and she'd been tattooed all over her body with purple ink in a scrollwork design. She hit

the potted azalea, trembled there for a moment like a botched
angel, and fell.

He said, I guess we're safe.

5.
The Female Body has many uses. It's been used as a door knocker,
a bottle opener, as a clock with a ticking belly, as something to
hold up lampshades, as a nutcracker, just squeeze the brass legs
together and out comes your nut. It bears torches, lifts victorious
wreaths, grows copper wings and raises aloft a ring of neon stars;
whole buildings rest on its marble heads.

It sells cars, beer, shaving lotion, cigarettes, hard liquor; it sells
diet plans and diamonds, and desire in tiny crystal bottles. Is this
the face that launched a thousand products? You bet it is, but
don't get any funny big ideas, honey, that smile is a dime a dozen.

It does not merely sell, it is sold. Money flows into this country or
that country, flies in, practically crawls in, suitful after suitful, lured
by all those hairless pre-teen legs. Listen, you want to reduce the
national debt, don't you? Aren't you patriotic? That's the spirit.
That's my girl.

She's a natural resource, a renewable one luckily, because those
things wear out so quickly. They don't make 'em like they used
to. Shoddy goods.

6.
One and one equals another one. Pleasure in the female is not a
requirement. Pair-bonding is stronger in geese. We're not talking about love, we're talking about biology. That's how we all got
here, daughter.

Snails do it differently. They're hermaphrodites, and work in
threes.

7.
Each Female Body contains a female brain. Handy. Makes things
work. Stick pins in it and you get amazing results. Old popular
songs. Short circuits. Bad dreams.

Anyway: each of these brains has two halves. They're joined together by a thick cord; neural pathways flow from one to the other, sparkles of electric information washing to and fro. Like light on waves. Like a conversation. How does a woman know? She listens. She listens in.

The male brain, now, that's a different matter. Only a thin connection. Space over here, time over there, music and arithmetic in their own sealed compartments. The right brain doesn't know what the left brain is doing. Good for aiming though, for hitting the target when you pull the trigger. What's the target? Who's the target? Who cares? What matters is hitting it. That's the male brain for you. Objective.

This is why men are so sad, why they feel so cut off, why they think of themselves as orphans cast adrift, footloose and stringless in the deep void. What void? she asks. What are you talking about? The void of the universe, he says, and she says Oh and looks out the window and tries to get a handle on it, but it's no use, there's too much going on, too many rustlings in the leaves, too many voices, so she says, Would you like a cheese sandwich, a piece of cake, a cup of tea? And he grinds his teeth because she doesn't understand, and wanders off, not just alone but Alone, lost in the dark, lost in the skull, searching for the other half, the twin who could complete him.

Then it comes to him: he's lost the Female Body! Look, it shines in the gloom, far ahead, a vision of wholeness, ripeness, like a giant melon, like an apple, like a metaphor for "breast" in a bad sex novel; it shines like a balloon, like a foggy noon, a watery moon, shimmering in its egg of light.

Catch it. Put it in a pumpkin, in a high tower, in a compound, in a chamber, in a house, in a room. Quick, stick a leash on it, a lock, a chain, some pain, settle it down, so it can never get away from you again.

# JOHN UPDIKE

## The Female Body

FROM MICHIGAN QUARTERLY REVIEW

"THY NAVEL is like a round goblet, which wanteth not liquor," says the male voice in the Song of Solomon, "thy belly is like a heap of wheat set about with lilies. Thy two breasts are like two young roes that are twins." Robert Graves, in *Watch the Northwind Rise*, quotes a vernacular rendering of these verses which goes, "Your belly's like a heap of wheat, / Your breasts like two young roes. / O come to bed with me, my sweet, / And take off all your clo'es!" A naked woman is, for most men, the most beautiful thing they will ever see. On this planet, the female body is the prime aesthetic object, re-created not only in statuary and painting but in the form of door knockers, nutcrackers, lamp stands, and caryatids. For the Victorians, it was everywhere, naked in brass, while their real women were swaddled and padded and reinforced like furniture; in this century, the female body haunts merchandising from top to bottom, from the silky epidermal feel of a soft cigarette pack to the rumpy curves of a Porsche. The female body is a masterpiece of market design, persuading the race to procreate generation after generation, extracting semen from mesmerized men with the ease of a pickpocket at a girlie show.

This captivating mechanism pays a price for its own complexity: cancer attacks breasts and ovaries, menstrual cramps and hysteria impair performance. Its season of bloom, of potential fertility, is shorter than that of the male body, though more piquant and powerful. Kafka, in a letter to Max Brod, unchivalrously remarked of women, "Not until summer does one really see their curious kind of flesh in quantities. It is soft flesh, retentive of a great deal of water, slightly puffy, and keeps its freshness only a few days." He goes on, with his scrupulous fairness: "Actually, of course, it stands up pretty well, but that is only proof of the brevity of human life." Just so, the actuarial longer-lastingness of the female body demonstrates the relative biological disposability of the male and the salubrious effects of lifelong exercise in the form of housework.

If the main social fact about the female body is its attractiveness, the main political fact is its weakness, compared with the male body. There may be some feminists ardent enough to dispute this, but the truth is elemental. As Elizabeth Hardwick, reviewing Simone de Beauvoir's *The Second Sex,* put it with admirable firmness, "Women are certainly physically inferior to men and if this were not the case the whole history of the world would be different. . . . Any woman who ever had her wrist twisted by a man recognizes a fact of nature as humbling as a cyclone to a frail tree branch." This fact lies behind many facts of feminine circumstance, such as the use of women as domestic drudges and beasts of burden in the world's fundamental economy, and the superior attentiveness and subtlety of women in the private maneuvers of advanced societies. "The fastidiousness of women," Stendhal wrote in *On Love,* "is the result of that perilous situation in which they find themselves placed so early, and of the necessity they are under of spending their lives among cruel and charming enemies."

This physical weakness and the cruelties that result are the truth but not all the truth, and from the standpoint of the species not even the main truth. An interesting thought-experiment, for an adult male, is to try to look at a prepubescent girl, one of ten or eleven, say, with the eyes again of a boy the same age. The relative weakness, the arresting curves, the female fastidiousness, are not yet in place, but the magic is — the siren song, the strange simultaneous call to be kind and to conquer, the swooning wish to place one's life *beside* this other. To be sure, cultural inducements to heterosexuality bombard us from infancy; but they fall, generally, upon terrifically receptive ground.

The female body is, in its ability to conceive and carry a fetus and to nurse an infant, our life's vehicle — it is the engine and the tracks. Male sexuality, then, returning to this primal source, drinks at the spring of being and enters the murky region, where up is down and death is life, of mythology. The paradoxical contradictoriness of male attitudes toward the female and her body — the impulses to exalt and debase, to serve and enslave, to injure and comfort, to reverence and mock — goes back to some point of origin where emotions are not yet differentiated and energy has no distinct direction. The sex act itself, from the male point of view, is a paradox, a transformation of his thrusts into pleasure, a poke in the gut that is gratefully received. Sadism and masochism naturally flirt on the edges of our, as Katherine Mansfield said, "profound and terrible . . . desire to establish contact."

And naturally modern women feel a personal impatience with being mythologized, with being envisioned (talk about hysteria!) as madonnas and whores, earth-mothers and vampires, helpless little girls and implacable dominatrices, and with male inability to see sex simply for what it is. What is it? A biological function and procedure, presumably, on a plane with eating and defecation, just as women are, properly regarded, equally entitled human beings and political entities with minds of their own. Well, men *have* been known, inadvertently, in lapses of distraction or satiety, to see the female body as just a body, very like their own, built for locomotion as well as procreation, an upright watery stalk temporarily withstanding, with its miraculous molecular chain reactions, the forces of gravity and entropy. It is a lucid but dispirited moment, seeing a nude woman as a kind of man, only smaller, lighter-framed, without a beard, but matching men tuft for tuft otherwise, and with bumps, soft swellings, unmale emphases stiffened with fat, softly swayed by gravity . . . a heap of wheat set about with lilies . . . those catenary curves, that curious, considerate absence . . . the moment of lucid vision passes.

In asking forgiveness of women for our mythologizing of their bodies, for being *unreal* about them, we can only appeal to their own sexuality, which is different but not basically different, perhaps, from our own. For women, too, there seems to be that tangle of supplication and possessiveness, that descent toward infantile undifferentiation, that omnipotent helplessness, that merger with the cosmic mother-warmth, that flushed pulse-quickened leap into overestimation, projection, general mix-up.

The Song of Solomon has two voices; there is a female extoller as well. She claims, "My beloved is white and ruddy, the chiefest among ten thousand. His head is as the most fine gold, his locks are bushy, and black as a raven. . . . His belly is as bright ivory overlaid with sapphires," etc. Can it be that the male body — its bulky shoulders, its narrow hips, its thick-veined feet and hands, its defenseless boneless belly above the one-eyed priapic oddity — may also loom as a glorious message from the deep? In Margaret Atwood's last novel, *Cat's Eye,* the heroine, in one of the many striking passages about growing up female and human, reflects upon the teenage boys she talks to on the telephone: "The serious part is their bodies. I sit in the hall with the cradled telephone, and what I hear is their bodies. I don't listen much to the words but to the silences, and in the silences these bodies recreate themselves, are created by me, take form." Some of this is sexual, she reflects, and some is not. Some is purely visual: "The faces of the boys change so much, they soften, open up, they ache. The body is pure energy, solidified light." For male and female alike, the bodies of the other sex are messages signaling what we must do — they are glowing signifiers of our own necessities.

JUDITH ORTIZ COFER

# Silent Dancing

FROM THE GEORGIA REVIEW

*We have a home movie of this party. Several times my mother and I have
watched it together, and I have asked questions about the silent revelers
coming in and out of focus. It is grainy and of short duration, but it's a
great visual aid to my memory of life at that time. And it is in color — the
only complete scene in color I can recall from those years.*

We lived in Puerto Rico until my brother was born in 1954. Soon
after, because of economic pressures on our growing family, my
father joined the United States Navy. He was assigned to duty on
a ship in Brooklyn Yard — a place of cement and steel that was
to be his home base in the States until his retirement more than
twenty years later. He left the Island first, alone, going to New
York City and tracking down his uncle who lived with his family
across the Hudson River in Paterson, New Jersey. There my father found a tiny apartment in a huge tenement that had once
housed Jewish families but was just being taken over and transformed by Puerto Ricans, overflowing from New York City. In
1955 he sent for us. My mother was only twenty years old, I was
not quite three, and my brother was a toddler when we arrived
at El Building, as the place had been christened by its newest residents.

My memories of life in Paterson during those first few years
are all in shades of gray. Maybe I was too young to absorb vivid
colors and details, or to discriminate between the slate blue of the
winter sky and the darker hues of the snow-bearing clouds, but
that single color washes over the whole period. The building we

lived in was gray, as were the streets, filled with slush the first few months of my life there. The coat my father had bought for me was similar in color and too big; it sat heavily on my thin frame.

I do remember the way the heater pipes banged and rattled, startling all of us out of sleep until we got so used to the sound that we automatically shut it out or raised our voices above the racket. The hiss from the valve punctuated my sleep (which has always been fitful) like a nonhuman presence in the room — a dragon sleeping at the entrance of my childhood. But the pipes were also a connection to all the other lives being lived around us. Having come from a house designed for a single family back in Puerto Rico — my mother's extended-family home — it was curious to know that strangers lived under our floor and above our heads, and that the heater pipe went through everyone's apartment. (My first spanking in Paterson came as a result of playing tunes on the pipes in my room to see if there would be an answer.) My mother was as new to this concept of beehive life as I was, but she had been given strict orders by my father to keep the doors locked, the noise down, ourselves to ourselves.

It seems that Father had learned some painful lessons about prejudice while searching for an apartment in Paterson. Not until years later did I hear how much resistance he had encountered with landlords who were panicking at the influx of Latinos into a neighborhood that had been Jewish for a couple of generations. It made no difference that it was the American phenomenon of ethnic turnover which was changing the urban core of Paterson, and that the human flood could not be held back with an accusing finger.

"You Cuban?" one man had asked my father, pointing at his name tag on the navy uniform — even though my father had the fair skin and light brown hair of his northern Spanish background, and the name Ortiz is as common in Puerto Rico as Johnson is in the United States.

"No," my father had answered, looking past the finger into his adversary's angry eyes. "I'm Puerto Rican."

"Same shit." And the door closed.

My father could have passed as European, but we couldn't. My brother and I both have our mother's black hair and olive skin, and so we lived in El Building and visited our great-uncle and his fair children on the next block. It was their private joke that they were the German branch of the family. Not many years later that area too would be mainly Puerto Rican. It was as if the heart of the city map were being gradually colored brown — *café con leche* brown. Our color.

*The movie opens with a sweep of the living room. It is "typical" immigrant Puerto Rican decor for the time: the sofa and chairs are square and hard-looking, upholstered in bright colors (blue and yellow in this instance) and covered with the transparent plastic that furniture salesmen then were so adept at convincing women to buy. The linoleum on the floor is light blue; where it had been subjected to spike heels, as it was in most places, there were dime-size indentations all over it that cannot be seen in this movie. The room is full of people dressed up: dark suits for the men, red dresses for the women. When I have asked my mother why most of the women are in red that night, she has shrugged and said, "I don't remember. Just a coincidence." She doesn't have my obsession for assigning symbolism to everything.*

*The three women in red sitting on the couch are my mother, my eighteen-year-old cousin, and her brother's girlfriend. The* novia *is just up from the Island, which is apparent in her body language. She sits up formally, her dress pulled over her knees. She is a pretty girl, but her posture makes her look insecure, lost in her full-skirted dress, which she has carefully tucked around her to make room for my gorgeous cousin, her future sister-in-law. My cousin has grown up in Paterson and is in her last year of high school. She doesn't have a trace of what Puerto Ricans call* la mancha *(literally, the stain: the mark of the new immigrant — something about the posture, the voice, or the humble demeanor that makes it obvious to everyone the person has just arrived on the mainland). My cousin is wearing a tight, sequined, cocktail dress. Her brown hair has been lightened with peroxide around the bangs, and she is holding a cigarette expertly between her fingers, bringing it up to her mouth in a sensuous arc of her arm as she talks animatedly. My mother, who has come up to sit between the two women, both only a few years younger than herself, is somewhere between the poles they represent in our culture.*

It became my father's obsession to get out of the barrio, and thus we were never permitted to form bonds with the place or with the people who lived there. Yet El Building was a comfort to my

mother, who never got over yearning for *la isla*. She felt surrounded by her language: the walls were thin, and voices speaking and arguing in Spanish could be heard all day. *Salsas* blasted
out of radios, turned on early in the morning and left on for
company. Women seemed to cook rice and beans perpetually —
the strong aroma of boiling red kidney beans permeated the
hallways.

Though Father preferred that we do our grocery shopping at
the supermarket when he came home on weekend leaves, my
mother insisted that she could cook only with products whose labels she could read. Consequently, during the week I accompanied her and my little brother to La Bodega — a hole-in-the-wall
grocery store across the street from El Building. There we
squeezed down three narrow aisles jammed with various products. Goya and Libby's — those were the trademarks that were
trusted by her *mamá*, so my mother bought many cans of Goya
beans, soups, and condiments, as well as little cans of Libby's fruit
juices for us. And she also bought Colgate toothpaste and Palm-
olive soap. (The final *e* is pronounced in both these products in
Spanish, so for many years I believed that they were manufactured on the Island. I remember my surprise at first hearing a
commercial on television in which "Colgate" rhymed with "ate.")
We always lingered at La Bodega, for it was there that Mother
breathed best, taking in the familiar aromas of the foods she knew
from Mamá's kitchen. It was also there that she got to speak to
the other women of El Building without violating outright Father's dictates against fraternizing with our neighbors.

Yet Father did his best to make our "assimilation" painless. I
can still see him carrying a real Christmas tree up several flights
of stairs to our apartment, leaving a trail of aromatic pine. He
carried it formally, as if it were a flag in a parade. We were the
only ones in El Building that I knew of who got presents on both
Christmas and *día de Reyes*, the day when the Three Kings brought
gifts to Christ and to Hispanic children.

Our supreme luxury in El Building was having our own television set. It must have been a result of Father's guilt feelings
over the isolation he had imposed on us, but we were among the
first in the barrio to have one. My brother quickly became an avid
watcher of Captain Kangaroo and Jungle Jim, while I loved all

the series showing families. By the time I started first grade, I could have drawn a map of Middle America as exemplified by the lives of characters in *Father Knows Best, The Donna Reed Show, Leave It to Beaver, My Three Sons,* and (my favorite) *Bachelor Father,* where John Forsythe treated his adopted teenage daughter like a princess because he was rich and had a Chinese houseboy to do everything for him. In truth, compared to our neighbors in El Building, *we* were rich. My father's navy check provided us with financial security and a standard of living that the factory workers envied. The only thing his money could not buy us was a place to live away from the barrio — his greatest wish, Mother's greatest fear.

*In the home movie the men are shown next, sitting around a card table set up in one corner of the living room, playing dominoes. The clack of the ivory pieces was a familiar sound. I heard it in many houses on the Island and in many apartments in Paterson. In* Leave It to Beaver, *the Cleavers played bridge in every other episode; in my childhood, the men started every social occasion with a hotly debated round of dominoes. The women would sit around and watch, but they never participated in the games.*

*Here and there you can see a small child. Children were always brought to parties and, whenever they got sleepy, were put to bed in the host's bedroom. Babysitting was a concept unrecognized by the Puerto Rican women I knew: a responsible mother did not leave her children with any stranger. And in a culture where children are not considered intrusive, there was no need to leave the children at home. We went where our mother went.*

Of my preschool years I have only impressions: the sharp bite of the wind in December as we walked with our parents toward the brightly lit stores downtown; how I felt like a stuffed doll in my heavy coat, boots, and mittens; how good it was to walk into the five-and-dime and sit at the counter drinking hot chocolate. On Saturdays our whole family would walk downtown to shop at the big department stores on Broadway. Mother bought all our clothes at Penney's and Sears, and she liked to buy her dresses at the women's specialty shops like Lerner's and Diana's. At some point we'd go into Woolworth's and sit at the soda fountain to eat.

We never ran into other Latinos at these stores or when eating out, and it became clear to me only years later that the women from El Building shopped mainly in other places — stores owned by other Puerto Ricans or by Jewish merchants who had philosophically accepted our presence in the city and decided to make us their good customers, if not real neighbors and friends. These establishments were located not downtown but in the blocks around our street, and they were referred to generically as La Tienda, El Bazar, La Bodega, La Botánica. Everyone knew what was meant. These were the stores where your face did not turn a clerk to stone, where your money was as green as anyone else's.

One New Year's Eve we were dressed up like child models in the Sears catalogue: my brother in a miniature man's suit and bow tie, and I in black patent-leather shoes and a frilly dress with several layers of crinoline underneath. My mother wore a bright red dress that night, I remember, and spike heels; her long black hair hung to her waist. Father, who usually wore his navy uniform during his short visits home, had put on a dark civilian suit for the occasion: we had been invited to his uncle's house for a big celebration. Everyone was excited because my mother's brother Hernan — a bachelor who could indulge himself with luxuries — had bought a home movie camera, which he would be trying out that night.

Even the home movie cannot fill in the sensory details such a gathering left imprinted in a child's brain. The thick sweetness of women's perfumes mixing with the ever-present smells of food cooking in the kitchen: meat and plantain *pasteles,* as well as the ubiquitous rice dish made special with pigeon peas — *gandules* — and seasoned with precious *sofrito* sent up from the Island by somebody's mother or smuggled in by a recent traveler. *Sofrito* was one of the items that women hoarded, since it was hardly ever in stock at La Bodega. It was the flavor of Puerto Rico.

The men drank Palo Viejo rum, and some of the younger ones got weepy. The first time I saw a grown man cry was at a New Year's Eve party: he had been reminded of his mother by the smells in the kitchen. But what I remember most were the boiled *pasteles,* plantain or yucca rectangles stuffed with corned beef or other meats, olives, and many other savory ingredients, all wrapped in banana leaves. Everybody had to fish one out with a fork. There was always a "trick" *pastel* — one without stuffing — and whoever got that one was the "New Year's Fool."

There was also the music. Long-playing albums were treated like precious china in these homes. Mexican recordings were popular, but the songs that brought tears to my mother's eyes were sung by the melancholy Daniel Santos, whose life as a drug addict was the stuff of legend. Felipe Rodríguez was a particular favorite of couples, since he sang about faithless women and brokenhearted men. There is a snatch of one lyric that has stuck in my mind like a needle on a worn groove: *De piedra ha de ser mi cama, de piedra la cabezera . . . la mujer que a mi me quiera . . . ha de quererme de veras. Ay, Ay, Ay, corazón, porque no amas . . .* I must have heard it a thousand times since the idea of a bed made of stone, and its connection to love, first troubled me with its disturbing images.

The five-minute home movie ends with people dancing in a circle — the creative filmmaker must have set it up, so that all of them could file past him. It is both comical and sad to watch silent dancing. Since there is no justification for the absurd movements that music provides for some of us, people appear frantic, their faces embarrassingly intense. It's as if you were watching sex. Yet for years, I've had dreams in the form of this home movie. In a recurring scene, familiar faces push themselves forward into my mind's eye, plastering their features into distorted close-ups. And I'm asking them: "Who is *she*? Who is the old woman I don't recognize? Is she an aunt? Somebody's wife? Tell me who she is."

"See the beauty mark on her cheek as big as a hill on the lunar landscape of her face — well, that runs in the family. The women on your father's side of the family wrinkle early; it's the price they pay for that fair skin. The young girl with the green stain on her wedding dress is *la novia* — just up from the Island. See, she lowers her eyes when she approaches the camera, as she's supposed to. Decent girls never look at you directly in the face. *Humilde*, humble, a girl should express humility in all her actions. She will make a good wife for your cousin. He should consider himself lucky to have met her only weeks after she arrived here. If he marries her quickly, she will make him a good Puerto Rican–style wife; but if he waits too long, she will be corrupted by the city, just like your cousin there."

"She means me. I do what I want. This is not some primitive island I live on. Do they expect me to wear a black mantilla on my head and go to mass every day? Not me. I'm an American woman, and I will do as I please. I can type faster than anyone in my senior class at Central High, and I'm going to be a secretary to a lawyer when I graduate. I can pass for an American girl anywhere — I've tried it. At least for Italian, anyway — I never speak Spanish in public. I hate these parties, but I wanted the dress. I look better than any of these *humildes* here. *My* life is going to be different. I have an American boyfriend. He is older and has a car. My parents don't know it, but I sneak out of the house late at night sometimes to be with him. If I marry him, even my name will be American. I hate rice and beans — that's what makes these women fat."

"Your *prima* is pregnant by that man she's been sneaking around with. Would I lie to you? I'm your *tiá política*, your great-uncle's common-law wife — the one he abandoned on the Island to go marry your cousin's mother. *I* was not invited to this party, of course, but I came anyway. I came to tell you that story about your cousin that you've always wanted to hear. Do you remember the comment your mother made to a neighbor that has always haunted you? The only thing you heard was your cousin's name, and then you saw your mother pick up your doll from the couch and say: 'It was as big as this doll when they flushed it down the toilet.' This image has bothered you for years, hasn't it? You had nightmares about babies being flushed down the toilet, and you wondered why anyone would do such a horrible thing. You didn't dare ask your mother about it. She would only tell you that you had not heard her right, and yell at you for listening to adult conversations. But later, when you were old enough to know about abortions, you suspected.

"I am here to tell you that you were right. Your cousin was growing an *americanito* in her belly when this movie was made. Soon after, she put something long and pointy into her pretty self, thinking maybe she could get rid of the problem before breakfast and still make it to her first class at the high school. Well, *niña*, her screams could be heard downtown. Your aunt, her *mamá*, who had been a midwife on the Island, managed to pull the little thing out. Yes, they probably flushed it down the toilet. What else could they do with it — give it a Christian burial in a little white casket with blue bows and ribbons? Nobody wanted that baby — least of all the father, a teacher at her school with a house in West Paterson that he was filling with real children, and a wife who was a natural blonde.

"Girl, the scandal sent your uncle back to the bottle. And guess where your cousin ended up? Irony of ironies. She was sent to a village in Puerto Rico to live with a relative on her mother's side: a place so far away from civilization that you have to ride a mule to reach it. A real change in scenery. She found a man there — women like that cannot live without male company — but believe me, the men in Puerto Rico know how to put a saddle on a woman like her. *La gringa,* they call her. Ha, ha, ha. *La gringa* is what she always wanted to be . . ."

The old woman's mouth becomes a cavernous black hole I fall into. And as I fall, I can feel the reverberations of her laughter. I hear the echoes of her last mocking words: *la gringa, la gringa!* And the conga line keeps moving silently past me. There is no music in my dream for the dancers.

When Odysseus visits Hades to see the spirit of his mother, he makes an offering of sacrificial blood, but since all the souls crave an audience with the living, he has to listen to many of them before he can ask questions. I, too, have to hear the dead and the forgotten speak in my dream. Those who are still part of my life remain silent, going around and around in their dance. The others keep pressing their faces forward to say things about the past.

My father's uncle is last in line. He is dying of alcoholism, shrunken and shriveled like a monkey, his face a mass of wrinkles and broken arteries. As he comes closer I realize that in his features I can see my whole family. If you were to stretch that rubbery flesh, you could find my father's face, and deep within *that* face — my own. I don't want to look into those eyes ringed in purple. In a few years he will retreat into silence, and take a long, long time to die. *Move back, Tío,* I tell him. *I don't want to hear what you have to say. Give the dancers room to move. Soon it will be midnight. Who is the New Year's Fool this time?*

FRANK CONROY

# *Running the Table*

FROM GQ

WHEN I was fifteen and living in New York City, I was supposed
to be going to Stuyvesant High School and in fact I did actually
show up three or four times a week, full of gloom, anger and
adolescent narcissism. The world was a dark place for me in those
days. I lived in a kind of tunnel of melancholy, constantly in trouble at home, in school and occasionally with the police. (Pitching
pennies, sneaking into movies, jumping the turnstile in the subway, stealing paperback books — fairly serious stuff in that earlier, more innocent time.) I was haunted by a sense of chaos, chaos
within and chaos without. Which is perhaps why the orderliness
of pool, the Euclidean cleanness of it, so appealed to me. The
formality of pool struck me as soothing and reassuring, a sort of
oasis of coolness, utterly rational and yet not without its elegant
little mysteries. But I'm getting ahead of myself.

One day, meandering around 14th Street, I stepped through
the open doors on an impulse and mounted the long, broad
stairway. Halfway up I heard the click of the balls. What a marvelous sound! Precise, sharp, crisp, and yet somehow mellow.
There was an intimacy to the sound that thrilled me. At the top
of the stairs I pushed through saloon-style swinging doors and
entered a vast, hushed, dim hall. Rows of pool tables stretched
away in every direction, almost all of them empty at this early
hour, but here and there in the distance, a pool of light, figures
in silhouette circling, bending, taking shots. Nearby, two old men
were playing a game I would later learn to be billiards on a large
table without pockets. The click of the three balls, two white, one

red, was what I had heard on the stairs. The men played unhurriedly, pausing now and then with their cues held like walking sticks to stare down at the street below. Cigar smoke swirled in the air.

I had walked into Julian's, little knowing that it was one of the most important pool halls on the East Coast. I was impressed by the stark functionality of the place — the absence of decoration of any kind. It seemed almost institutional in its atmosphere, right down to the large poster hung on the cashier's cage setting out the rules and regulations. No drinking, no eating, no sitting on the edges of the tables, no spitting except in the cuspidors, no massé shots, etc. Tables were twenty-five cents an hour. Cue sticks were to be found on racks against the walls. Balls available from the cashier as he clocked you in.

"How do you play?" I asked.

The cashier was bald and overweight. He wore, for some reason, a green eyeshade. "You from Stuyvesant?"

I nodded, and he grunted, reached down to some hidden shelf and gave me a small paper pamphlet, pushing it forward across the worn wooden counter. I scanned it quickly. Basic information about straight pool, eight ball, nine ball, billiards, snooker and a few other games. "Start with straight pool," he said. "Go over there and watch those guys on twenty-two for a while. Sit still, don't talk, and don't move around."

I did as I was told, sitting on a kind of mini-bleachers against the wall, my chin in my hands. The two men playing were in their twenties, an Abbott-and-Costello duo, thin Bud wearing a vest and smoking constantly, pudgy Lou moving delicately around the table, using the bridge now and then because of his short arms. They paid no attention to me and played with concentration, silent except for calling combinations.

"Six off the thirteen," Lou said.

Bud nodded. They only called combinations. All straight shots, no matter how difficult, were presumably obvious. After a while, with a few discreet glances at my pamphlet, I began to get the hang of it. All the balls, striped and solid, were fair game. You simply kept shooting until you missed, and then it was the other guy's turn. After each run, you moved some beads on a wire overhead with the tip of your cue, marking up the number of balls you'd sunk. So much for the rules. What was amazing was the shooting.

Object balls clipped so fine they moved sideways. Bank shots off the cushion into a pocket. Long combinations. Breakout shots in which a whole cluster of balls would explode in all directions while one from the middle would limp into a nearby pocket. And it didn't take long to realize that making a given shot was only part of what was going on. Controlling the position of the cue ball after the shot was equally important, so as to have a makable next shot. I could see that strategy was involved, although how they made the cue ball behave so differently in similar situations seemed nothing short of magical. Lou completed a run of nine or ten balls and reached fifty on the wire overhead. He had won, apparently.

"Double or nothing?"

Bud shook his head. Money changed hands. Lou put the balls in a tray, turned out the light over the table, and both men checked out at the cashier's. I sat for a while, thinking over what I had seen, reading the pamphlet again. I didn't have enough money to play that day, but I knew I was coming back.

Sometime in the late sixties, as an adult, I went to the Botanic Garden in Brooklyn to visit the recently completed Zen rock garden. It was a meticulous re-creation of a particular installation from a particular Japanese monastery. No one else was there. I sat on the bench gazing at the spiral patterns in the sand, looking at the black rocks set like volcanic islands in a white sea. Peace. Tranquility. As absurd as it may sound, I was reminded of my childhood experience of Julian's on a quiet afternoon — a sense of harmony, of an entirely disinterested material world entirely unaffected by one's perception of it.

For me, at fifteen, Julian's was a sort of retreat, a withdrawal from the world. I would shoot for hours at a time, racking up, breaking, shooting, racking up, breaking, shooting, in a solitary trance. Or I would surrender to the ritual of practice — setting up long shots over the length of the table again and again, trying to sink a shot with the same configuration ten times in a row, and then twenty, and then a more difficult configuration to a different pocket three times in a row, and then five, etc. I did not get

bored with the repetition. Every time a ball went in the pocket I
felt satisfaction. When I missed I simply ignored the fact, reset
the shot and tried again. This went on for several weeks at a remote table in a far corner of the hall — table nineteen — which
nobody else ever seemed to want. Once in a while I'd play with
another kid, usually also from Stuyvesant, and split the time. After
a couple of months I would sometimes play for the time — loser
pays — against opponents who looked even weaker than myself.
But most of the time I played alone.

Late one afternoon, racking up on table nineteen for perhaps
the tenth time, I noticed a man sitting in the gloom up against
the wall. He was extremely thin, with a narrow face and a protruding brow. He wore a double-breasted suit and two-tone shoes,
one leg dangling languidly over the other. He gave me an almost
imperceptible nod. I chalked the tip of my cue, went to the head
of the table and stroked a clean break. Aware that I was being
watched, I studied the lie of the balls for a moment and proceeded to sink seven in a row, everything going according to plan,
until I scratched. I pulled up the cue ball and the object ball, re-
created the shot and scratched again.

"Why don't you use English?" he asked quietly.

I stared at the table. "What's English?"

A moment's pause. "Set it up again," he said.

I did so.

"Aim, but don't hit. Pretend you're going to shoot."

I made a bridge with my left hand, aimed at the object ball and
held the tip of my stick right behind the center of the cue ball.

"All right. All lined up?"

"Yes," I said, almost flat on the table.

"Do not change the line. Are you aiming at the center of the
cue ball?"

"Yes."

"Aim a quarter of an inch higher."

"You mean I should . . ." For some reason what he was sug-
gesting seemed almost sacrilegious.

"Yes, yes. Don't hit the cue ball in the center. Strike a quarter
of an inch above. Now go ahead. Shoot."

I made my stroke, watched the object ball go in, and watched
the cue ball take a different path after impact than it had before.

It didn't scratch this time, but missed the pocket, bounced smartly off the cushion and rolled to a stop near the center of the table for an easy next shot.

"Hey. That's terrific!" I said.

"That's English." He unfolded his legs and stood up. He came over and took the pool cue from my hands. "If a person pays attention," he said, "a person can learn about ninety-five percent of what he needs to know in about ten minutes. Ten minutes for the principles, then who knows how many years for the practice." His dark, deep-set eyes gave his face a vaguely ominous cast. "You want to learn?"

"Absolutely," I said without hesitation. "Yes."

As it turned out, it took about half an hour. The man teaching me was called Smilin' Jack, after the comic-strip character and presumably because of his glum demeanor. He was a Julian's regular, and it was my good luck to have caught him when somebody had stood him up for what was to have been a money game. I could sense that he enjoyed going through the drill — articulate, methodical, explicating on cause and effect with quiet relish, moving the balls around the table with no wasted motion whatsoever, executing the demo shots with a stroke as smooth as powdered silk — it was an elegant dance, with commentary. A sort of offering to the gods of pool.

I cannot possibly recount here what I learned. Follow, draw, left and right English and how they affect the movement of the cue ball after impact. The object ball picking up opposite English from the cue ball. The effectiveness of different kinds of English as a function of distance (between cue ball and object ball) and of speed. *Sliding* the cue ball. Playing the diamond points. Shooting a ball frozen on the cushion. How to read combinations, and on and on. I paid very close attention and jotted down what notes I could. (*Over*shoot bank shots to the side pockets. *Under*shoot bank shots to the corner pockets.) At the end of the half hour my head ached. In addition to trying to grasp the principles, I'd been trying to film the whole thing, to superimpose an eidetic memory on the cells of my brain, so I could retrieve what I'd seen at will. I was exhausted.

He handed me the stick, shot his cuffs and adjusted the front of his jacket with a slight forward movement of his shoulders.

"That should keep you busy for a while." Then he simply walked away.

"Thanks," I called after him.

Without looking back, he raised his hand and gave a laconic little wave.

Practice, practice. Months of practice. It was a delicate business, English, affected by things like the relative roughness of the cue tip and its ability to hold chalk, or the condition of the felt, or infinitesimal degrees of table lean. But it worked. There was no doubt about it, when you got the feel of it you greatly increased your power over the all-important position of the cue ball. There was a word for it — the "leave," as in "good shot, but a tough leave." And of course the more you could control the leave, the more deeply involved was the strategy — planning out how to sink twelve balls in a row, rather than just five or six. Progress was slow, but it was tangible, and very, very satisfying. I began to beat people. I moved off table nineteen up toward the middle of the hall and began to beat almost everybody from Stuyvesant.

The most important hurdle for a straight-pool player involves being able to run into the second rack. You have to sink fourteen balls and leave the fifteenth ball and the cue ball positioned in such a way as to be able to sink the last ball (breaking open the new rack at the same time) and have a good enough leave to start all over again. I achieved this shortly before my sixteenth birthday, with a run of twenty-three.

The owners of Julian's recognized the accomplishment as a significant rite of passage and awarded certain privileges to those who had achieved it. During my last year of high school a cue of my own selection, with my name taped to the handle, was kept in a special rack behind the cashier's cage. No one else could use that particular cue stick. It was reserved, along with thirty or forty others for young players who had distinguished themselves.

I was a nonentity at school, but I could walk up to the cage at Julian's and the cashier would reach back for my stick and say, "Hey, Frank. How's it going?"

What a splendid place it was.

There's a lot to feel in pool, a physical aspect to the game, which means you have to play all the time to stay good. I've lost most of my chops (to borrow a word from jazz), but I still drop down to my local bar, the Foxhead, every now and then to play on the undersize table. It's a challenge arrangement. Put your name on the chalkboard, slip two quarters in the slot when it's your turn, and try to win.

There's a good deal more chance in eight ball, your basic bar game, than in straight pool, but it's fun. We've got some regulars. Jerry, a middle-aged man with a gorgeous stroke (a nationally ranked player in his youth), can beat anybody who walks into the place if he isn't furious at having to play doubles, at kids slopping beer onto the felt, or some other infraction of civilized behavior. There's Doug, a graduate student who always looks as if he'd spent the previous night in a cardboard box in an alley and who hits every shot as hard as he can, leaving the question of where the cue ball is going to end up more or less to the gods, in the hope that they will thus tangibly express the favor in which they hold him. (He is a poet.) We have George, an engineer, who exhausts our patience by approaching each situation with extreme care, circling the table several times, leaning over to stare down at a cluster of balls in what appears to be a hypnotic trance, chalking up with the care of Vermeer at the easel and running through a complicated series of various facial and physical tics before committing himself. There's Henry, who programs the jukebox to play "Brown Sugar" ten times in a row before he racks up. We've got students, working people, teachers, nurses (Yes. Women! Smilin' Jack would be scandalized) and barflies. We've got everybody at the Foxhead.

There are nights when I can hold the table for a couple of hours, but not very often. My touch is mostly gone, and bifocals make things difficult. Still, a bit of Julian's is still with me and, at the very least, I talk a good game.

GERALD EARLY

# Life with Daughters: Watching the Miss America Pageant

FROM THE KENYON REVIEW

The theater is an expression of our dream life — of our unconscious aspirations.
> — David Mamet, "A Tradition of the Theater as Art," *Writing in Restaurants*

Aunt Hester went out one night, — where or for what I do not
know, — and happened to be absent when my master desired her
presence.
> — Frederick Douglass, *Narrative of the Life of Frederick Douglass*

Adults, older girls, shops, magazines, newspapers, window
signs — all the world had agreed that a blue-eyed, yellow-haired,
pink-skinned doll was what every girl child treasured.
> — Toni Morrison, *The Bluest Eye*

IT IS NOW fast become a tradition — if one can use that word
to describe a habit about which I still feel a certain amount of
shamefacedness — for our household to watch the Miss America
contest on television every year. The source of my embarrass-
ment is that this program remains, despite its attempts in recent
years to modernize its frightfully antique quality of "women on
parade," a kind of maddeningly barbarous example of the persistent, hard, crass urge to sell: from the plugs for the sponsor
that are made a part of the script (that being an antique of fifties
and sixties television; the show does not remember its history so
much as it seems bent on repeating it) to the constant references

to the success of some of the previous contestants and the re-
minders that this is some sort of scholarship competition, the
program has all the cheap earnestness of a social uplift project
being played as a musical revue in Las Vegas. Paradoxically, it
wishes to convince the public that it is a common entertainment
while simultaneously wishing to convey that it is more than mere
entertainment. The Miss America pageant is the worst sort of
"Americanism," the soft smile of sex and the hard sell of toothpaste and hair dye ads wrapped in the dreamy ideological gauze
of "making it through one's own effort." In a perverse way, I like
the show; it is the only live television left other than sports, news
broadcasts, performing arts awards programs, and speeches by
the president. I miss live TV. It was the closest thing to theater
for the masses. And the Miss America contest is, as it has been
for some time, the most perfectly rendered theater in our culture, for it so perfectly captures what we yearn for: a low-class
ritual, a polished restatement of vulgarity, that wants to open the
door to high-class respectability by way of plain middle-class anxiety and ambition. Am I doing all right? the contestants seem to
ask in a kind of reassuring, if numbed, way. The contest brings
together all the American classes in a show-biz spectacle of class-
lessness and tastelessness.

My wife has been interested in the Miss America contest since
childhood, and so I ascribe her uninterrupted engagement with
America's cultural passage into fall (Miss America, like college
and pro football, signifies for us as a nation the end of summer;
the contest was invented, back in 1921, by Atlantic City merchants to prolong the summer season past Labor Day) as something mystically and uniquely female. She, as a black woman, had
a long-standing quarrel with the contest until Vanessa Williams
was chosen the first black Miss America in September 1983.
Somehow she felt vindicated by Williams for all those years as a
black girl in Dallas, watching white women win the crown and
thumb their noses at her, at her blackness, at her straightened
hair, her thick lips, her wide nose. She played with white Barbie
dolls as a little girl and had, I suppose, a "natural," or at least an
understandable and predictable, interest in seeing the National
White Barbie Doll chosen every year because for such a long time,
of course, the Miss America contest, with few exceptions, was a

totemic preoccupation with and representation of a particularly stilted form of patriarchal white supremacy. In short, it was a national white doll contest. And well we know that every black girl growing up in the fifties and early sixties had her peculiar love-hate affair with white dolls, with mythicized white femininity. I am reminded of this historical instance: everyone knows that in the Brown versus Topeka Board of Education case (the case that resulted in the Supreme Court decision to integrate public schools) part of the sociological evidence used by the plaintiffs to show the psychological damage suffered by blacks because of Jim Crow was an account by Kenneth Clarke of how, when offered a choice between a black doll and a white doll, little black girls invariably chose the white doll because they thought it "prettier."

On the front page of the January 6, 1962, *Pittsburgh Courier,* a black weekly, is a picture of a hospitalized black girl named Connie Smith holding a white doll sent to her by Attorney General Robert Kennedy. Something had occurred between 1954, when the Supreme Court made its decision, and 1962 which made it impossible for Kennedy to send the girl a black doll, and this impossibility was to signal, ironically, that the terms of segregation and the terms of racial integration, the very icon of them, were to be exactly the same. Kennedy could not send the girl a black doll, as it would have implied, in the age of integration, that he was, in effect, sending her a Jim Crow toy, a toy that would emphasize the girl's race. In the early sixties such a gesture would have been considered condescending. To give the black girl a white doll in the early sixties was to mainstream the black girl into the culture, to say that she was worthy of the same kind of doll that a white girl would have. But how can it be that conservatism and liberalism, segregation and integration, could produce, fantastically, the same results, the identical iconography: a black girl hugging a white doll because everyone thinks it is best for her to have it? How can it be that at one time the white doll is the sign of the black girl's rejection and inferiority and fewer than ten years later it is the sign of her acceptance and redemption? Those who are knowledgeable about certain aspects of the black mind or the collective black consciousness realize, of course, that the issues of segregation and integration, of conservatism and liberalism, of acceptance and rejection, of redemption and inferior-

ity, are all restatements of the same immovable and relentless
reality of the meaning of American blackness; that this is all a
matter of the harrowing and compelling intensity that is called,
quaintly, race pride. And in this context, the issue of white dolls,
this fetishization of young white feminine beauty, and the complexity of black girlhood becomes an unresolved theme stated in
a strident key. Blacks have preached for a long time about how
to heal their daughters of whiteness: in the November 1908 issue
of *The Colored American Magazine*, E. A. Johnson wrote an article
entitled, "Negro Dolls for Negro Babies," in which he said, "I am
convinced that one of the best ways to teach Negro children to
respect their own color would be to see to it that the children be
given colored dolls to play with. . . . To give a Negro child a white
doll means to create in it a prejudice against its own color, which
will cling to it through life." Lots of black people believed this
and, for all I know, probably still do, as race pride, or the lack
thereof, burns and crackles like a current through most African-
American public and private discourse. Besides, it is no easy matter to wish white dolls away.

A few years ago I was thumbing through an album of old family photographs and saw one of me and my oldest sister taken
when I was four and she was nine. It struck me, transfixed me
really, as it was a color photo and most of the old family pictures
taken when I was a boy were black-and-white because my mother
could not afford to have color pictures developed. We, my sister
and I, are sitting on an old stuffed blue chair and she is holding
a white doll in her hand, displaying it for the picture. I remember the occasion very well, as my sister was to be confirmed in our
small, all-black Episcopal church that day, and she was, naturally,
proud of the moment and wanted to share it with her favorite
toy. That, I remembered, was why these were color pictures. It
was a special day for the family, a day my mother wanted to celebrate by taking special pictures. My mother is a very dark woman
who has a great deal of race pride and often speaks about my
sisters' having black dolls. I was surprised, in looking at the picture recently, that they ever owned a white one, that indeed a
white one had been a favorite.

My wife grew up — enjoyed the primary years of black girlhood, so to speak — during the years 1954 through 1962; she

was about five or six years younger than my oldest sister. She lived
in a southern state, or a state that was a reasonable facsimile of a
southern state. She remembers that signs for colored and white
bathrooms and water fountains persisted well into the mid-sixties in Texas. She remembers also Phyllis George, the Miss America
from Denton, Texas, who went on to become a television personality for several years. She has always been very interested in
George's career, and she has always disliked her. "She sounds just
like a white girl from Texas," my wife likes to say, always reminding me that while both blacks and whites in Texas have accents,
they do not sound alike. George won the contest in 1971, my wife's
freshman year at the University of Pennsylvania and around the
time she began to wear an Afro, a popular hairstyle for young
black women in the days of "our terrible blackness" or "our black
terribleness." It was a year fraught with complex passages into
black womanhood for her. To think that a white woman from
Texas should win the Miss America title that year! For my wife,
the years of watching the Miss America contest were nothing more,
in some sense continue to be nothing more, than an expression
of anger made all the worse by the very unconscious or semicon-
scious nature of it. But if the anger has been persistent, so has
her enormous capacity to "take it"; for in all these years it has
never occurred to her to refuse to watch because, like the black
girl being offered the white doll, like all black folk being offered
white gifts, she has absolutely no idea how that is done, and she
is not naïve enough to think that a simple refusal would be an act
of empowerment. Empowerment comes only through making
demands of our bogeymen, not by trying to convince ourselves
we are not tormented. Yet, paradoxically, among blacks there is
the bitter hope that a simplistic race pride will save us, a creed
that masks its complex contradictions beneath lapping waves of
bourgeois optimism and bourgeois anguish; for race pride clings
to the opposing notions that the great hope (but secret fear) of
an African-American future is, first, that blacks will always remain black and, second, that the great fear (but secret hope) of
an African-American future is that blacks will not always remain
black but evolve into something else. Race pride, which at its most
insistent argues that blackness is everything, becomes, in its attempt to be the psychological quest for sanity, a form of demen-

tia that exists as a response to that form of white dementia that
says blackness is nothing. Existing as it does as a reactive force
battling against a white preemptive presumption, race pride begins to take on the vices of an unthinking dogma and the virtues
of a disciplined religious faith, all in the same instance. With so
much at stake, race pride becomes both the act of making a virtue of a necessity and making a necessity of a virtue and, finally,
making a profound and touching absurdity of both virtue and
necessity. In some ways my wife learned her lessons well in her
youth: she never buys our daughters white dolls.

My daughters, Linnet, age ten, and Rosalind, age seven, have
become staunch fans of beauty contests in the last three years. In
that time they have watched, in their entirety, several Miss America pageants, one Miss Black America contest, and one Miss USA.
At first, I ascribed this to the same impulse that made my wife
interested in such events when she was little: something secretly
female, just as an interest in professional sports might be ascribed to something peculiarly male. Probably it is a sort of resentment that black girls harbor toward these contests. But that
could not really be the case with my daughters. After all, they
have seen several black entrants in these contests and have even
seen black winners. They also have black dolls.

Back in the fall of 1983 when Vanessa Williams became Miss
America, we, as a family, had our picture taken with her when
she visited St. Louis. We went, my wife and I, to celebrate the
grand moment when white American popular culture decided to
embrace black women as something other than sexual subver-
sives or fat, kindly maids cleaning up and caring for white families. We had our own, well, royalty, and royal origins mean a great
deal to people who have been denied their myths and their right
to human blood. White women reformers may be ready to scrap
the Miss America contest. (And the contest has certainly re-
sponded to the criticism it has been subjected to in recent years
by muting some of the fleshier aspects of the program while, in
its attempts to be even more the anxiety-ridden middle-class
dream-wish, emphasizing more and more the magic of education and scholarly attainments.) It is now the contest that signifies
the quest for professionalism among bourgeois women, and the
first achievement of the professional career is to win something

in a competition. But if there is a movement afoot to bring down
the curtain finally on Miss America, my wife wants no part of it:
"Whites always want to reform and end things when black people start getting on the gravy train they've been enjoying for years.
What harm does the Miss America contest do?" None, I suppose,
especially since black women have been winning lately.

Linnet and Rosalind were too young when we met Vanessa
Williams to recall anything about the pictures, but they are amazed
to see themselves in a bright, color Polaroid picture with a famous person, being part of an event which does not strike a chord
in their consciousness because they cannot remember being alive
when it happened. I often wonder if they attach any significance
to the pictures at all. They think Vanessa is very pretty, prettier
than their mother, but they attach no significance to being pretty —
that is to say, no real value; they would not admire someone simply because he or she was good-looking. They think Williams is
beautiful, but they do not wish that she was their mother. And
this issue of being beautiful is not to be taken lightly in the life of
a black girl. About two years ago Linnet started coming home
from school wishing aloud that her hair was long and blond so
that she could fling it about, the way she saw many of her white
classmates doing. As she attends a school that is more than 90
percent white, it seemed inevitable to my wife that one of our
daughters would become sensitive about her appearance. At this
time Linnet's hair was not straightened and she wore it in braids.
Oddly, despite the fact that she wanted a different hairstyle that
would permit her hair to "blow in the wind," so to speak, she ve-
hemently opposed having it straightened, although my wife has
straightened hair, after having worn an Afro for several years. I
am not sure why Linnet did not want her hair straightened; perhaps, after seeing her teenage cousin have her hair straightened
on several occasions, the process of hair straightening seemed
distasteful or disheartening or frightening. Actually, I do not think
Linnet wanted to change her hair to be beautiful; she wanted to
be like everyone else. But perhaps this is simply wishful thinking
here or playing with words because Linnet must have felt her
difference as being a kind of ugliness. Yet she is not a girl who is
subject to illusion. Once, about a year earlier, when she had had
a particularly rough day in school, I told her, in a father's patron-

izing way with a daughter, that I thought she was the most beautiful girl in the world. She looked at me strangely when I said that and then replied matter-of-factly: "I don't think I'm beautiful at all. I think I'm just ordinary. There is nothing wrong with that, is there, Daddy? Just to be ordinary?" "Are you unhappy to be ordinary?" I asked. She thought for a moment, then said quietly and finally, "No. Are you?"

Hair straightening, therefore, was not an option and would not have been even if Linnet had wanted it, because my wife was opposed to having Linnet's hair straightened at her age. At first, Linnet began going to school with her hair unbraided. Unfortunately, this turned out to be a disastrous hairdo, as her hair shrank during the course of a day to a tangled mess. Finally, my wife decided to have both Linnet and Rosalind get short Afro haircuts. Ostensibly, this was to ease the problem of taking swim lessons during the summer. In reality, it was to end Linnet's wishes for a white hairstyle by, in effect, foreclosing any possibility that she could remotely capture such a look. Rosalind's hair was cut so that Linnet would not feel that she was being singled out. (Alas, the trials of being both the second and the younger child!) At first, the haircuts caused many problems in school. Some of the children — both black and white — made fun of them. Brillo heads, they were called, and fungus and Afro heads. One group of black girls at school refused to play with Linnet. "You look so ugly with that short hair," they would say. "Why don't you wear your hair straight like your mom. Your mom's hair is so pretty." Then, for the first time, the girls were called niggers by a white child on their school bus, although I think neither the child nor my daughters completely understood the gravity of that obscenity. People in supermarkets would refer to them as boys unless they were wearing dresses. Both girls went through a period when they suffered most acutely from that particularly American disease, that particularly African-American disease, the conjunction of oppression and exhibitionistic desire: self-consciousness. They thought about their hair all the time. My wife called the parents of the children who teased them. The teasing stopped for the most part, although a few of the black girls remained so persistent that the white school counselor suggested that Linnet's and Rosalind's hair be straightened. "I'm white," he said, "and maybe I shouldn't get into this, but they might feel more comfortable if they wore a different hairstyle." My wife angrily rejected that bit of advice. She had them wear dresses more often to make them look unmistakably like girls, although she refused out of hand my suggestion of having their ears pierced. She is convinced that pierced ears are just a form of mutilation, primitive tattooing or scarring passing itself off as something fashionable. Eventually, the girls became used to their hair. Now, after more than a year, they hardly think about it, and even if Linnet wears a sweat suit or jeans, no one thinks she is a boy because she is budding breasts. Poor Rosalind still suffers on occasion in supermarkets because she shows no outward signs of sexual maturity. Once, while watching Linnet look at her mother's very long and silken straight hair, the hair that the other black girls at school admire, always calling it pretty, I asked her if she would like to have hers straightened.

"Not now," she said. "Maybe when I'm older. It'll be something different."

"Do you think you will like it?" I asked.

"Maybe," she said.

And in that "maybe," so calmly and evenly uttered, rests the complex contradictions, the uneasy tentative negotiations of that which cannot be compromised yet can never be realized in this flawed world as an ideal; there is, in that "maybe," the epistemology of race pride for black American women so paradoxically symbolized by their straightened hair. In the February 1939 issue of *The Atlantic Monthly,* a black woman named Kimbal Goffman (possibly a pseudonym) wrote an essay entitled "Black Pride" in which she accused blacks of being ashamed of their heritage and, even more damningly in some of her barbs obviously aimed at black women, of their looks:

> ... why are so many manufacturers becoming rich through the manufacture of bleaching preparations? Why are hair-straightening combs found in nearly every Negro home? Why is the following remark made so often to a newborn baby, when grandma or auntie visits it for the first time? "Tell Mother she must pinch your nose every morning. If she doesn't, you're gonna have a sure 'nough darky nose."

According to Goffman, blacks do not exploit what society has given them; they are simply ashamed to have what they have, tainted as it is with being associated with a degraded people, and long to be white or to have possessions that would accrue a kind of white status. In the essay, blacks in general receive their share of criticism but only black women are criticized in a gender-specific way that their neurotic sense of inferiority concerning physical appearance is a particularly dangerous form of reactionism as it stigmatizes each new generation. According to Goffman, it is black women, because they are mothers, who perpetuate their sense of inferiority by passing it on to their children. In this largely Du Boisian argument, Goffman advises, "Originality is the backbone of all progress." And, in this sense, originality means understanding blackness as something uncontrolled or uninfluenced by what whites say it is. This is the idealism of race pride that demands both purity and parity. Exactly one year later, in the February 1940 issue of *The Brown American,* a black magazine published in Philadelphia, Lillian Franklin McCall wrote an article about the history of black women beauty shop owners and entrepreneurs entitled "Appointment at Seven." The opening paragraph is filled with dollar signs:

> The business of straightening milady's insistent curls tinkles cash registers in the country to the tune of two million and a half dollars a year. And that covers merely the semi-monthly session with the hairdresser for the estimated four million of Eve's sepia adult daughters by national census. Today there is a growing trend to top off the regular, "Shampoo and wave," with a facial; and, perhaps, a manicure. New oil treatments and rinses prove a lure, too, so milady finds her beauty budget stepped up from approximately $39 yearly for an average $1.25 or $1.50 "hair-do," to $52.00 per year if she adds a facial to the beauty rite, and $10 more, for the manicure.

In a Booker T. Washington tone, McCall goes on to describe how the establishment of a black beauty culture serves as a source of empowerment for black women:

> Brown business it is, in all its magnitude for Miss Brown America receives her treatments from the hands of Negro beauticians and her hair preparations and skin dreams come, usually from Negro laboratories.

She then tells the reader that leading companies in this field were founded by black women: Madam C. J. Walker, Mrs. Annie Turbo

Malone, Madame Sara Spencer Washington. And one is struck by the absences that this essay evokes, not only in comparison to Goffman's piece but also to Elsie Johnson McDougald's major manifesto on black women, "The Task of Negro Womanhood," that appeared in Alain Locke's seminal 1925 anthology of African-American thought, *The New Negro*. In McDougald's piece, which outlines all the economic status and achievements of black women at the time, there is absolutely no mention of black beauty culture, no mention of Madame C. J. Walker, although her newspaper ads were among the biggest in black newspapers nationwide during the twenties. (And why did McDougald not mention black women's beauty workers and businesspeople culture along with the nurses, domestics, clerks, and teachers she discusses at length? It can scarcely be because she, as a trained and experienced writer on black sociological matters, did not think of it.) It is not simply money or black woman's industry or endeavor that makes the black woman present or a presence; it is beauty culture generally which finally brings her into being, and specifically, her presence is generated by her hair. What for one black woman writer, Goffman, is an absence and thus a sign of degradation, is for another a presence and a sign of economic possibilities inherent in feminine aesthetics.

What did I see as a boy when I passed the large black beauty shop on Broad and South streets in Philadelphia where the name of its owner, Adele Reese, commanded such respect or provoked such jealousy? What did I see there but a long row of black women dressed immaculately in white tunics, washing and styling the hair of other black women. That was a sign of what culture, of what set of politics? The sheen of those straightened heads, the entire enterprise of the making of black feminine beauty: was it an enactment of a degradation inspirited by a bitter inferiority or was it a womanly laying on of hands where black women were, in their way, helping themselves to live through and transcend their degradation? As a boy, I used to watch and wonder as my mother straightened my sisters' hair every Saturday night for church on Sunday morning. Under a low flame on the stove, the hot comb would glow dully; from an open jar of Apex bergamot hair oil or Dixie Peach, my mother would extract blobs and place them on the back of one hand, deftly applying the oil to strands of my sisters' hair with the other. And the strange talk about a "light press" or a "heavy press" or a "close press" to get the edges and the ends; the concern about the hair "going back" if caught in the rain. Going back where, I wondered. To Africa? To the bush? And the constant worry and vigil about burning, getting too close to the scalp. I can remember hearing my sisters' hair sizzle and crackle as the comb passed through with a kind of pungent smell of actually burning hair. And I, like an intentional moth, with lonely narrow arcs, hovered near this flame of femininity with a fascinated impertinence. Had I witnessed the debilitating nullity of absence or was it the affirmation of an inescapable presence? Had I witnessed a mutilation or a rite of devotion? Black women's hair is, I decided even as a boy, unintelligible. And now I wonder, is the acceptance of the reigns of black women as Miss America a sign that black beauty has become part of the mainstream culture? Is the black woman now truly a presence?

We, I and my wife and our daughters, sat together and watched the latest Miss America contest. We did what we usually do. We ate popcorn. We laughed at all the talent numbers, particularly the ones when the contestants were opera singers or dancers. We laughed when the girls tried to answer grand social questions — such as "How can we inspire children to achieve and stay in school?" or "How can we address the problem of mainstreaming physically disadvantaged people?" — in thirty seconds. In fact, as Rosalind told me after the show, the main reason my daughters watch the Miss America pageant is that "it's funny." My daughters laugh because they cannot understand why the women are doing what they are doing, why they are trying so hard to please, to be pleasing. This must certainly be a refreshing bit of sanity, as the only proper response for such a contest is simply to dismiss it as hilarious; this grandiose version of an elocution, charm school, dance and music recital, which is not a revelation of talent but a reaffirmation of bourgeois cultural conditioning. And this bit of sanity on my daughters' part may prove hopeful for our future, for our American future, for our African-American future, if black girls are, unlike my wife when she was young, no longer angry. When it was announced that Miss Missouri, Debbye Turner, the third black to be Miss America, was the winner, my children were indifferent. It hardly mattered to them who

won, and a black woman's victory meant no more than if any other
contestant had prevailed. "She's pretty," Linnet said. She won two
dollars in a bet with my wife, who did not think it possible that
another black Miss America would be chosen. "Vanessa screwed
up for the whole race," she told me once. "It's the race burden,
the sins of the one become the original sins of us all." Linnet said
simply, "She'll win because she is the best." Meritocracy is still a
valid concept with the young.

For me, it was almost to be expected that Miss Turner would
win. First, she received more precontest publicity than any other
contestant in recent years, with the possible exception of the black
woman who was chosen Miss Mississippi a few years ago. Second,
after the reign of Vanessa Williams, one would think that the Miss
America powers that be very much wanted to have another black
win and have a successful reign so that the contest itself could
both prove its good faith (to blacks) and forestall criticism from
white feminists and liberals (who are always put in a difficult position when the object of their disapproval is a black woman). As
with the selection of Williams, the contest gained a veneer of
postmodernist social and political relevance not only by selecting
a black again but by having an Asian, a kidney donor, and a hear-
ing-impaired woman among the top ten finalists. This all smacks
of affirmative action or the let's-play-fair-with-the-underrepre-
sented doctrine, which, as Miss Virginia pointed out after the
contest, smacks of politics. But the point she missed, of course, is
the point that all people who oppose affirmative action miss. The
selection process for the Miss America contest has always been
political. Back in the days when only white college women, whose
main interest in most instances was a degree in MRS, could win,
the contest was indeed just as political as it is now, a clear ideological bow to both patriarchal ideals and racism. It is simply a matter of which politics you prefer, and while no politics are perfect,
some are clearly better than others. But in America, it must be
added, the doctrine of fair play should not even be graced with
such a sophisticated term as "political." It is more our small-town,
bourgeois Christian, muscular myth of ethical rectitude, the tremendous need Americans feel to be decent. So Miss Turner is
intended to be both the supersession of Vanessa Williams — a
religious vet student whose ambitions are properly, well, post-

modernist Victorianism, preach do-goodism, evoke the name of God whenever you speak of your ambitions, and live with smug humility — and the redemption of the image of black women in American popular culture, since the Miss America contest is one of the few vehicles of display and competition for women in popular culture.

And if my daughters have come to one profound penetration of this cultural rite, it is that the contest ought to be laughed at in some ways, as most of the manifestations of popular culture ought to be for being the shoddy illusions that they are. For one always ought to laugh at someone or a group of someones who are trying to convince you that nothing is something — and that is not really the same as someone trying to convince you that you can have something for nothing, because in the popular culture business, the price for nothing is the same as the price for something; this "nothing is something" is, in fact, in most cases what the merchandising of popular culture is all about. (But as Mother reminded me as a boy: nothing is nothing and something is something. Accept no substitutes!) For my children, the contest can be laughed at because it is so completely meaningless to them; they know it is an illusion despite its veneer as a competition. And it is that magical word, competition, which is used over and over again all night long by the host and hostesses of the Miss America show (a contest, like most others these days, from the SATs to professional sports, that is made up of a series of competitions within the framework of larger competitions in such a pyramid that the entire structure of the outside world, for the bourgeois mind, is a frightful maze, a strangulating skein of competitions), that is the touchstone of reality, the momentous signifier that the sponsors of the pageant hope will give this extravaganza new significance and new life. For everything that we feel is important now is a matter of competition, beating out someone else for a prize, for some cheap prestige, a moment of notice before descending to cipherhood again; competition ranging from high culture (literary prizes, which seem to be awarded every day in the week, and classical music competitions for every instrument in a symphony orchestra, because of course for high culture one can never have enough art) to mid-culture (the entire phenomenon of American education, from academic honors to entrance require-

ments for prestigious schools, because of course for the middle
class one can never have enough education or enough professionalism) to low culture (playing the lottery and various forms
of gambling, because of course for the lower class one can never
hope enough for money). And the more stringent and compul-
sively expressed the competition is (and the Miss America contest
has reached a new height of hysteria in both the stridency and
compulsion of the competition), the more legitimate and note-
worthy it is.

Everyone in our culture wants to win a prize. Perhaps that is
the grand lesson we have taken with us from kindergarten in the
age of the perversions of Dewey-style education: everyone gets a
ribbon, and praise becomes a meaningless narcotic to soothe
egoistic distemper. And in our bourgeois coming-of-age, we simply crave more and more ribbons and praise, the attainment of
which becomes all the more delightful and satisfying if they are
gotten at someone else's expense. Competition, therefore, becomes in the end a kind of laissez-faire psychotherapy that structures and orders our impossible rages of ambition, our rages to
be noticed. But competition does not produce better people (a
myth we have swallowed whole); it does not even produce better
candidates; it simply produces more desperately grasping com-
petitors. The "quality" of the average Miss America contestant is
not significantly better now than it was twenty-five years ago, although the desires of today's contestants may meet with our ap-
proval (who could possibly disapprove of a black woman who
wishes to be a vet in this day of careerism as the expression of
independence and political empowerment), but then the women
of twenty-five years ago wanted what their audiences approved
of as well. That is not necessarily an advance or progress; that is
simply a recognition that we are all bound by the mood and tem-
per of our time. So, in this vast competition, this fierce theatrical
warfare where all the women are supposed to love their neighbor while they wish to beat her brains out, this warfare so pointedly exposed before the nation, what we have chosen is not the
Royal American Daughter (although the contest's preoccupation
with the terminology of aristocracy mirrors the public's need for
such a person as the American princess) but rather the Cosmopolitan Girl. As the magazine ad states:

Can a girl be too Busy? I'm taking seventeen units at Princeton, pushing on with my career during vacations and school breaks, study singing and dancing when I can, try never to lose track of my five closest
chums, steal the time for Michael Jackson and Thomas Hardy, work
for an anti-drug program for kids and, oh yes, I hang out with three
horses, three cats, two birds and my dog Jack. My favorite magazine
says "too busy" just means you don't want to miss anything . . . I love
that magazine. I guess you can say I'm That Cosmopolitan Girl.

When one reads about these women in the Miss America contest,
that is precisely what they sound like: the Cosmopolitan Girl who
knows how to have serious fun, and she has virtually nothing with
which to claim our attention except a moralistic bourgeois dili-
gence. To use a twenties term: she sounds "swell." She is an amal-
gam of both lead characters portrayed by Patty Duke on her old
TV show: the studious, serious kid and the "typical" wacky but
good-hearted suburban teenager, or, to borrow Ann Douglas's
concept, she is the Teen Angel: the bourgeois girl who can do
everything, is completely self-absorbed with her leisure, and has
a heart of gold. Once again, with the Miss America contest we
have America's vehement preoccupation with innocence, with its
inability to deal with the darkness of youth, the darkness of its
own uselessly expressed ambition, the dark complexity of its own
simplistic morality of sunshine and success, the darkness, righteous rage, and bitter depth of its own daughters. Once again,
when the new Miss America, victorious and smiling, walks down
the runway, we know that runway, that victory march, to be the
American catwalk of supreme bourgeois self-consciousness and
supreme illusion. We are still being told that nothing is something.

    Nonetheless, the fact that Miss Turner won struck both my wife
and me as important, as something important for the race. We
laughed during the contest, but we did not laugh when she was
chosen. We wanted her to win very much; it is impossible to escape that need to see the race uplifted, to thumb your nose at
whites in a competition. It is impossible for blacks not to want to
see their black daughters elevated to the platforms where white
women are. Perhaps this tainted desire, an echoing "Ballad of
the Brown Girl" that resounds in the unconscious psyche of all
black people, is the unity of feeling which is the only race pride

blacks have ever had since they became Americans; for race pride for the African American, finally, is something that can only be understood as existing on the edge of tragedy and history and is, finally, that which binds both together to make the African American the darkly and richly complicated person he or she is. In the end, both black women magazine writers quoted earlier were right: race pride is transcending your degradation while learning to live in it and with it. To paraphrase an idea of Dorothy Sayers, race pride must teach blacks that they are not to be saved *from* degradation but saved *in* it.

A few days after the contest I watched both my daughters playing Barbies, as they call it. They squat on the floor on their knees, moving their dolls around through an imaginary town and in imaginary houses. I decided to join them and squatted down too, asking them the rules of their game, which they patiently explained as though they did not mind having me, the strange adult, invade their children's world. I told them it was hard for me to squat and asked if I could simply sit down, but they said that one always plays Barbies while squatting. It was a rule that had to be obeyed. As they went along, explaining relationships among their myriad dolls and the several landscapes, as complicated a genealogy as anything Faulkner ever dreamed up, a theater as vast as the entire girlhood of the world, they told me that one particular black Ken doll and one particular black Barbie doll were married and that the dolls had a child. Then Rosalind held up a white doll that someone, probably a grandparent, had given them (my wife is fairly strict on the point of our daughters' not having white dolls, but I guess a few have slipped through), explaining that this doll was the daughter of the black Ken and Barbie.

"But," I said, "how could two black dolls have a white daughter?"

"Oh," said Rosalind, looking at me as if I were an object deserving of only her indulgent pity, "we're not racial. That's old-fashioned. Don't you think so, Daddy? Aren't you tired of all that racial stuff?"

Bowing to that wisdom which, it is said, is the only kind that will lead us to Christ and to ourselves, I decided to get up and leave them to their play. My knees had begun to hurt and I real-

ized, painfully, that I was much too old, much too at peace with
stiffness and inflexibility, for children's games.

### N O T E S

1. Richard Wright tells a story in his 1956 account of the Bandung conference,
   entitled *The Color Curtain,* that emphasizes the absence of the black woman.
   He relates how a white woman journalist knocks on his hotel room door during the course of the conference and confides the strange behavior of her
   roommate — a black woman journalist from Boston. Her roommate walks
   around in the middle of the night and the white woman often covertly spies
   her in "a dark corner of the room . . . bent over a tiny blue light, a very low
   and a very blue flame. . . . It seemed like she was combing her hair, but I wasn't
   sure. Her right arm was moving and now and then she would look over her
   shoulder toward my bed." The white woman thinks that the black woman is
   practicing voodoo. But Wright soon explains that the black woman is simply
   straightening her hair.

   "But why would she straighten her hair? Her hair seems all right" [the
   white woman journalist asks].
   "Her hair is all right. But it's not straight. It's kinky. But she does not
   want you, a white woman, to see her when she straightens her hair. She
   would feel embarrassed —"
   "Why?"
   "Because you were born with straight hair, and she wants to look as much
   like you as possible. . . ."
   The woman stared at me, then clapped her hands to her eyes and ex-
   claimed:
   "Oh!"
   I leaned back and thought: here in Asia, where everybody was dark, the
   poor American Negro woman was worried about the hair she was born with.
   Here, where practically nobody was white, her hair would have been acceptable; no one would have found her "inferior" because her hair was kinky;
   on the contrary, the Indonesians would perhaps have found her different
   and charming.

   The conversation continues with an account of the black woman's secretive
   skin lightening treatments. What is revealing in this dialogue which takes on
   both political and psychoanalytic proportions is the utter absence of the black
   woman's voice, her presence. She is simply the dark, neurotic ghost that flits
   in the other room while the black male and the white female, both in the same
   room, one with dispassionate curtness and the other with sentimentalized guilt,
   consider the illness that is enacted before them as a kind of bad theater. Once
   again, the psychopathology of the black American is symbolized by the black
   woman's straightened hair, by her beauty culture.

2. Jacques Barzun, "Culture High and Dry," *The Culture We Deserve* (Middle-
   town, Conn., Wesleyan University Press, 1989).

GRETEL EHRLICH

## *This Autumn Morning*

FROM ANTAEUS

WHEN DID all this happen, this rain and snow bending green branches, this turning of light to shadow in my throat, these bird-notes going flat, and how did these sawtooth willow leaves unscrew themselves from the twig, and the hard, bright paths trampled into the hills loosen themselves to mud? When did the wind begin churning inside trees, and why did the sixty-million-year-old mountains start looking like two uplifted hands holding and releasing the gargled, whistling, echoing grunts of bull elk, and when did the loose fires inside me begin *not* to burn?

Wasn't it only last week, in August, that I saw the stained glass of a monarch butterfly clasping a purple thistle flower, then rising as if a whole cathedral had taken flight?

Now what looks like smoke is only mare's tails — clouds streaming — and as the season changes, my young dog and I wonder if raindrops might not be shattered lightning.

It's September. At this time of year light is on the wane. There is no fresh green breast of earth to embrace. None of that. Just to breathe is a kind of violence against death. To long for love, to have experienced passion's deep pleasure, even once, is to understand the mercilessness of having a human body whose memory rides desire's back unanchored from season to season.

Last night while driving to town I hit a deer. She jumped into my path from behind bushes so close I could not stop. A piece of red flesh flew up and hit the windshield. I watched as she ran off limping. There was nothing I could do. Much later, on the way home, I looked for her again. I could see where a deer had bed-

ded down beside a tree, but there was no sign of a wounded animal, so I continued on.

Halfway up our mountain road a falling star burned a red line
across the sky — a meteorite, a pristine piece of galactic debris
that came into existence billions of years before our solar system
was made. The tail stretched out gold and slid. I stopped the truck,
then realized I was at the exact place where, years ago, I declared
love to a friend as a meteor shower burst over us. At dawn, a
belted kingfisher peered down into water as if reading a message
to us about how to live, about what would suffice.

Tonight on the same road in a different year I see only the
zigzagging of foxes whose red tails are long floats that give their
small bodies buoyancy. No friends meet me to view the stars. The
nights have turned cold. The crickets' summer mating songs have
hardened into drumbeats and dark rays of light pole out from
under clouds as if steadying the flapping tent of the sky.

Even when the air is still I keep hearing a breeze, the way it
shinnies up the bones of things, up the bark of trees. A hard frost
pales the hayfields. Tucked into the flickering universe of a cottonwood tree, yellow leaves shaped like gloved hands reach across
the green umbrella for autumn.

It's said that after fruition nothing will suffice, there is no more,
but who can know the answer? I've decided to begin at the end,
where the earth is black and barren. I want to see how death is
mixed in, how the final plurals are taken back to single things —
if they are; how and where life stirs out of ash.

On May 5, the first day the roads opened, my husband and I
drove to Yellowstone Park. Twenty miles before the east entrance, we were greeted by buffalo: four mother cows, one yearling, and a newly born calf. At Sylvan Pass a young couple were
skiing down a precipitous snow-covered landslide, then trudging
up the nearly vertical slope carrying their skis. Just before we
reached Yellowstone Lake, a pair of blue grouse, in the midst of
a courting display, could not be moved from the center of the
road. Neck and tail feathers plumed and fanned out; we waited.
The lake was all ice. Far out, a logjam — upended, splintered,
frozen in place — was the eye's only resting place in all that white.

Around the next bend I came on a primordial scene: north of

Mary's Bay, wide, ice-covered meadows were full of dead buffalo, and searching for grass in among the carcasses were the barely
live bison who had survived a rigorous winter, so thin they looked
like cardboard cutouts, a deep hollow between their withers and
ribs.

We drove on. More dead bison, and dead elk. The park biologists were saying that roughly 28 percent of both herds wintered-
killed this year, not only because the fires diminished some of
their forage but also because the drought had brought us five
years of mild winters, thus allowing the old and sick animals to
survive.

Between Madison Junction and the Firehold River we stood in
the charred ruins of a lodgepole pine forest. The hollow trunks
of burned-out trees looked as if they had been picked up and
dropped, coming to rest at every possible angle. The ground was
black. Where the fire had burned underground, smoldering root
systems upended trees; where there had once been a pond or a
bog with ducks and swans was now a waterless depression. Way
back in the trees, a geyser hissed, its plume of white steam a ghost
of last year's hundred-mile-long streamer of smoke.

Later we returned to the lake and sat on the end of a long spit
of land that angles out into water. From there it's difficult to tell
there was a fire. Lodgepole pines fringe the shore. A cloud that
had moved off Mount Sheridan to the south rolled toward us, its
front edge buffeted by a north wind. In ancient Greece it's said
that Boreas, god of the north wind, became jealous of his lover,
Pitys, who had been flirting with Pan, and threw her against a
rocky ledge. In that moment she turned into a pine tree. The
amber drops of sap at the breaks of limbs are her tears.

Boreas shattered the cloud above me and blew it over the lake,
and the trees at the edge took on wild shapes. The Buriats in
eastern Siberia considered groves of pines sacred and always rode
through them in silence. A trumpeter swan glided by, then a tribe
of golden-eye ducks headed for a sheltered inlet.

Pines are such ancient trees, first appearing 170 million years
ago. But what does Boreas care? He cut through the cloud and
sent a bulbous chunk toward me until it broke off that fragile tail
of land as if it had been a tree.

*

That was May, and now it's September and already frost is breaking down the green in leaves, then clotting like blood as tannin, anthocyanin, carotene, and xanthophyll. If pines represent continuance, then cottonwood leaves show me how the illusion of time punctuates space, how we fill those dusty, gaseous voids with escapades of life and death, dropping the tiny spans of human days into them.

This morning I found a yearling heifer, bred by a fence-jumping bull out of season, trying to calve. I saw her high up on a sage-covered slope, lying down, flicking her tail, and thought she must have colic. But I was wrong. The calf's front feet and head had already pushed out, who knows how many hours before, and it was dead.

I walked her down the mountain to the calving shed, where a friend, Ben, and I winched the dead calf out. We doctored the heifer for uterine infections, and I made a bed of straw, brought fresh creek water and hay. The heifer ate and rested. By evening she had revived, but by the next morning she seemed to have contracted pneumonia. Immediately I gave her a huge shot of penicillin. She worsened. The antibiotics didn't kick in.

That night she lay on her straw bed emitting grunts and high-pitched squeals. The vet came at midnight. We considered every possibility — infection, pneumonia, poisoning — what else could it be? Another day and her condition worsened. Not any one symptom, but a steady decline. I emptied more medicine into her, knowing it was doing no good, but my conscience forbade me to do less. The vet came again and left. He suggested it might be "hardware disease," a euphemism for an ingested piece of metal, a nail or barbed wire, cutting into her throat or stomach or heart. I put a magnet down her throat. Strange as it seems, it sometimes picks up the metal, taking it all the way through the digestive tract. No response. I sat with her. I played music, Merle Haggard and Mozart, wondering if my presence consoled or irritated her. This was not a cow we had raised, and she seemed unsure of me. Could a calf-puller, a shot-giver, *not* mean harm?

In the morning I found she had not eaten or taken any water. Her breathing was worse. I lay on the straw beside her and slept. Before coming to the barn I had smelled something acrid — an old, familiar smell of death's presence, although she was still alive. Yet the sounds she made now had changed from grunting to a

low moan, the kind of sound one makes when giving in to something. By nightfall she was dead.

Today yellow is combed all through the trees, and the heart-
shaped cottonwood leaves spin downward to nothingness. I know
how death is made — not why — but where in the body it begins,
its lurking presence before the fact, its strangled music as if the
neck of a violin were being choked; I know how breathing begins
to catch on each rib, how the look of the eye flattens, gives up its
depth, no longer sees past itself; I know how easily existence is
squandered, how noiselessly love is dropped to the ground.

When I go to town I notice the feed store calendar: a cornu-
copia bursting with the produce of the season — nuts, apples,
wheat, corn, pumpkins, beans. I've seen death eat away at the
edges of plenty. Now I want to watch life fill in the fractal geo-
metries of what exists no more.

Now I walk to the ranch graveyard. On a ranch, death is as
much a constant as birth. The heifer is there with her calf, legs
stretched out straight, belly bloated . . . but the white droppings
of ravens, who are making a meal of her, cascade down her rib
cage like a waterfall.

I wander through the scattered bones of other animals who
have died. Two carcasses are still intact: Blue and Lawyer, saddle
horses who put in many good years. Manes, tails, hair gone, their
skin has hardened to rawhide, dried to a tautness, peeling back
just slightly from ribs, noses, and hooves, revealing a hollow interior as if letting me see that the souls are really gone.

After fruition, after death, after black ash, perhaps there is
something more, even if it is only the droppings of a scavenger,
or bones pointing every which way as if to say, "Touch here, touch
here," and the velocity of the abyss when a loved one goes his
way, and the way wind stirs hard over fresh graves, and the emptying out of souls into rooms and the mischief they get into, flip-
ping switches, opening windows, knocking candles out of silver
holders, and after, shimmering on water like leaked gas ready to
explode.

Mid-September. Afternoons I paddle my blue canoe across our
nine-acre lake, letting water take me where it will. The canoe was
a gift: eight dollars at the local thrift store.

As I drift aimlessly, ducks move out from the reeds, all mallards. Adaptable, omnivorous, and hardy, they nest here every year on the two tiny islands in the lake. After communal courtship and mating, the extra male ducks are chased away, but this year one stayed behind. Perhaps he fathered a clutch on the sly or was too young to know where else to go. When the ducklings hatched and began swimming, he often tagged along, keeping them loosely together until the official father sent him away. Then he'd swim the whole circumference of the lake alone, too bewildered and dignified to show defeat.

A green net of aquatic weeds knots the water, holding and releasing me as if I were weightless, as if I were loose change. Raised on the Pacific, I can row a boat, but I hardly know how to paddle. The water is either ink or a clear, bloodless liquid, and the black water snakes that writhe as I plunge my paddle are trying to write words.

Evening. In Kyoto I was taken to a moon-viewing room atop an ancient house on temple grounds. The room was square and the windows on four sides were rice-paper cutouts framed by bamboo, rounds split down the center, allowing the viewer to recreate the moon's phase. To view the moon, one had to look through the moon of the window.

Tonight the lake is a mirror. The moon swims across. Every now and then I slide my paddle into its face. Last week I saw the moon rise twice in one night: once, heavy and orange — a harvest moon — heaving over the valley, and later, in the mountains, it rose small, tight, and bright. But in August the moon went blind. I sat outside with a bottle of wine and watched a shade pull across its difficult, cratered solitude. Earlier, while thumbing through a book of late Tang poets, I came on this: "But this night, the fifteenth of the eighth month, was not like other nights; for now we saw a strange thing: the rim was as though a strong man hacked off pieces with an axe," and "Darkness smeared the whole sky like soot, and then it seemed for thousands of ages the sky would never open." That was 810. Over a thousand years later, a lunar eclipse happened again: same day, same month.

Now a half-moon slants down light, and shadows move desolation all over the place. At dawn a flicker knocks. The hollow sound of his labor makes leaves drop in yellow skirts around the trunks of trees. Water bends daylight. Thoughts shift like whitecaps, wild and bitter. My gut is a harp. Its strings get plucked in advance of any two-way communication by people I love, so that I know when attentions wane or bloom, when someone dear goes from me. From the same battered book I read this by Meng Chiao: "The danger of the road is not in the distance, ten yards is far enough to break a wheel. The peril of love is not in loving too often. A single evening can leave its wound in the soul."

Tonight thin spines of boreal light pin down thoughts as if skewered on the ends of thrown quills. I'm trying to understand how an empty tube behind a flower swells to fruit, how leaves twisting from trees are pieces of last year's fire spoiling to humus. Now trees are orange globes, their brightness billowing into cumulus clouds. As the sun rises, the barometer drops. Wind swings around, blasting me from the east, and every tin roof shudders to a new tune.

Stripped of leaves, stripped of love, I run my hands over my single wound and remember how one man was like a light going up inside me, not flesh. Wind comes like horn blasts: the whole mountain range is gathered in one sucking breath. Leaves keep coming off trees as if circulating through a fountain; aspens growing in steep groves glow.

I search for the possible in the impossible. Nothing. Then I try for the opposite, but the yellow leaves in trees — shaped like mouths — just laugh. Tell me, how can I shut out the longing to comprehend?

Wind slices off pondswells, laying them sharp and flat. I paddle and paddle. Rain fires into the water all around me, denting the mirror. The pond goes colorless. It is blue or gray or black. Where the warm spring feeds in, a narrow lane has been cut through aquatic flowers to the deep end. I slide my canoe into the channel. Tendrils of duckweed wave green arms. Are they saying hello or goodbye?

Willows, clouds, and mountains lie in the lake's mirror, although they look as if they're standing. I dip my paddle and glide — I think I'm getting the hang of it now — and slide over great folds of time, through lapping depositions of memory, over Precambrian rock, then move inward, up a narrow gorge where a hidden waterfall gleams. After fruition, water mirrors water.

The canoe slides to shore and I get out. The way a cloud tears, letting sun through, then closes again, I know that every truth flies. I get down on my hands and knees and touch my tongue to water: the lake divides. Its body is only chasm after chasm. Like water I have no skin, only surface tension. How exposed I feel. Where a duck tips down to feed, one small ripple causes random turbidity, ceaseless chaos, and the lake won't stop breaking . . . I can punch my finger through anything . . .

Much later, in the night, in the dark, I shine a flashlight down: my single wound is a bright scar that gives off hooked light like a new moon.

I try to cut things out of my heart, but the pack rat who has invaded my study won't let me. He has made himself the curator of my effects, my despair, my questioning, my memory. Every day a new show is installed. As if courting, he brings me bouquets of purple aster and sage gone to seed, cottonwood twigs whose leaves are the color of pumpkins. His scat is scattered like black rain: books, photographs, and manuscripts are covered. The small offering I set out years ago when I began using this room — a fistful of magpie feathers and the orange husks of two tangerines — has been gnawed into. Only the carved stone figure of a monk my mother gave me during tumultuous teenage years stands solid. The top of the narrow French desk where I write is strewn with torn-off cactus paddles, all lined up end to end, as if to remind me of how prickly the practice of vandalizing one's consciousness can be, how what seems inexpressible is like a thorn torn off under the skin.

The pack rat keeps me honest and this is how: he reminds me that I've left something out. Last August I returned to Yellowstone Park. I wanted to begin again in barrenness, I wanted to understand ash. This time the carcasses were gone — some eaten by bears, coyotes, eagles, and ravens; others taken away by the park. Those charnel grounds where only a green haze of vegetation showed had become tall stands of grass. And the bison — those who survived — were fat.

In a grassland at the northern end of the park I stood in fairy rings of ash where sagebrush had burned hot, and saw how mauve lupine seeds had been thrown by twisted pods into those bare spots. At the edges were thumbnail-size sage seedlings. Under a stand of charred Douglas firs was a carpet of purple asters and knee-high pine grass in bloom for the first time in two hundred years — its inflorescence had been stimulated by fire. I saw a low-lying wild geranium that appears only after a fire, then goes into dormancy again, exhibiting a kind of patience I know nothing of. In another blackened stand of trees it was possible to follow the exact course of the fire by stepping only where pine grass was in flower; I could see how groundfire had moved like rivulets of water. In places where the fire burned hottest there was no grass, because the organic matter in the soil had burned away, but there were hundreds of lodgepole pine seedlings; the black hills were covered with dark pink fireweed.

Just when all is black ash, something new happens. Ash, of course, is a natural fertilizer, and it's now thought to have a water-holding capacity: black ground is self-irrigating in a self-regulating universe. How quickly "barrenness becomes a thousand things and so exists no more."

Now it's October. I'm on the pond again, that dumping ground for thought. Water clanks against the patched hull. It is my favorite music, like that made by halyards against aluminum masts. It is the music emptiness would compose if emptiness could change into something. The seat of my pants is wet because the broken seat in the canoe is a sponge holding last week's rainwater. All around me sun-parched meadows are green again.

In the evening the face of the mountain looks like a ruined city. Branches stripped bare of leaves are skeletons hung from a gray sky and next to them are tall buildings of trees still on fire. Bands and bars of color are like layers of thought, moving the way stream water does, bending at point bars, eroding cutbanks. I lay my paddle down, letting the canoe drift. I can't help wondering how many ways water shapes the body, how the body shapes desire, how desire moves water, how water stirs color, how thought rises from land, how wind polishes thought, how spirit shapes matter, how a stream that carves through rock is shaped by rock.

Now the lake is flat but the boat's wake — such as it is — pushes water into a confusion of changing patterns, new creations: black ink shifting to silver, and tiny riptides breaking forward-moving swells.

I glide across rolling clouds and ponder what my astronomer friend told me: that in those mysterious moments before the big bang there was no beginning, no tuning up of the orchestra, only a featureless simplicity, a stretch of emptiness more vast than a hundred billion Wyoming skies. By chance this quantum vacuum blipped or burped as if a bar towel had been snapped, and resulted in a cosmic plasma that fluctuated into and out of existence, finally moving in the direction of life.

"But where did the bar towel come from?" I asked my friend in a small voice. No answer. Somehow life proceeded from artlessness and instability, burping into a wild diversity that follows no linear rules. Yet, in all this indeterminacy, life keeps opting for life. Galactic clouds show a propensity to become organic, not inorganic, matter; carbon-rich meteorites have seeded our earthly oasis with rich carbon-based compounds; sea vents let out juvenile water warm enough to make things grow, and sea meadows brew up a marine plasma — matter that is a thousandth of a millimeter wide — and thus give rise to all plant life and the fish, insects, and animals with which it coevolved.

I dip my paddle. The canoe pivots around. Somewhere out there in the cosmos, shock waves collapsed gas and dust into a swirl of matter made of star-grains so delicate as to resemble smoke, slowly aggregating, gradually sweeping up and colliding with enough material to become a planet like ours.

Dusk. A bubble of cloud rises over the mountains. It looks like the moon, then a rock tooth pierces it and wind burnishes the pieces into soft puffs of mist. Forms dissolve into other forms: a horse head becomes a frog; the frog becomes stick figures scrawled across the sky. I watch our single sun drop. Beyond the water, a tree's yellow leaves are hung like butterlamps high up near the trunk. As the sun sinks, the tree appears to be lit from the inside.

Another day. Listen, it's nothing fancy. Just a man-made pond in the center of the ranch, which is at the northern, mountainous edge of a desolate state. And it's fall, not too much different from the last fourteen autumns I've lived through here, maybe warmer at times, maybe windier, maybe rainier. I've always wondered why people sit at the edge of water and throw rocks. Better to toss stones at the car that brought you, then sit quietly.

This lake is a knowing eye that keeps tabs on me. I try to behave. Last summer I swam in its stream of white blossoms contemplating "the floating life." Now I lie on its undulant surface.

For a moment the lake is a boat sliding hard to the bottom of a deep trough, then it is a lover's body reshaping me. Whenever I try to splice discipline into my heart, the lake throws diamonds at me, but I persist, staring into its dangerous light as if into the sun. On its silvered surface I finally locate desire deep in the eye, to use Wallace Stevens's words, "behind all actual seeing."

Now wind pinches water into peaked roofs as if this were a distant city at my feet. I slide my canoe onto one of the tiny, humpbacked islands. The rind of earth at water's edge shows me where deer have come to drink and ducks have found shelter. It's not shelter I seek but a way of going to the end of thought.

I sit the way a monk taught me: legs crossed, hands cupped, thumbs touching, palms upward. The posture has a purpose — it helps transform breathing into energy — but the pose, as it must appear to the onlooker, is a ruse. There is no such thing as stillness, of course, since life progresses by vibration — the constant flexing and releasing of muscles, the liquid pulse, the chemical storms in the brain. I use this island only to make my body stop, this posture to lower the mind's high-decibel racket.

The ground is cold. All week blasts of Arctic air have braided into lingering warmth. Sometimes a lip of ice grows outward from shore, but afternoon sun burns it back. Water rubs against earth as if trying to make a spark. Nothing. The fountain of leaves in trees has stopped. But how weightless everything appears without the burden of leaves.

At last light, my friend the bachelor duck makes a last spin around the lake's perimeter. When the breeze that sweeps up from the south turns on itself, he swims against the current, dipping out of sight behind a gold-tinged swell. Fruition comes to this, then: not barrenness but lambency.

November 1. The ducks are gone. A lip of ice grew grotesquely fast during the night and now stretches across the water. I *can't* sit. Even the desire to be still, to take refuge from despair in the extremes of diversity, to bow down to light, is a mockery. Nothing moves. Looking out across the lake is like viewing a corpse: no resemblance to the living body. I go to the house despondent. When news of the California earthquake came I thought about stillness and movement, how their juxtaposition creates an equilibrium, how their constant rubbing sparks life and imposes death.

But now I don't know. Now the island is like a wobbly tooth, hung by a fine thread to the earth's mantle, and the lake is a solid thing, a pane of glass that falls vertically, cutting autumn off.

A week later. It has snowed and I'm sitting on the white hump of the island. My thrift-store canoe is hopelessly locked in ice. Today the frozen lake is the color of my mother's eyes, slate blue but without the sparkle. Snow under me, ice at my feet, no mesmerizing continuum of ripples forwarding memory, no moving lines in which to write music. And yet . . .

I put my nose to ice. It's the only way I'll know what I'm facing. At first it looks flat and featureless, like an unborn cosmos, but closer I see its surface is dented and pocked, and across the middle, where the water is deepest, there are white splotches radiating arms like starfish. It's like looking up the spiral arm of a galaxy.

At midday the barometer drops and the radio carries stockmen's warnings: high winds, snow and blowing snow in the northern mountains. That's us. Sure enough the wind comes, but it's a warm chinook. Instead of snow, rain undulates across the face of the mountains. Then the storm blows east.

In the morning I go to the lake. Drifts of snow dapple the white surface like sand dunes, and between, dead leaves scud across the ones trapped under ice. But at the north end, where the warm spring feeds in, there is open water — a tiny oval cut like a gem. Something catches my eye: a duck swims out from the reeds, all alone. Is it my bachelor duck? Around and around he goes, then climbs onto the lip of ice and faces the warm sun.

How fragile death is, how easily it opens back into life. Inside the oval, water ripples, then lies flat. The mirror it creates is so small I can see only a strip of mountains and the duck's fat chest bulging. I want to call out to him: "Look this way, I'm here too this autumn morning," but I'm afraid I'll scare him.

He goes anyway, first sliding into the water, then swimming anxious laps. When he takes off, his head is like a green flame. He circles so close I can hear the wing-creak and rasp of feathers. Over the lake he flies, crossing the spillway and dam bank, then up through a snowy saddle, not south as I would have expected, but northwest, in the direction of oncoming storms.

DIANA HUME GEORGE

# Wounded Chevy
# at Wounded Knee

FROM THE MISSOURI REVIEW

*Pine Ridge Sioux Reservation, July 1989*
"IF YOU break down on that reservation, your car belongs to the
Indians. They don't like white people out there." This was our
amiable motel proprietor in Custer, South Dakota, who asked
where we were headed and then propped a conspiratorial white
elbow on the counter and said we'd better make sure our vehicle
was in good shape. To get to Wounded Knee, site of the last cavalry massacre of the Lakota in 1890 and of more recent confron-
tations between the FBI and the American Indian Movement,
you take a road out of Pine Ridge on the Lakota reservation and
go about eight miles. If you weren't watching for it you could
miss it, because nothing is there but a hill, a painted board explaining what happened, a tiny church, and a cemetery.

The motel man told us stories about his trucking times, when
by day his gas stops were friendly, but by night groups of Indian
men who'd been drinking used to circle his truck looking for
something to steal — or so he assumed. He began carrying a .357
Magnum with him "just in case." Once he took his wife out to
Pine Ridge. "She broke out in hives before we even got there."
And when they were stopped on the roadside and a reservation
policeman asked if they needed help, she was sure he was going
to order her out of the car, steal it, and, I suppose, rape and scalp
her while he was at it. As the motel man told us these contradic-
tory stories, he seemed to be unaware of the irony of warning us

that the Indians would steal our car if they got a chance and following with a story about an Indian who tried to help them just in case they might be having trouble.

He did make a distinction between the reservation toughs and the police. He wasn't a racist creep, but rather a basically decent fellow whose view of the world was narrowly white. I briefly entertained the notion of staying awhile, pouring another cup of coffee, and asking him a few questions that would make him address the assumptions behind his little sermon, but I really wanted to get on my way, and I knew he wasn't going to change his mind about Indians here in the middle of his life in the middle of the Black Hills.

Mac and I exchanged a few rueful remarks about it while we drove. But we both knew that the real resistance to dealing with Indian culture on these trips that have taken us through both Pueblo and Plains Indian territories hasn't come from outside of our car or our minds, but rather from within them. More specifically, from within me. For years Mac has read about the Plains Indians with real attentiveness and with an openness to learning what he can about the indigenous peoples of North America. He reads histories, biographies, novels, and essays, thinks carefully about the issues involved, remembers what he has read, informs himself with curiosity and respect about tribes that have occupied the areas we visit. For a couple of years he urged me toward these materials, many of which have been visible around our home for years: *Black Elk Speaks, In a Sacred Manner We Live, Bury My Heart at Wounded Knee,* studies of Indian spiritual and cultural life. While we were in Lakota country this time, he was reading Mari Sandoz's biography of Crazy Horse. But he has long since given up on getting me to pay sustained attention to these rich materials, because my resistance has been firm and long-standing. I am probably better informed about Indian life than most Americans ever thought of being, but not informed enough for a thoughtful reader and writer. My resistance has taken the form of a mixture of pride and contempt: pride that I already know more than these books can tell me, and contempt for the white liberal intellectual's romance with all things Indian. But my position has been very strange perhaps, given that I was married to an American Indian for five years, lived on a reservation, and am the mother of a half-Indian son.

I've been mostly wrong in my attitudes, but it's taken me years to understand that. Wounded Knee is where I came to terms with my confusion, rejection, and ambivalence, and it happened in a direct confrontation with past events that are now twenty years old. My resistance broke down because of an encounter with a young Lakota named Mark, who is just about my own son's age.

I grew up in the 1950s and 1960s in a small white community on the edge of the Cattaraugus Seneca Indian Reservation in western New York State. Relations between Indians and whites in my world were bitter, and in many respects replicated the dynamics between whites and blacks in the South, with many exceptions due to the very different functions and circumstances of these two groups of people of color in white America. The school system had recently been integrated after the closing of the Thomas Indian School on the reservation. The middle-class whites wanted nothing to do with the Indians, whom they saw as drunkards and degenerates, in many cases subhuman. When I rebelled against the restraints of my white upbringing, the medium for asserting myself against my parents and my world was ready-made, and I grabbed it.

I began hanging out on the reserve with young Indians and shifted my social and sexual arena entirely to the Indian world. I fell in love with an idea of noble darkness in the form of an Indian carnival worker, got pregnant by him, married him, left the white world completely, and moved into his. Despite the fact that this was the sixties, my actions weren't politically motivated; or, rather, my politics were entirely personal at that point. While my more aware counterparts might have done some of the same things as conscious political and spiritual statements, I was fifteen when I started my romance with Indians, and I only knew that I was in love with life outside the constricting white mainstream, and with all the energy that vibrates on the outer reaches of cultural stability. My heart and what would later become my politics were definitely in the right place, and I have never regretted where I went or what I came to know. But for twenty years that knowledge spoiled me for another kind of knowing.

Whatever my romantic notions were about the ideal forms of American Indian wisdom — closeness to the land, respect for other living creatures, a sense of harmony with natural cycles, a way of walking lightly in the world, a manner of living that could

make the ordinary and profane into the sacred — I learned that
on the reservation I was inhabiting a world that was contrary to
all these values. American Indian culture at the end of the road
has virtually none of these qualities. White America has destroyed them. Any culture in its death throes is a grim spectacle,
and there can be no grimmer reality than that endured by people
on their way to annihilation.

I did not live among the scattered wise people or political activ-
ists of the Seneca Nation. I did not marry a nominal American
Indian from a middle-class family. I married an illiterate man
who dropped out of school in the seventh grade and was in school
only intermittently before that. He traveled around the East with
carnivals, running a Ferris wheel during the summer months, and
logged wood on the reservation during the winter — when he
could get work. Home base was an old trailer without plumbing
in the woods, where his mother lived. He drank sporadically but
heavily, and his weekends, often his weekdays, were full of pool
tables, bar brawls, the endlessness of hanging out with little to do.
He didn't talk much. How I built this dismal life into a romanti-
cized myth about still waters running deep gives me an enduring
respect for the mythopoeic, self-deluding power of desire, wish,
will.

When I was married to him my world was a blur of old cars
driven by drunk men in the middle of the night, of honky-tonk
bars, country music, late night fights with furniture flying, food
stamps and welfare lines, stories of injury and death. The smell
of beer still sickens me slightly. I was sober as a saint through all
of this, so I didn't have the insulation of liquor, only of love. I
lived the contrary of every white myth about Indian life, both the
myths of the small-town white racists and those of the smitten
hippies. When I finally left that life behind, extricating myself
and my child in the certain knowledge that to stay would mean
something very like death for both of us, I removed myself in
every respect. I knew how stupid white prejudice was, understood the real story about why Indians drank and wasted their
lives, felt the complexities so keenly that I couldn't even try to
explain them to anyone white. But similarly, I knew how bird-
brained the lovechild generation's romance with Indian culture
was.

My husband went on to a career of raping white women that had begun during — or maybe before — our marriage. When he was finally caught, convicted, and sent to Attica, I was long since done with that part of my life. My son pulled me back toward it with his own love for his father, and I still keep in touch with my husband's mother on the reservation, sometimes helping her to handle white bureaucracy, but that's all. I heard at a remove of miles, of eons, it seemed, about the early deaths of young men I'd known well — deaths due to diabetes, to lost limbs, or to car wrecks at high speed — and I felt something, but I didn't have to deal with it. When I tried to think about that past life in order to put it into some kind of perspective, no whole picture emerged. When I tried to write about it, no words would come. And when I tried to be open to learning something new about Indians in America on my trips, my heart closed up tight, and with it my mind. When I went to Wounded Knee, the wounds of these other Indians half a continent and half a lifetime away were a part of the landscape.

We pull off to the side of the road to read the billboard that tells what happened here. "Massacre of Wounded Knee" is the header, but upon close inspection you see that "Massacre" is a new addition, painted over something else. "Battle," perhaps? What did it used to say, I wonder, and hope I'll run into a local who can tell me. While I'm puzzling over this, an old Chevy sputters into the pull-off and shakes to a stop. It's loaded with dark faces, a young man and an older woman with many small children. The man gets out and walks slowly to the front of the car, rolling up his T-shirt over his stomach to get air on his skin. As he raises the hood, a Comanche truck pulls in beside him with one woman inside. It's very hot, and I weave a little in the glare of sun. Suddenly I see the past, superimposed on this hot moment. I've seen it before, again and again, cars full of little Indian kids in the heat of summer on the sides of roads. I glance again, see the woman in the front seat, know that she's their mother or their aunt. She looks weary and resigned, not really sad. She expects this.

And then in another blink it's not only that I have seen this woman; I have *been* this woman, my old car or someone else's packed with little kids who are almost preternaturally quiet, wide-eyed and dark-skinned and already knowing that this is a big part of what life is about, sitting in boiling back seats, their arms jammed against the arms of their brother, their sister, their cousin. There is no use asking when they'll get there, wherever "there" is. It will happen when it happens, when the adults as helpless as they figure out what to do. In the meantime they sweat and stare. But I am not this woman anymore, not responsible for these children, some of whose intelligent faces will blank into a permanent sheen of resignation before they're five. I am a tourist in a new Plymouth Voyager, my luggage rack packed with fine camping equipment, my Minolta in my hand to snap pictures of the places I can afford to go.

When Mac suggests that we offer to help them, I am not surprised at my flat negative feeling. He doesn't know what that means, I surmise, and I don't have any way to tell him. Help them? Do you want to get anywhere today, do you have the whole afternoon? The young man's shoulders bend over the motor. He is fit and beautiful, his good torso moves knowingly but powerlessly over the heat rising from beneath the hood. I recognize him, as well as the woman. He has no job. He talks about getting off the reservation, finding work, living the dreams he still has. He'll talk this way for a few more years, then give up entirely. He drinks too much. He has nothing to do. Drinking is the only thing that makes him really laugh, and his only way to release rage. I also know that whatever else is wrong with it the car is out of gas, and that these people have no money. Okay, sure, I say to Mac, standing to one side while he asks how we can help. Close to the car now, I see that the woman is the young man's mother. These kids are his brothers and sisters.

The car is out of gas and it needs a jump. The battery is bad. The woman in the other car is the young man's aunt, who can give him a jump but has no money to give him for gas — or so she says. I know her, too. She is more prosperous than her relatives, and has learned the hard way never to give them any money because she needs it herself, and if she gives it to them she'll never see it again. She made her policy years ago, and makes it stick no matter what. She has to.

Well, then, we'll take them to the nearest gas station. Do they have a gas can? No, just a plastic washer-fluid jug with no top. Okay, that will have to do. How far is the nearest gas? Just up the road a couple of miles. But they don't have any money because they were on their way to cash his mother's unemployment check when they ran out of gas, and the town where they can do that is many miles away. So can we loan them some money for gas? We can. He gets in the front seat. I get in the back, and as we pull away from the windy parking area, I look at the woman and the kids who will be sitting in the car waiting until we return. She knows she can't figure out how soon that will be. She stares straight ahead. I don't want to catch her eye, nor will she catch mine.

Right here up this road. Mark is in his early twenties. Mac asks him questions. He is careful and restrained in his answers at first, then begins to open up. No there's no work around here. Sometimes he does a little horse breaking or fence mending for the ranchers. All the ranches here are run by whites who had the money to make the grim land yield a living. They lease it from the Lakota. Mark went away to a Job Corps camp last year, but he had to come back because his twenty-one-year-old brother died last winter, leaving his mother alone with the little ones. He froze to death. He was drinking at a party and went outside to take a leak. Mark said they figured he must have just stopped for a minute to rest, and then he fell asleep. They found him frozen in the morning. Mark had to come back home to bury his brother and help his mother with the kids.

As we bounce over the dirt road, I stare at the back of Mark's head and at his good Indian profile when he turns toward Mac to speak. He is so familiar to me that I could almost reach out to touch his black straight hair, his brown shoulder. He is my husband, he is my son. I want to give him hope. He speaks about getting out of here, going to "Rapid" — Lakota shorthand for Rapid City — and making a life. He is sick of having nothing to do, he wants work, wants an apartment. But he can't leave yet; he has to stay to help his mother. But things are going to be okay, because he has just won a hundred thousand dollars and is waiting for them to send the check.

What?

"You know the Baja Sweepstakes?" He pronounces it "Bay-jah." "Well, I won it, I think I won it, I got a letter. My little brother

sent in the entry form we got with my CD club and he put my
name on it, and it came back saying that I'm one of a select few
chosen people who've won a hundred thousand dollars. That's
what it said, it said that, and I had to scratch out the letters and if
three of them matched it means I win, and they matched, and so
I sent it back in and now I'm just waiting for my money. It should
come pretty soon and then everything will be okay." He repeats
it over and over again in the next few minutes: he's one of a select
few chosen people.

As he speaks of this, his flat voice becomes animated. Slowly I
begin to believe that he believes this. Whatever part of him
knows better is firmly shelved for now. This hope, this belief that
hundreds of thousands of dollars are on the way, is what keeps
him going, what keeps him from walking out into the sky — or
to the outhouse in the winter to take a leak and a nap in the snow.
What will you do with the money, I ask. Well, first he is going to
buy his mother and the kids a house.

The first gas stop is a little shack that's closed when we finally
get there. Sandy wind and no sign of life. Miles on down the road
is a small Lakota grocery store with only a few items on the shelves
and a sign that reads "Stealing is not the Lakota way." Mac hands
Mark a five dollar bill. You can kiss that five bucks goodbye, I say
to Mac. I know, he nods. When Mark comes back out he has the
gas, and also a big cup of 7-Up and a bag of nachos. You want
some, he asks me? He hands Mac a buck fifty in change. On the
way back I hold the gas can in the back seat, placing my hand
over the opening. Despite the open windows, the van fills with
fumes. My head begins to ache. I am riding in a dream of flatness, ranch fences, Mark's dark head in front of me wishing away
his life, waiting for the break that takes him to Rapid. Later I
learn that we are in Manderson, and this is the road where Black
Elk lived.

Mark is talking about white people now. Yes, they get along
okay. For "yes" he has an expression of affirmation that sounds
sort of like "huh." Mari Sandoz spells it "hou" in her books on
the Lakota. The Lakota are infiltrated in every way by whites,
according to Mark. Lots of people in charge are white, the ranchers are white. And there's a place in Rapid called Lakota Hills,
fancy houses meant for Lakotas, but whites live in them. Later it

occurs to us that this is probably a development named Lakota Hills that has nothing at all to do with the Indians, but it has their name and so Mark thinks it belongs to them. I am angry for him that we borrow their name this way and paste it on our air-conditioned prosperity. I don't have anything to say to him. I lean back and close my eyes. It would be easy to be one of them again. I remember now how it's done. You just let everything flatten inside.

And when we return to Wounded Knee, the pull-off is empty. Mother, children, car, aunt, all are gone. There's nothing but wind and dust. This doesn't surprise me. Mark's mother knows better than to wait for her son's return if other help comes along. Mark means well, but maybe she has learned that sometimes it's hours before he gets back with gas — hours and a couple of six-packs if he has the chance. Now we face the prospect of driving Mark around the reservation until we can find them. I have just resigned myself to this when his aunt pulls back in and says they're broken down again a couple of miles up. We can leave now. Mark thanks us, smiles, and shyly allows us the liberty of having his aunt take a picture of all three of us. I am feeling a strange kind of shame, as though I had seen him naked, because he told us his secret and I knew it was a lie.

Unemployment, high rates of suicide and infant mortality, fetal alcohol syndrome, death by accident, and drinking-related diseases such as diabetes: these are now the ways that American Indians are approaching their collective demise. Over a century ago, American whites began this destruction by displacing and killing the *pte,* the Indian name for the buffalo the Plains Indians depended upon. We herded them together in far crueler ways than they had herded the bison, whose sacredness the Indians respected even as they killed them for food and shelter. The history of our genocide is available in many historical and imaginative sources. What is still elusive, still amazingly misunderstood, is how and why the Indians seem to have participated in their own destruction by their failure to adapt to changed circumstances.

Whites can point to the phenomenal adjustments of other non-Caucasian groups in America, most recently the Asians, who were badly mistreated and who have nevertheless not only adapted but excelled. Indians even come off badly in comparison to the group in some respects most parallel to them, American blacks, whose slowness in adapting seems at first glance to have more justification. Blacks were, after all, our slaves, brought here against their will, without close cultural ties to keep them bound together in a tradition of strength; and on the whole blacks are doing better than Indians. However slowly, a black middle class is emerging in America. What's the matter with Indians? Why haven't they adjusted better as a group?

The American Indian Movement is of course strong in some areas, and Indians have articulate, tough leaders and savvy representatives of their cause who are fighting hard against the tide of despair gripping the heart of their race. But they're still losing, and they know it. Estimates of unemployment on the Pine Ridge and Rosebud reservations run as high as 85 percent. Health officials at Pine Ridge estimate that as many as 25 percent of babies born on the reservation now have fetal alcohol syndrome. This culturally lethal condition cannot be overemphasized, since it means that the next generation of Lakota are genetically as well as socioeconomically crippled; one of the consequences of fetal alcohol syndrome is not only physical disability but mental retardation. The prospects are extremely depressing for Lakota leaders whose traditional values are associated with mental acuity and imaginative wisdom. Mark is vastly ignorant and gullible, but he is intelligent enough. Many of his younger brothers and sisters are not only underprivileged and without educational advantages, but also — let the word be spoken — stupid. When the light of inquiry, curiosity, mental energy, dies out in the eyes of young Indians early in their stunted lives because they have nowhere to go and nothing to do, it is one kind of tragedy. When it is never present to die out in the first place, the magnitude of the waste and devastation is exponentially increased. Indian leaders who are now concentrating on anti-alcohol campaigns among their people are doing so for good reasons.

Indian leaders disagree about culpability at this point. Essentially the arguments become theories of genocide or suicide. On one end of the spectrum of blame is the theory that it is all the fault of white America. The evidence that can be marshaled for

this point of view is massive: broken treaties, complete destruction of the Indian ways of life, welfare dependency established
as the cheapest and easiest form of guilt payment, continued un-
dermining of Indian autonomy and rights. The problem with this
perspective, say others, is that it perpetuates Indian desperation
and permits the easy way out — spend your life complaining that
white America put you here, and drink yourself into the oblivion
of martyrdom instead of taking responsibility for your own life.
Some Indians say they've heard enough about white America's
culpability, and prefer to transfer responsibility — not blame,
but responsibility — to the shoulders of their own people.
"White people aren't doing this to us — we're doing it to ourselves," said one Pine Ridge health official on National Public Radio's *Morning Edition* recently. She sees the victim stance as the
lethal enemy now.

The situation is as nearly hopeless as it is possible to be. Assimilation failed the first time and would fail if tried concertedly again,
because Indian culture is rural and tribal and tied to open land,
not urban airlessness. The Indian model is the encampment or
village — the latter more recently and under duress — and not
the city. Even the more stationary pueblo model is by definition
not urban. The only real hope for Indian prosperity would be
connected to vast tracts of land — not wasteland, but rich land.
Nor are most Indians farmers in the sense that white America
defines the farm. Though they might be, and have been, successful farmers under pressure, this is not their traditional milieu.
Supposing that many tribes could adapt to the farming model
over hunting and gathering, they would need large tracts of fine
land to farm, and there are none left to grant them.

When the American government gave the Lakota 160 acres
apiece and said "Farm this," they misunderstood the Indians
completely; and even if Indians had been able to adapt readily —
a change approximately as difficult as asking a yuppie to become
a nomad moving from encampment to encampment — the land
they were given was inadequate to the purpose. Grubbing a living out of the land we have given them, in what John Wesley
Powell called "the arid region" west of the one hundredth merid-
ian — takes a kind of know-how developed and perfected by white
Americans, and it also takes capital. It is no coincidence that the

large ranches on Pine Ridge are almost entirely leased by whites who had the initial wherewithal to make the land yield.

The Sioux were a people whose lives were shaped by a sense of seeking and vision that white America could barely understand even if we were to try, and we do not try. The life of a Sioux of a century and a half ago was framed by the Vision Quest, a search for goals, identity, purpose. One primary means of fulfillment was self-sacrifice. Now, as Royal Hassrick has written, "No longer is there anything which they can deny themselves, and so they have sacrificed themselves in pity." Whereas they were once people whose idea of being human was bound to creative self-expression, their faces now reflect what Hassrick calls "apathy and psychic emaciation." Collectively and individually they have become a people without a vision.

Why do they drink themselves into obliteration and erasure? Why not? When white America approaches the problem from within our own ethnocentric biases, we can't see why people would allow themselves to be wasted in this way, why they would not take the initiative to better themselves, to save themselves through the capitalist individuality that says, "*I* will make it out of this." But in fact part of their problem is that they have tried to do this, as have most Indian peoples. They've bought the American dream in part, and become greedy for money and material goods. Life on an Indian reservation — almost any reservation — is a despairing imitation of white middle-class values. In this respect Indians are like all other minority groups in ghettos in America, and this explains why Mark has a CD player instead of the more modest possessions we would not have begrudged him. If he is anything like the Indians I lived with, he also has a color TV, though he may well live in a shack or trailer without plumbing and without siding.

Their own dreams have evaded them, and so have ours. Mark and his brothers and sisters have been nourished on memories of a culture that vanished long before they were born and on the promises of a different one, from whose advantages they are forever excluded. Does Mark really believe he has won the sweepstakes? What he got was obviously one of those computer letters that invite the recipient to believe he has won something. Without the education that could teach him to read its language critically, or to read it adequately at all, he has been deceived into

believing that a *deus ex machina* in the form of the Baja Sweepstakes will take him out of his despair.

In 1890, the year of the final defeat of the Sioux at Wounded
Knee, the Ghost Dance was sweeping the plains. Begun by a few
leaders, especially the Paiute seer Wovoka, the Ghost Dance
promised its practitioners among the warriors that the buffalo
would return and the white man would be defeated. Ghost Dancers
believed that their ceremonial dancing and the shirts they wore
would make them proof against the white man's bullets. Among
the Sioux warriors at Wounded Knee, the willing suspension of
disbelief was complete. It made the warriors reckless and abandoned, throwing normal caution and survival strategy to the wind.

A tragically inverted form of the self-delusion embodied in the
Ghost Dance is practiced today on the Pine Ridge and other Sioux
reservations. The original Ghost Dance has beauty and vitality,
as well as desperation, as its sources. Now many Sioux men who
would have been warriors in another time behave as though liquor and passivity will not kill them. Mark chooses to suspend
his disbelief in white promises and to wait for a hundred thousand dollars to arrive in the mail.

Hank Doctor was my husband's best friend on the Seneca reservation. He was raunchy, hard drinking, outrageous in behavior and looks. His hair was long and scraggly, his nearly black
eyes were genuinely wild, and his blue jeans were always caked
with dust and falling down his hips. His wit was wicked, his laugh
raucous, dangerous, infectious. Hank was merciless toward me,
always making white-girl jokes, telling me maybe I better go
home to my mama, where I'd be safe from all these dark men.
He wanted me to feel a little afraid in his world, told me horrible
stories about ghost-dogs that would get me on the reservation if
I ventured out at night — and then he'd laugh in a way that said
hey, white girl, just joking, but not entirely. He alternated his affection toward me with edgy threats, made fun of the too-white
way I talked or walked, took every opportunity to make me feel
foolish and out of place. He was suspicious that I was just slum-
ming it as a temporary rebellion — maybe taking notes in my
head — and that I'd probably run for home when the going got
too tough. Of course he was right, even though I didn't know it
at the time. I liked him a lot.

A few years ago, my son Bernie went through a period when

he chose to remove himself from my world and go live in his father's, from which I'd taken him when he was three. I didn't try to stop him, even though I knew he was hanging out with people who lived dangerously. I used to lie in bed unable to go to sleep because I was wondering what tree he'd end up wrapped around with his dad. He was a minor, but I was essentially helpless to prevent this. If I'd forced the issue, it would only have made his desire to know a forbidden world more intense. He lived there for months, and I slowly learned to get to sleep at night. Mothers can't save their children. And he had a right.

The day I knew he'd ultimately be okay was when he came home and told me about Hank. He wondered if I'd known Hank. He'd never met him before because Hank had been out west for years. Now he was back home, living in a shack way out in the country, terribly crippled with diabetes and other ailments from drinking, barely able to walk. Hank would have been in his mid-forties at this time. Bernie and his dad took rabbits to Hank when they went hunting so that Hank would have something to eat. During these visits, Hank talked nonstop about the old days, reminding big Bernard of all their bar brawls, crowing to young Bernie that the two of them could beat anyone then they fought as a team, recounting the times they'd dismantled the insides of buildings at four in the morning. He told his stories in vivid, loving detail. His gift for metaphor was precise and fine, his memory perfect even if hyperbolic. He recalled the conversations leading up to fights, the way a person had leaned over the bar, and who had said what to whom just before the furniture flew.

Bernie was impressed with him, but mostly he thought it was pathetic, this not-yet-old man who looked like he was in his seventies, with nothing to remember but brawls. I told Bernie to value Hank for the way he remembered, the way he could make a night from twenty years ago intensely present again, his gift for swagger and characterization, his poetry, his laughter. In another time Hank would have been a tribal narrator, a story catcher with better exploits to recount. He would have occupied a special place in Seneca life because of his gifts.

My son left the reservation valuing and understanding important things about his father's world, but not interested in living in its grip. He lives in Florida where he's a chef in a resort, and he's going to college. A month ago his daughter, my grand-daughter, was born. She is named Sequoia, after the Cherokee chief who gave his people an alphabet and a written language. Bernie took her to the reservation on his recent visit north and introduced the infant Sequoia to her great-grandmother. My husband's mother says that big Bernard is drinking again, using up her money, and she doesn't know how much more she can take. I know she'll take as much as she has to. I hope I'll see Bernard someday soon to say hello, and maybe we can bend together over our granddaughter, for whom I know we both have many hopes.

Just before we leave Wounded Knee, I walk over to Aunt Lena's Comanche and point to the tribal sign that tells the story. "It says 'Massacre' there, but it used to say something else." I ask her if she knows what it said before. She looks over my shoulder and laughs. "That's funny," she says, "I've lived here all my life, but you know, I never did read that sign." We're miles down the road before I realize that I never finished reading it myself.

STEPHEN JAY GOULD

# Counters and Cable Cars

FROM NATURAL HISTORY

*San Francisco, October 11, 1989*
IN A distinctive linguistic regionalism, New Yorkers like me stand
"on line," while the rest of the nation waits patiently "in line."
Actually, I spend a good part of my life trying to avoid that particular activity altogether, no matter what preposition it may bear.
I am a firm supporter of the Yogi Berra principle regarding once
fashionable restaurants: "No one goes there anymore; it's too
crowded."

Consequently, in San Francisco this morning, I awoke before
sunrise in order to get my breakfast of Sears's famous eighteen
pancakes (marvel not, they're very small) before the morning crush
of more amenable hours rendered the restaurant uninhabitable
on Berra's maxim. Then out the door by 7:30 to the cable car
stop at Union Square for a ride that thrills me no less in middle
life than on my first trip as a boy. What moment in public trans-
portation could possibly surpass that final steep descent down
Russian Hill? (For a distant second and third in America, I nom-
inate the Saint Charles streetcar of New Orleans, last of the old-
time trolley lines, as it passes by the antebellum houses of the garden district; and the Staten Island Ferry, only a nickel in my youth
and the world's most distinguished cheap date, as it skirts the
Statue of Liberty by moonlight.) I travel during the last minutes
of comfort and accessibility. By 9 A.M., long lines of tourists will
form and no one will want to ride anymore.

We paleontologists are driven, almost by professional definition, to an abiding respect for items and institutions that have

prevailed and prospered with integrity in an unending sea of change (although I trust that we can also welcome, even foster, intellectual innovation). I love Sears restaurant with its familiar, uniformly excellent, and utterly nonyuppie breakfast menu. And I adore those Victorian cars with their wooden seats and their distinctive sounds — the two-clang signal to move, the hum of the cable perpetually running underground, the grasp of the grip as it takes hold to pull the passive car along.

As I ride, I ponder a psychological puzzle that has long intrigued me: why does authenticity — as a purely conceptual theme — exert such a hold upon us? An identical restaurant with the same food, newly built in the San Francisco segment of a Great Cities Theme Park, would supply me with nothing but calories; a perfect replica of a cable car, following an even hillier route in Disneyland, would be a silly bauble.

Authenticity has many guises, each contributing something essential to our calm satisfaction with the truly genuine. Authenticity of *object* fascinates me most deeply because its pull is entirely abstract and conceptual. The art of replica making has reached such sophistication that only the most astute professional can now tell the difference between, say, a genuine dinosaur skeleton and a well-made cast. The real and the replica are effectively alike in all but our abstract knowledge of authenticity, yet we feel awe in the presence of bone once truly clothed in dinosaur flesh and mere interest in fiberglass of identical appearance.

If I may repeat, because it touched me so deeply, a story on this subject told once before in this forum (November 1984). A group of blind visitors met with the director of the Air and Space Museum in Washington to discuss greater accessibility, especially of the large objects hanging from the ceiling of the great atrium and perceptible only by sight. The director asked his guests whether a scale model of Lindbergh's *Spirit of St. Louis,* mounted and fully touchable, might alleviate the frustration of nonaccess to the real McCoy. The visitors replied that such a solution would be most welcome, but only if the model was placed directly beneath the invisible original. Simple knowledge of the imperceptible presence of authenticity can move us to tears.

We also respect an authenticity of *place.* Genuine objects out of context and milieu may foster intrigue, but rarely inspiration.

London Bridge dismantled and reassembled in America becomes a mere curiosity. I love to watch giraffes in zoo cages, but
their jerky, yet somehow graceful, progress over the African veld
provokes a more satisfying feeling of awe.

Yet, until today, I had not appreciated the power of a third
authenticity, that of *use*. Genuine objects in their proper place
can be devalued by altered use — particularly when our avid ap-
petite for casual and ephemeral leisure overwhelms an original
use in the honorable world of daily work.

Lord knows, being one myself, I have no right to complain about
tourists mobbing cable cars. Visitors have an inalienable right to
reach Fisherman's Wharf and Ghirardelli Square by any legal
means sanctioned and maintained by the city of San Francisco.
Still, I love to ride incognito at 7:30 A.M. with native San Franciscans using the cable car as a public conveyance to their place of
work — Asian students embarking on their way to school as the
car skirts by Chinatown; smartly dressed executives with their
monthly transit passes.

But I write this essay because I experienced a different, unan-
ticipated, and most pleasant example of authenticity of use in Sears
this morning. (I could not have asked for a better context. The
Bay Area, this week, is experiencing a bonanza in authenticity of
place — as the Oakland A's and the San Francisco Giants prepare for the first single-area World Series since 1956, when the
seventh and last "subway series" of ten glorious childhood years
in New York, 1947 to 1956, produced Don Larsen's perfect game
and the revenge of my beloved Yankees for their only defeat, the
year before, by the Dodgers in their true home in Brooklyn. Think
what we would lose if, in deference to October weather and a
misplaced sense of even opportunity, the World Series moved
from the home cities of full-season drama to some neutral turf in
balmy Miami or New Orleans.)

I have always gone to Sears with other people and sat at a table.
This time I went alone and ate at the counter. I had not known
that the counter is a domain of regulars, native San Franciscans
on their way to work. One man gets up and says to the waitress,
"Real good, maybe I'll come back again sometime." "He's in here
every morning," whispers the waitress to me. Another man takes
the empty seat, saying "Hi, honey" to the woman on the next stool.

"You're pretty early today," she replies. "The works!" he says as the waitress passes by. "You got it," she replies. A few minutes later, she returns with a plate of pancakes and a dish of scrambled eggs. But first she slides the eggs off the plate onto a napkin, blotting away the butter. "No good for him," she explains. He begins a discussion on the relative merits of cloth napkins and paper towels in such an enterprise. Good fellowship in authenticity of use; people taking care of each other in small ways of enduring significance.

As I present talks on evolutionary subjects all around America, I can be sure of certain questions following any speech: Where is human evolution going? What about genetic engineering? Are blacks really better at basketball? (Both the dumb and the profound share this character of inevitability.) High on the list of these perennial inquiries, I must rank the ecological question, usually asked with compassion but sometimes with pugnacity: Why do we need to save all these species anyway?

I know the conventional answers rooted in practicality. I even believe in them: you never know what medical or agricultural use might emerge from species currently unknown or ignored; beneficial diversity of gene pools in cultivated species can often be fostered by interbreeding with wild relatives; interconnectedness of ecological webs may lead to dire and unintended consequences for "valued" species when "insignificant" creatures are rubbed out. Still, I prefer to answer with an ethical, more accurately a viscerally aesthetic, statement espoused by nearly all evolutionary biologists as a virtual psychic necessity for wanting to enter the field in the first place: we relish diversity; we love every slightly different way, every nuance of form and behavior; and we know that the loss of a significant fraction of this gorgeous variety will quench our senses and our satisfactions for any future worth contemplating in human terms (potential recovery of diversity several million years down the road is too abstract and conjectural for this legitimately selfish argument). What in the world could possibly be more magnificent than the fact that beetle anatomy presents itself in more than half a million separate packages called species?

I have always been especially wary of "soft" and overly pat analogies between biological evolution and human cultural change.

(Some comparisons are apt and informative, for all modes of change must hold features in common; but the mechanisms of biological evolution and cultural change are so different that close analogies usually confuse far more than they enlighten.) Nonetheless, aesthetic statements may claim a more legitimate universality, especially when an overt form rather than the underlying mechanism of production becomes the subject of our consideration. If you feel aesthetic pleasure in proportions set by the "golden section," then you may gain similar satisfaction from a nautilus shell or a Greek building despite their maximally different methods and causes of construction. I do, therefore, feel justified in writing an essay on the moral and aesthetic value of diversity both in natural and in human works — and in trying to link the genesis and defense of diversity with various meanings of authenticity. (In addition, *Natural History* has been breaking ground within its genre for many years by including the diversity of human works under its mantle, and by recognizing that the life of modern cities belongs as firmly to natural history as the overphotographed and overromanticized ways of the few human groups still living as hunters and gatherers in pristine habitats.)

(Finally, if I may make a terrible confession for a working biologist and a natural historian: I grew up on the streets of New York, and I suppose that one never loses a primary affection for things first familiar — call it authenticity of place if you wish. I do think that America's southwestern desert, in the four corners region around Monument Valley, is the most sublime spot on earth. But when I crave diversity rather than majesty, I choose cities and the products of human labor, as they resist conformity and embody authenticity of object, place, and use. My motto must be the couplet of Milton's "L'Allegro" and "Il Penseroso" — from the happy rather than the pensive side: "Towered cities please us then / And the busy hum of men." Several years ago I visited India on a trip sponsored by Harvard's natural history museum. My colleagues delighted in arising at 4 A.M., piling into a bus, driving to a nature reserve, and trying to spot the dot of a tiger at some absurd distance, rendered only slightly more interesting by binoculars. I yearned to be let off the bus alone in the middle of any bazaar in any town.)

Natural diversity exists at several levels. Variety permeates any nonclonal population from within. Even our tightest genealogical groups contain fat people and thin people, tall and short. The primal folk wisdom of the ages proclaims the enormous differences in temperament among siblings of a single family. But the greatest dollop of natural diversity arises from our geographical divisions — the differences from place to place as we adapt to varying environments and accumulate our distinctiveness by limited contact with other regions. If all species, like rats and pigeons, lived all over the world, our planet would contain but a tiny fraction of its actual diversity.

I therefore tend to revel most in the distinctive diversity of geographical regions when I contemplate the aesthetic pleasure of differences. Since I am most drawn to human works, I find my greatest joy in learning to recognize local accents, regional customs of greeting and dining, styles of architecture linked to distinctive times and places. I also, at least in my head if not often enough in overt action, think of myself as a watchdog for the preservation of this fragile variety and an implacable foe of standardization and homogenization.

I recognize, of course, that official programs of urban layout and road building must produce more elements of commonality than a strict aesthetic of maximal diversity might welcome. After all, criteria of design have a universality that becomes more and more pressing at upper limits of size and speed. If you have to move a certain number of cars through a given region at a stated speed, the road can't meander along the riverbanks or run through the main streets of old market towns. Public buildings and city street grids beg for an optimal efficiency that imposes some acceptable degree of uniformity.

But the sacred task of regionalism must be to fill in the spaces between with a riotous diversity of distinctive local traditions — preferably of productive work, not only of leisure. With this model of a potentially standardized framework for roads and public spaces filled in, softened, and humanized by local products made by local people for local purposes — authenticity of object, place, and use — I think that I can finally articulate why I love the Sears counter and the cable cars in the early morning. They embody all the authenticities, but they also welcome the respectful stranger. (Again, nature and human life jibe in obedience to basic principles of structural organization. Ecological rules and principles — flow of energy across trophic levels, webs of interaction that define the "balance of nature" — have generality corresponding to permissible uniformity in the framework of public space. But local diversity prevails because different organisms embody the rules from place to place — lions or tigers or bears as predictable carnivores of three separate continents — just as uniquely local businesses should fill the slots within a more uniform framework.)

I also now understand, with an intellectual argument to back a previous feeling, what I find so troubling about the drive for standardization, on either vernacular (McDonald's) or boutique levels (Ghirardelli Square or Harborside or Quincy Market or how can you tell which is where when all have their gourmet chocolate chip cookie cart and their Crabtree & Evelyn soap store). I cannot object to the homogenization per se, for I accept such uniformity in the essential framework of public spaces. But McDonald's introduces standardization at the wrong level, for it usurps the smaller spaces of immediate and daily use, the places that cry out for local distinction and its attendant sense of community. McDonald's is a flock of pigeons ordering all endemic birds to the block, a horde of rats wiping out all the mice, gerbils, hamsters, chinchillas, squirrels, beavers, and capybaras. The Mom-and-Pop chain stores of Phoenix and Tucson are almost a cruel joke, a contradiction in terms.

I grew up in Queens, next to a fine establishment called the T-Bone Diner (it is still there, *mirabile dictu*). The contrast between railroad-car-style diners of my youth and McDonald's of my midlife brings us to the heart of the dilemma. Diners were manufactured in a few standardized sizes and shapes — many by the Worcester Car Company in my adopted state — and then shipped to their prospective homes. Owners then took their standard issue and proceeded to cultivate the distinctness that defines this precious item of American culture: menus abounding with local products and suited to the skills and tastes of owners; waiters and waitresses with a flair for uniqueness, even eccentricity, of verve, sassiness, or simple friendliness; above all, a regular clientele forged into a community of common care. McDonald's works in precisely the opposite way and becomes perverse in its incongruity. It enters the small-scale domain of appropriate uniqueness within the interstices of an allowable uniform framework. It even occupies spaces of widely differing designs, placements, and previous uses. It then forges this diversity into a crushing uniformity that permits not a millimeter of variation in the width of a fry from Oakland to Ogunquit.

But we are not defeated. Uniqueness has a habit of crawling back in and around the uniformities of central planning. Uniqueness also has staying power against all the practical odds of commercial culture because authenticities speak to the human soul. Many of those old diners are still flourishing in New England. I am at least a semiregular at one of the finest. On my last visit, the counter lady pointed to a jar with dollar bills. A regular customer, she told me, had a sick child in need of an operation, and everyone was kicking in, if only as a symbol of support and community. No one even mentioned the jar to casual customers on that particular morning; but I was simply told to contribute. No pleas, no harangues, no explanations beyond the simple facts of the case. Our communities are many, overlapping, and of various strengths. I am proud to be part of this aggregate, forged to a coherent species by a common place of local integrity. So long as these tiny communities continue to form in the interstices of conformity, I will remain optimistic about the power of diversity. And I will remember Elijah's discovery during his flight from Jezebel (1 Kings 19:11–12): "After the wind an earthquake. . . . And after the earthquake a fire. . . . And after the fire a still, small voice."

POSTSCRIPT: As the dateline indicates, I wrote this essay just a week before the great San Francisco earthquake of October 17. This violently altered circumstance has converted my closing line into an utterance that, if intended after the fact rather than written unwittingly before, might seem overly pointed, if not verging on cruel. In using Elijah to reemphasize my central contrast between small-scale, local, and distinctive diversity (the "still, small voice") and global effects (well represented by general catastrophes), I was, I freely confess, also trying to make a small joke about San Francisco as the location of my essay — for the 1906 earthquake did wreak its main destruction with a tremor followed by fire.

Little did I know that my attempt at humor would soon be turned so sour by nature. I could, of course, just change the ending, sink this postscript, and fudge a fine fit with history — the virtue of working with a magazine's three-month, rather than a newspaper's one-day, lead time. But I would rather show what I wrote originally — appropriate to its moment, but not a week later — as a testimony to nature's continuing power over our fortunes, and as a working example of another theme so often addressed in this series: the quirky role of unique historical events both in nature and in human life.

The earthquake has also illuminated several other points that I raised about authenticity and local diversity. The World Series, although delayed, was not moved to neutral turf but was played by honoring baseball's powerful tradition for authenticity of place, despite the practical difficulties. My line about "people taking care of each other in small ways of enduring significance," although meant only as a comment about the Sears counter, soon extended to the whole region. Every fire or flood provokes endless rumination and pious commentary about why we seem to need disaster to bring out the best in us. But clichés are hackneyed because they are true; and the framework of this essay does put a different twist upon a commonplace: just as McDonald's marks the dark side by bringing the allowable conformity of large-scale public space into the inappropriate arena of local distinctiveness, human kindness after disaster, on the bright side, has a precisely opposite effect, for it promotes the usual caring of small and local communities to the large and overt domain of anonymity and callousness. Now how can this still, small voice be heard and felt at all scales all the time?

ELIZABETH HARDWICK

# New York City: Crash Course

FROM GRANTA

THE OLD New York airport was once called Idlewild, a pastoral welcome to the gate of a zoological garden of free-ranging species. Or so it seemed to say before the names were changed to those of politicians, those who won. Kennedy Airport, international arrival to our hysterical, battered and battering, potholed, bankrupt metropolis. A spectacular warehouse this city is; folk from anywhere, especially from those sunny sovereignties to the south of us, coming to peer out of blackened windows, each one in his shelter of sorts.

In 1879 a curious urban structure called the "dumb-bell tenement" won a prize as the most imaginative and useful design for the hordes seeking shelter. Windows looked out upon a rubbish-strewn courtyard, black and empty, giving neither light nor air but surely an improvement on something not previously thought of. Shelter: beautiful word, like dwelling. "Wuthering Heights is the name of Mr. Heathcliff's dwelling." But utter not the word shelter just now, here where it has acquired or grown a scrofulous hide.

Will you not come with me to the Shelter on this icy evening, dear, old homeless one, stuffed into your bag of rags and surrounded by upstanding pieces of cardboard, making as it were a sort of private room on the freeze of concrete near a corner or before a storefront? No, you f—ing little rat-faced volunteer on vacation from the country club of Wellesley College or piling up credit at the Fordham School of Social Work. I'll die before I'll take my bag upon bag of nameless litter, my mangy head, my own, my leprous legs, purple, scabbed and swollen, my numbed, crooked fingers, myself, to the City Shelter, or flophouse, whatever you call it.

It's a battle, and the blue and white salvation van makes off slowly, idly offering in the gloom of perplexity the wide, public, rectangular barns, the dormitories with their rows of iron beds, muslin sheets, and flattened pillow, and somewhere down a corridor a lukewarm shower. The trouble is, among others, that if you nod off, what you're there for, you might become separated from your wealth of trash, robbed of your cache of mementos — an old key, a newspaper item perhaps of some paranoid interest, a safety pin, an arcane Welfare Department communication without name or number — things folded into layers of astounding clothing; and worst of all, to be with others.

The 1990 census is trying to take note of them, on the streets, in the tunnels of the subways, hiding behind a bush in the park, or on the lonesome late nights of the West Side Highway in the traffic divider, standing by a metal can burning trash for warmth . . . Well, there's no news in that, not here in New York . . . When you get right down to it, the van driver said, the homeless people are just a bunch of clichés. Are they ever, said the volunteer girl.

In our antiquity, not so many hundred years ago, this place was lying here, entrance to the dreaming acres north, south, and west, lying here waiting for something to happen, for what's new? Waiting for the worn-down explorers trying to get to the Orient, waiting for them to alight from their obdurate, temperamental ships, waiting for a sort of opening night in Manhattan. At last they paddled ashore to our bay and didn't find much, indeed "no indigenous civilization," or so they said. Not much except the usual basking verdure, several dozen or so small, wind-rattled shelters made of tree bark and "the poor Indian." (Columbus, around Santo Domingo or thereabouts, took several of these solemn, long-faced, reddish-brown bodies back to Europe for the curiosity of it and perhaps to amuse his wife, "the wellborn Dona Filipa Perestrello e Moniz"; and as a sort of wampum offering the transported native stock was to receive Christian baptism, to implant in innocent minds the Happy Hunting Ground complexities of the Resurrection.)

It was to be New Amsterdam with the Dutch putting up lots

for sale and beginning to imagine our fate-laden checkerboard destiny. They bought, in a manner of speaking, the place and strangely the straggling settlers from the Zuider Zee, or IJsselmeer, initiated by a squatter's rights over the succeeding English, our aristocracy, "old new York," born in the memory perhaps of the murdered William the Silent. Van Rensselaer, Schuyler, and Schermerhorn, names with a somewhat heraldic resonance, supplanted the Oneida and the Algonquin. And were themselves supplanted in the porous atmosphere of New York which will, by a vivacious regicide, crown more kings and queens in a year than history knows of.

A gray Sunday afternoon, smoky light, and a sanctified drowsing between our rivers east and west, a quiet except for the sacrificial athleticism of the joggers, running or preparing to run in the park, as a rabbit out of its hutch will surely hop off. And some comfortable cows still lolling in their stalls on Central Park West. All of this before the tiny white lights come on, a cheerful, if unnatural, decoration strung on the winter tree branches. Cottony brilliant leaves they are as the grinding bus, with a few Sunday evening travelers, makes its way through the underpass in the soft, waxy beauty of the urban evening.

At the Lincoln Center Opera House, papier-mâché stone battlements by the ineffable Zeffirelli worth, or cost, a couple of million, a piece of the rock. Baudelaire said that what he liked best about the opera was the *chandelier,* and here some invisible hand lowers the large bunch of little globes and raises them before dimming in a pretty display of mechanical superfluity. In 1849, at the Astor Place Opera House, there was a ferocious outbreak of riot, one of peculiar import. On the heath, thunder and lightning, torches and baseball bats "hover through the fog and filthy air." The occasion was a performance of Shakespeare's *Macbeth,* in the theater which was then a shrine for the patrons who would trip in satin slippers through the horse droppings at the curb, having emerged from the carriage to leave the coachman in chimney-sweep black outfittings to rust in the long wait for the final curtain. And then it would be off to the houses, the mansions, edging ever upward from the Thirties streets near Madison to the Fifties on Fifth Avenue, the way things were going. In the old postcards of the city everything appears gay, small, empty, and tranquil. The swish of long skirts and the gothic ascension of many wonderful hats, worthy people treading the streets, down Broadway, and keeping away from the Plug-Uglies, the Dead Rabbits, citizen gangs with their own rancorous claims.

For the *Macbeth* performance the Anglophiles had brought across the Atlantic a star, William Macready, an innocent elocutionist, on tour. This was seen as an insult to our own master of fustian, Edwin Forrest, and the mob mounted a patriotic stone-throwing, window-smashing, outraged, red-faced, beer-encouraged assault. Poor Macready, eloquence trembling through the dagger irresolution and the pacing melancholy of tomorrow and tomorrow, and at last having surrendered his head to Macduff, was to slink through the back door with a cortège, front and back, of high prestige, among them Washington Irving and John Jacob Astor. Still, the contract was in place and at a later performance thousands gathered to storm the building, stones flying like some hellish hail storm of local resentment. The rioters were met with three hundred policemen and two hundred state militia who fired into the crowd, killing almost two dozen of the rebels. Macbeth Macready decamped on the next boat to England, but the theatrical criticism of the populace, the class gap, the canals of separation, already impassable, represented by the rioters and the merchant class, represented by the point-blank fire, occasioned the usual bitter civic debate, howls ending in a draw.

Herman Melville, home from the cannibals and acquainted with mutiny, getting on fairly well with *Omoo* and *Typee*, signed like a good PEN member the first petition favoring the appearance of Macready on the boards. This was before the militia assault, and what he might have thought about the state's forceful, explosive protection of the right to speechifying is not certain. Melville's mother was a Gansevoort, an "old New Yorker."

The emergency ambulance shrills through the night — or is it a fire truck, all glistening red and burnished brass shining in the murk, arriving in multiplication like a tank parade, the men in their black and yellow rubber mantles and their smart, brim-back hats, pirate hats, answering with good fortune this time only a wastebasket conflagration in the banal, sleepless interiors of ABC-

TV. As early as seven in the morning, in the winds of winter or the breathless air of summer, the crowds gather outside the building to see great Pompey pass the streets of Rome — that is, to see whoever might be interviewed on the morning show.

In 1838, on an arctic evening with temperatures sliding down to seventeen below zero, as if in the brush-strewn fields of Minnesota under a high, cold moon, there was a four-alarm flaming that swept through the stone and timber of the financial district. Thirteen acres turned to frozen rubble. They were soon back on the trading floor, as they are ever to be, mysterious men, *condottierri*, nowadays tanned from battle in the financing trenches, trim from the rigors of the conference call, nervous and powerful on their steeds, lances drawn, rulers of principalities in the Hamptons or in Beverly Hills. Should they be thrown from their horses they will be bathed in unguents, the precious oils of severance pay and bankruptcy bonuses, settlements. "Day after day the columns of the press revealed fresh scandals to the astonished public, which at last grew indifferent to such revelations. Beneath all the wrangling of the courts, however, while the popular attention was distracted by the clatter of lawyers' tongues, the leaders in the controversy were quietly approaching a settlement" (Charles Francis Adams on the Erie Railroad scandals of 1868). A golden age it has been the last few years, and about some of the financiers, soon to be tried and those tried before, you might say they wrote the script and played all the parts.

The men make and the wives spend, indeed are chosen for their talents in consumption, a contract historical, imitative, and pleasurable as the sunshine. But, think what an occupation it is to fill the cathedrals, the vaults and domes on Park Avenue and Fifth. Ten coats of paint on the glaze of the walls, and even then, so often, not quite right. A burdensome eclecticism of track lighting and electrified ceiling ornamentations transported from the castles of Europe. In an entrance hall, four or five eighteenth-century Dutch interiors; up higher on the avenue the collector is, as we say, "into" contemporary, and thus a Jasper Johns, bought yesterday, hangs over a leather sofa. Everywhere, gregarious tables to hold quaint miniatures, inlaid boxes, Georgian silver items; grand carpets from Xanadu, chairs from France, desks from England, and in the dining hall, large enough for the knights in a saga, rare, fragile practicalities in lots of twenty-four for receiving food and drink. Unassuaged longings and who would imagine there was so much provenance left or waiting to be sold or traded. "Stone by stone we shall remove the Alhambra, the Kremlin and the Louvre and build them anew on the banks of the Hudson" (Benjamin de Casseres, *Mirrors of New York*). A billion dollars is buying, arranging, dusting and polishing and insuring.

As for a mere million or two: nothing much came forth from the red lips, the lithe, stalky, skin-and-bone woman in a mink tent getting out of the long, black, hired car. She emerges from the tomb and from the defiant optics of the black limousine windows, opaque as death on the outside, but from which she, inside, can look out to see a white poodle on its leash. I wish I had one, she says, and he, from the hearse in which they are driven, says, If you want one, buy one, for God's sake.

The black tube waits at the curb while they enter and loll for an hour or so, as if in a sudden resurrection, among the tropical plants of the lead-paned restaurant. The little French lamps on the table reveal luscious cakes waiting for the knife. But not for them. Perhaps for the two plump wage earners from the "boroughs," maliciously defining address, perhaps for them the infantile fatality of the gorgeous concoctions, all cream and gurgle and clog, life threatening and shaming. The tomb dwellers look on from their decaf espressos.

The delivery boy from the Food Emporium is at the door. Theatrical youth, delivery youth, scarcely a boy. High-top running shoes with the laces slack, in the fashion, hair, also in the fashion, shaved from the nape of the neck to end in a pile at the top of the head beaming straight up as if struck by a thunderbolt — some name-brand mousse or spray helping to defy gravity. Around the streets they go, pushing their archival load: low-sodium seltzer water, kosher hot dogs, low-cholesterol mayo, Perdue chicken breasts, Weight Watchers margarine, four-grain bread, Ben and Jerry's chocolate cherry ice cream, Paul Newman's marinara sauce . . . What the deliverer gets from the $2.50 charge for service is a corporate secret, but here he is, deer-fleet, smelling briskly of cologne, on the job.

Slavery came to the Manhattan shores with great promptitude, came to New Amsterdam with black souls gathered up by the prudent Dutch at Curaçao, another of the country's far-flung "interests." And more were to arrive later, after Amsterdam gave way to New York. A pitiful insurrection among the slaves of the city took place in 1712, a dream-heavy insufficiency of Black Power it was. A few dozen from Africa, with a musket here and there, went on a rampage, set a few fires, killed a few whites. You see the insurrectionists glistening and trembling, large, agonized, bewildered figures like the Emperor Jones, trying to run for cover up a tree, in a swamp, and soon overcome by the city militia. And taught a lesson, yes, strung up for public viewing, burned, tortured on the wheel. Consequent fear on the streets, in the houses, no place is safe, muggers (derivation unknown) on every corner, too many of them . . . and so on and so on.

There appeared in the fearful city a most extraordinary white lunatic, one Mary Burton, indentured — that is, a citizen from the British Isles working to pay off the cost of the passage to the New World, pay on the credit card more or less, many of them of course declining in clever ways after reaching their destination, here. When fires and robberies broke out, Mary B. began to offer her inside dope gained in taverns, her dense knowledge of barroom alliances for felony. She took her interesting, fevered tales to the courts and thus set the slaveholders on edge for protection and revenge. Slaves hanged, burned at the stake, sent off somewhere, until Mary, wonderfully alert to the great industry of New York, alert to publicity, the magic of it, went astray, far afield, accusing respectable whites, whoever, and at last that was that for Mary. Slavery abolished in New York in 1799, too risky, not worth the bother, bottom line.

City of journalism, the lone suitable literary art to catch up, take in this treasure island, open-faced, each street a logo, Fifth Avenue or Tenth Avenue, Duke Ellington Boulevard or Gramercy Park, East Side and West Side, the Village, a transparency, laid out, as easy to read as an advertisement, nothing hidden. You know where you are and who will be there with you, a sort of suburbanism in the air. Someone must be doing the work, coming in of a morning, double-parking, arriving over the bridges and expressways to fix the leaking pipe, to paint the high-gloss walls, lay the Italian tiles, scrape the floors in a gas mask, deliver the heating oil flowing in the long, fat coils. They run the elevators, stand importantly in their tuxedos in the old-fashioned restaurants and at midnight take the subway train back to Brooklyn or Queens or Flushing or some other stop.

Nothing here in the brilliant inner city for the family man, place of torture and bankruptcy for the guards of the flaking, tedious columns of the Temple of Dendur at the Metropolitan Museum, for the news dealers, the movie ushers, the night workers with their pails and Dustbusters neatening at Rockefeller Center. The old shops in the West Thirties and on Seventh Avenue with their filthy windows announcing Wholesale — dusty ribbons for unwanted hats, plastic flowers, buttons and buttonholes, bolts of figured cotton for the homemade house dress, thread for the Singer sewing machine, guitar strings: establishments sitting on prime real estate, a joke, you might say, of maladaptation and swept away in a quick fluid movement, as if by the hose from the sanitation truck.

The Italo-Americans on the street where the deputed mobster lives in a small bungalow with a Mercedes equal in size out front and little sign here of melting in the pot. The Salvadorans, the Dominicans, the Koreans in their fruit stores, the Asian Indians at the newspaper kiosk, hot dog vendors from Greece, huddling together somewhere, each one a secret, inviolable clan, getting by, offering product but, off the income bracket, un-Americanized, still breathing in the hills of home.

The Irish and many of the German immigrants to the city were not attracted to fighting for the Union and in honor of the Emancipation Proclamation. So when the Conscription Act was passed in 1863, falling largely on the working classes and the unemployed whites without the money to buy off, the great Draft Riots broke out. The Irish, objects of contempt in New York and Boston, did not always share the Yankee high-minded grief for the stain of slavery on the national psyche. The Rainbow Coalition of Protestant, well-to-do abolitionists and the black population was the same it is now at the reign of our first black mayor. A horror of class and race war fell on the streets of Manhattan in 1863 as the rioters attacked the police, set fire to the Colored Orphan Asylum, lynched, broke into white abolitionist homes, set upon Horace Greeley's left-wing paper, the *Tribune,* and sent him flying out the back door or hiding under a table in fear of his life. "It was the women who inflicted the most fiendish tortures upon Negroes, soldiers and policemen captured by the mob, slicing their flesh with butcher knives, ripping out eyes and tongues, and applying the torch after victims had been sprayed with oil and hanged on a tree" (*The Gangs of New York,* by Herbert Asbury).

The explorers seldom came to a good end. Columbus died in want, ignorant of the fame that would attach his name to New York City banks, avenues, universities, restaurants, dry-cleaning establishments, video centers, delis, and many more. Sir Walter Raleigh, after smoking tobacco and eating the corn of the New World in Virginia, got into trouble with the Spanish and was beheaded in London. "What a head fell there," said the executioner. Verrazano was killed by the natives in the West Indies. Henry Hudson and his son, after a leveraged buyout of the Hudson Bay Company, were cast adrift to die up near Labrador, never to see the Palisades again.

The truest New Yorker among the great seamen was Captain Kidd, who in his span of years kept going and coming here, married a respectable and prosperous widow, Sarah Oort, and had a daughter, built himself a brick house, and gathered up other properties. In the colonial period, Captain Kidd could be said to know everyone worth knowing; he knew the legislator Robert Livingston and the colonial governor of New England, Lord Bellamont, both of whom were mixed up in his affairs and maritime assignments and both abandoned him. Captain Kidd, sent out to hunt pirates, was accused of turning pirate himself and of murdering a troublesome seaman during a quarrel. The captain left some treasure from the legal looting of captured ships at Gardiners Island on Long Island and left in romantic minds the possibilities of hidden treasure elsewhere. Like our own, finally sentenced to death or long imprisonment, he has had his defenders, investigative reporters telling a different story. As for him, his defense is familiar to New York ears: "I am the innocentest person of them all, only I have been sworn against by perjured persons."

The noble mariners of old, taking off without a space suit and nobody back in Europe on Mission Control, endured great suffering and often with little profit to themselves. But, of course, they would discover this America and the other America, South. And yet imagine the United States at last, each state with its boundaries and climate, mountains or flatlands for wheat; imagine all the states with their borders and squawking pride without the immense, obstinate, unassimilable, violently fluent New York City. Imagine the sulky provinciality of a vast country freed from this "un-American" city with its intimidating statistics of bodies, crimes, dope, guns, homicide records, robberies, illiterates, poverty, its blank towers, mausoleums hanging over the edge of the two rivers and blighting the rigid intersections in between, and its turbulent campaigns of consumption in the imperial mode.

From where have you come and why are you here? Why does the hummingbird return to the north? A puzzle, each resident of the recalcitrant city a puzzle. Once here, a lingering infection seems to set in and the streets are filled with the complaints and whines of the hypochondriac who will not budge, will not face a fertile pasture. Here it is, that's all, the place itself, shadowy, ever promising and ever withholding, a bad mother, queen of the double bind . . . Nevertheless.

> Keep your fields of clover and timothy, and your cornfields and
>   orchards,
> Keep the blossoming buckwheat fields where the Ninth-month
>   bees hum;
> Give me faces and streets — give me these phantoms incessant
>   and endless along the trottoirs!
>
> —Whitman

The constellations are not visible in the evening sky because of our impressive interference. Perhaps there, suddenly, is the red star, Denab, United Airlines coming into port, edging down so gracefully with its rosy flickering lights, an everlasting beacon in the overloaded sky, saying, *prepare for landing*.

GARRETT HONGO

# *Kubota*

FROM PLOUGHSHARES

ON December 8, 1941, the day after the Japanese attack on Pearl Harbor in Hawaii, my grandfather barricaded himself with his family — my grandmother, my teenage mother, her two sisters and two brothers — inside of his home in La'ie, a sugar plantation village on Oahu's North Shore. This was my maternal grandfather, a man most villagers called by his last name, Kubota. It could mean either "Wayside Field" or else "Broken Dreams," depending on which ideograms he used. Kubota ran La'ie's general store, and the previous night, after a long day of bad news on the radio, some locals had come by, pounded on the front door, and made threats. One was said to have brandished a machete. They were angry and shocked, as the whole nation was in the aftermath of the surprise attack. Kubota was one of the few Japanese Americans in the village and president of the local Japanese language school. He had become a target for their rage and suspicion. A wise man, he locked all his doors and windows and did not open his store the next day, but stayed closed and waited for news from some official.

He was a *kibei,* a Japanese American born in Hawaii (a U.S. territory then, so he was thus a citizen) but who was subsequently sent back by his father for formal education in Hiroshima, Japan, their home province. *Kibei* is written with two ideograms in Japanese: one is the word for "return" and the other is the word for "rice." Poetically, it means one who returns from America, known as the Land of Rice in Japanese (by contrast, Chinese immigrants called their new home Mountain of Gold).

Kubota was graduated from a Japanese high school and then came back to Hawaii as a teenager. He spoke English — and a Hawaiian creole version of it at that — with a Japanese accent. But he was well liked and good at numbers, scrupulous and hard working like so many immigrants and children of immigrants. Castle & Cook, a grower's company that ran the sugarcane business along the North Shore, hired him on first as a stock boy and then appointed him to run one of its company stores. He did well, had the trust of management and labor — not an easy accomplishment in any day — married, had children, and had begun to exert himself in community affairs and excel in his own recreations. He put together a Japanese community organization that backed a Japanese language school for children and sponsored teachers from Japan. Kubota boarded many of them, in succession, in his own home. This made dinners a silent affair for his talkative, Hawaiian-bred children, as their stern *sensei*, or teacher, was nearly always at table and their own abilities in the Japanese language were as delinquent as their attendance. While Kubota and the *sensei* rattled on about things Japanese, speaking Japanese, his children hurried through their suppers and tried to run off early to listen to the radio shows.

After dinner, while the *sensei* graded exams seated in a wicker chair in the spare room and his wife and children gathered around the radio in the front parlor, Kubota sat on the screened porch outside, reading the local Japanese newspapers. He finished reading about the same time as he finished the tea he drank for his digestion — a habit he'd learned in Japan — and then he'd get out his fishing gear and spread it out on the plank floors. The wraps on his rods needed to be redone, gears in his reels needed oil, and, once through with those tasks, he'd painstakingly wind on hundreds of yards of new line. Fishing was his hobby and his passion. He spent weekends camping along the North Shore beaches with his children, setting up umbrella tents, packing a rice pot and hibachi along for meals. And he caught fish. *Ulu'a* mostly, the huge surf-feeding fish known on the mainland as the jack crevalle, but he'd go after almost anything in its season. In Kawela, a plantation-owned bay nearby, he fished for mullet Hawaiian-style with a throw net, stalking the bottom-hugging, gray-backed schools as they gathered at the stream mouths and in the freshwater springs. In an outrigger out beyond the reef, he'd try for *aku* — the skipjack tuna prized for steaks and, sliced raw and mixed with fresh seaweed and cut onions, for *sashimi* salad. In Kahaluu and Ka'awa and on an offshore rock locals called Goat Island, he loved to go torching, stringing lanterns on bamboo poles stuck in the sand to attract *kumu'u*, the red goatfish, as they schooled at night just inside the reef. But in Lai'e on Laniloa Point near Kahuku, the northernmost tip of Oahu, he cast twelve- and fourteen-foot surf rods for the huge, varicolored, and fast-running *ulu'a* as they ran for schools of squid and baitfish just beyond the biggest breakers and past the low sand flats wadable from the shore to nearly a half mile out. At sunset, against the western light, he looked as if he walked on water as he came back, fish and rods slung over his shoulders, stepping along the rock and coral path just inches under the surface of a running tide.

When it was torching season, in December or January, he'd drive out the afternoon before and stay with old friends, the Tanakas or Yoshikawas, shopkeepers like him who ran stores near the fishing grounds. They'd have been preparing for weeks, selecting and cutting their bamboo poles, cleaning the hurricane lanterns, tearing up burlap sacks for the cloths they'd soak with kerosene and tie onto sticks they'd poke into the soft sand of the shallows. Once lit, touched off with a Zippo lighter, these would be the torches they'd use as beacons to attract the schooling fish. In another time, they might have made up a dozen paper lanterns of the kind mostly used for decorating the summer folk dances outdoors on the grounds of the Buddhist church during O-Bon, the Festival for the Dead. But now, wealthy and modern and efficient killers of fish, Tanaka and Kubota used rag torches and Colemans and cast rods with tips made of Tonkin bamboo and butts of American-spun fiberglass. After just one good night, they might bring back a prize bounty of a dozen burlap bags filled with scores of bloody, rigid fish delicious to eat and even better to give away as gifts to friends, family, and special customers.

It was a Monday night, the day after Pearl Harbor, and there was a rattling knock at the front door. Two FBI agents presented themselves, showed identification, and took my grandfather in for questioning in Honolulu. He didn't return home for days. No one knew what had happened or what was wrong. But there

was a roundup going on of all those in the Japanese-American
community suspected of sympathizing with the enemy and worse.
My grandfather was suspected of espionage, of communicating
with offshore Japanese submarines launched from the attack fleet
days before war began. Torpedo planes and escort fighters, decorated with the insignia of the Rising Sun, had taken an approach route from northwest of Oahu directly across Kahuku
Point and on toward Pearl. They had strafed an auxiliary air station near the fishing grounds my grandfather loved and destroyed a small gun battery there, killing three men. Kubota was
known to have sponsored and harbored Japanese nationals in his
own home. He had a radio. He had wholesale access to firearms.
Circumstances and an undertone of racial resentment had combined with wartime hysteria in the aftermath of the tragic naval
battle to cast suspicion on the loyalties of my grandfather and all
other Japanese Americans. The FBI reached out and pulled
hundreds of them in for questioning in dragnets cast throughout
the West Coast and Hawaii.

My grandfather was lucky; he'd somehow been let go after only
a few days. Others were not as fortunate. Hundreds, from small
communities in Washington, California, Oregon, and Hawaii, were
rounded up and, after what appeared to be routine questioning,
shipped off under Justice Department orders to holding centers
in Leuppe on the Navaho reservation in Arizona, in Fort Mis-
soula in Montana, and on Sand Island in Honolulu Harbor. There
were other special camps on Maui in Ha'iku and on Hawaii —
the Big Island — in my own home village of Volcano.

Many of these men — it was exclusively the Japanese-American men suspected of ties to Japan who were initially rounded
up — did not see their families again for more than four years.
Under a suspension of due process that was only after the fact
ruled as warranted by military necessity, they were, if only temporarily, "disappeared" in Justice Department prison camps
scattered in particularly desolate areas of the United States designated as militarily "safe." These were grim forerunners of the
assembly centers and concentration camps for the 120,000 Japanese-American evacuees that were to come later.

I am Kubota's eldest grandchild, and I remember him as a
lonely, habitually silent old man who lived with us in our home

near Los Angeles for most of my childhood and adolescence. It was the fifties, and my parents had emigrated from Hawaii to the mainland in the hope of a better life away from the old sugar plantation. After some success, they had sent back for my grand-parents and taken them in. And it was my grandparents who did the work of the household while my mother and father worked their salaried city jobs. My grandmother cooked and sewed, washed our clothes, and knitted in the front room under the light of a huge lamp with a bright three-way bulb. Kubota raised a flower garden, read up on soils and grasses in gardening books, and planted a zoysia lawn in front and a dichondra one in back. He planted a small patch near the rear block wall with green onions, eggplant, white Japanese radishes, and cucumber. While he hoed and spaded the loamless, clayey earth of Los Angeles, he sang particularly plangent songs in Japanese about plum blossoms and bamboo groves.

Once, in the mid-sixties, after a dinner during which, as al-ways, he had been silent while he worked away at a meal of fish and rice spiced with dabs of Chinese mustard and catsup thinned with soy sauce, Kubota took his own dishes to the kitchen sink and washed them up. He took a clean jelly jar out of the cup-board — the glass was thick and its shape squatty like an old-fashioned. He reached around to the hutch below where he kept his bourbon. He made himself a drink and retired to the living room where I was expected to join him for "talk story," the Ha-waiian idiom for chewing the fat.

I was a teenager and, though I was bored listening to stories I'd heard often enough before at holiday dinners, I was dutiful. I took my spot on the couch next to Kubota and heard him out. Usually, he'd tell me about his schooling in Japan where he learned judo along with mathematics and literature. He'd learned the *so-roban* there — the abacus, which was the original pocket calcula-tor of the Far East — and that, along with his strong, judo-trained back, got him his first job in Hawaii. This was the moral. "Study *ha-ahd*," he'd say with pidgin emphasis. "Learn read good. Learn speak da kine *good* English." The message is the familiar one taught to any children of immigrants: succeed through education. And imitation. But this time, Kubota reached down into his past and told me a different story. I was thirteen by then, and I suppose he thought me ready for it. He told me about Pearl Harbor, how the planes flew in wing after wing of formations over his old house in La'ie in Hawaii, and how, the next day, after Roosevelt had made his famous "Day of Infamy" speech about the treachery of the Japanese, the FBI agents had come to his door and taken him in, hauled him off to Honolulu for questioning, and held him without charge for several days. I thought he was lying. I thought he was making up a kind of horror story to shock me and give his moral that much more starch. But it was true. I asked around. I brought it up during history class in junior high school, and my teacher, after silencing me and stepping me off to the back of the room, told me that it was indeed so. I asked my mother and she said it was true. I asked my schoolmates, who laughed and ridiculed me for being so ignorant. We lived in a Japanese-American community, and the parents of most of my classmates were the *nisei* who had been interned as teenagers all through the war. But there was a strange silence around all of this. There was a hush, as if one were invoking the ill powers of the dead when one brought it up. No one cared to speak about the evacuation and relocation for very long. It wasn't in our history books, though we were studying World War II at the time. It wasn't in the family albums of the people I knew and whom I'd visit staying over weekends with friends. And it wasn't anything that the family talked about or allowed me to keep bringing up either. I was given the facts, told sternly and pointedly that "it was war" and that "nothing could be done." *"Shikatta ga nai"* is the phrase in Japanese, a kind of resolute and determinist pronouncement on how to deal with inexplicable tragedy. I was to know it but not to dwell on it. Japanese Americans were busy trying to forget it ever happened and were having a hard enough time building their new lives after "camp." It was as if we had no history for four years and the relocation was something unspeakable.

But Kubota would not let it go. In session after session, for months it seemed, he pounded away at his story. He wanted to tell me the names of the FBI agents. He went over their questions and his responses again and again. He'd tell me how one would try to act friendly toward him, offering him cigarettes while the other, who hounded him with accusations and threats, left the interrogation room. Good cop, bad cop, I thought to myself,

already superficially streetwise from stories black classmates told
of the Watts riots and from my having watched too many epi-
sodes of *Dragnet* and *The Mod Squad*. But Kubota was not interested in my experiences. I was not made yet, and he was determined that his stories be part of my making. He spoke quietly at
first, mildly, but once into his narrative and after his drink was
down, his voice would rise and quaver with resentment and he'd
make his accusations. He gave his testimony to me and I held it
at first cautiously in my conscience like it was an heirloom too
delicate to expose to strangers and anyone outside of the world
Kubota made with his words. "I give you story now," he once said,
"and you learn speak good, eh?" It was my job, as the disciple of
his preaching I had then become, Ananda to his Buddha, to reassure him with a promise. "You learn speak good like the Dillingham," he'd say another time, referring to the wealthy scion
of the grower family who had once run, unsuccessfully, for one
of Hawaii's first senatorial seats. Or he'd then invoke a magical
name, the name of one of his heroes, a man he thought particularly exemplary and righteous. "Learn speak dah good Ing-rish
like *Mistah Inouye*," Kubota shouted. "He *lick* dah Dillingham even
in debate. I saw on *terre-bision* myself." He was remembering the
debates before the first senatorial election just before Hawaii was
admitted to the Union as its fiftieth state. "You *tell* story," Kubota
would end. And I had my injunction.

The town we settled in after the move from Hawaii is called
Gardena, the independently incorporated city south of Los Angeles and north of San Pedro harbor. At its northern limit, it borders on Watts and Compton, black towns. To the southwest are
Torrance and Redondo Beach, white towns. To the rest of L.A.,
Gardena is primarily famous for having legalized five-card draw
poker after the war. On Vermont Boulevard, its eastern border,
there is a dingy little Vegas-like strip of card clubs with huge
parking lots and flickering neon signs that spell out "The Rainbow" and "The Horseshoe" in timed sequences of varicolored
lights. The town is only secondarily famous as the largest community of Japanese Americans in the United States outside of
Honolulu, Hawaii. When I was in high school there, it seemed to
me that every *sansei* kid I knew wanted to be a doctor, an engineer, or a pharmacist. Our fathers were gardeners or electricians

or nurserymen or ran small businesses catering to other Japanese Americans. Our mothers worked in civil service for the city or as cashiers for Thrifty Drug. What the kids wanted was a good job, good pay, a fine home, and no troubles. No one wanted to mess with the law — from either side — and no one wanted to mess with language or art. They all talked about getting into the right clubs so that they could go to the right schools. There was a certain kind of sameness, an intensely enforced system of conformity. Style was all. Boys wore moccasin-sewn shoes from Flagg Brothers, black A-1 slacks, and Kensington shirts with high collars. Girls wore their hair up in stiff bouffants solidified in hairspray and knew all the latest dances from the slauson to the funky chicken. We did well in chemistry and in math, no one who was Japanese but me spoke in English class or in history unless called upon, and no one talked about World War II. The day after Robert Kennedy was assassinated, after winning the California Democratic primary, we worked on calculus and elected class coordinators for the prom, featuring the 5th Dimension. We avoided grief. We avoided government. We avoided strong feelings and dangers of any kind. Once punished, we tried to maintain a concerted emotional and social discipline and would not willingly seek to fall out of the narrow margin of protective favor again.

But when I was thirteen, in junior high, I'd not understood why it was so difficult for my classmates, those who were themselves Japanese American, to talk about the relocation. They had cringed, too, when I tried to bring it up during our discussions of World War II. I was Hawaiian-born. They were mainland-born. Their parents had been in camp, had been the ones to suffer the complicated experience of having to distance themselves from their own history and all things Japanese in order to make their way back and into the American social and economic mainstream. It was out of this sense of shame and a fear of stigma I was only beginning to understand that the *nisei* had silenced themselves. And, for their children, among whom I grew up, they wanted no heritage, no culture, no contact with a defiled history. I recall the silence very well. The Japanese-American children around me were burdened in a way I was not. Their injunction was silence. Mine was to speak.

Away at college, in another protected world in its own way as magical to me as the Hawaii of my childhood, I dreamed about my grandfather. Tired from studying languages, practicing German conjugations or scripting an army's worth of Chinese ideograms on a single sheet of paper, Kubota would come to me as I drifted off into sleep. Or I would walk across the newly mown ball field in back of my dormitory, cutting through a street-side phalanx of ancient eucalyptus trees on my way to visit friends off campus, and I would think of him, his anger, and his sadness.

I don't know myself what makes someone feel that kind of need to have a story they've lived through be deposited somewhere, but I can guess. I think about *The Illiad, The Odyssey, The Peloponnesian Wars* of Thucydides, and a myriad of the works of literature I've studied. A character, almost a *topoi* he occurs so often, is frequently the witness who gives personal testimony about an event the rest of his community cannot even imagine. The sibyl is such a character. And Procne, the maid whose tongue is cut out so that she will not tell that she has been raped by her own brother-in-law, the king of Thebes. There are the dime novels, the epic blockbusters Hollywood makes into miniseries, and then there are the plain, relentless stories of witnesses who have suffered through horrors major and minor that have marked and changed their lives. I myself haven't talked to Holocaust victims. But I've read their survival stories and their stories of witness and been revolted and moved by them. My father-in-law, Al Thiessen, tells me his war stories again and again and I listen. A Mennonite who set aside the strictures of his own church in order to serve, he was a Marine codeman in the Pacific during World War II, in the Signal Corps on Guadalcanal, Morotai, and Bougainville. He was part of the island-hopping maneuver MacArthur had devised to win the war in the Pacific. He saw friends die from bombs which exploded not ten yards away. When he was with the 298th Signal Corps attached to the Thirteenth Air Force, he saw plane after plane come in and crash, just short of the runway, killing their crews, setting the jungle ablaze with oil and gas fires. Emergency wagons would scramble, bouncing over newly bulldozed land men used just the afternoon before for a football game. Every time we go fishing together, whether it's in a McKenzie boat drifting for salmon in Tillamook Bay or taking a lunch break from wading the riffles of a stream in the Cascades, he tells me about what happened to him and the young men in his unit. One was a Jewish boy from Brooklyn. One was a foul-mouthed kid from Kansas. They died. And he *has* to tell me. And I *have* to listen. It's a ritual payment the young owe their elders who have survived. The evacuation and relocation is something like that.

Kubota, my grandfather, had been ill with Alzheimer's disease for some time before he died. At the house he'd built on Kamehameha Highway in Hau'ula, a seacoast village just down the road from La'ie where he had his store, he'd wander out from the garage or greenhouse where he'd set up a workbench, and trudge down to the beach or up toward the line of pines he'd planted while employed by the Work Projects Administration during the thirties. Kubota thought he was going fishing. Or he thought he was back at work for Roosevelt, planting pines as a windbreak or soilbreak on the windward flank of the Ko'olau Mountains, emerald monoliths rising out of sea and cane fields from Waialua to Kaneohe. When I visited, my grandmother would send me down to the beach to fetch him. Or I'd run down Kam Highway a quarter mile or so and find him hiding in the cane field by the roadside, counting stalks, measuring circumferences in the claw of his thumb and forefinger. The look on his face was confused or concentrated, I didn't know which. But I guessed he was going fishing again. I'd grab him and walk him back to his house on the highway. My grandmother would shut him in a room.

Within a few years, Kubota had a stroke and survived it, then he had another one and was completely debilitated. The family decided to put him in a nursing home in Kahuku, just set back from the highway, within a mile or so of Kahuku Point and the Tanaka Store where he had his first job as a stock boy. He lived there three years, and I visited him once with my aunt. He was like a potato that had been worn down by cooking. Everything on him — his eyes, his teeth, his legs and torso — seemed like it had been sloughed away. What he had been was mostly gone now and I was looking at the nub of a man. In a wheelchair, he grasped my hands and tugged on them — violently. His hands were still thick and, I believed, strong enough to lift me out of my own seat into his lap. He murmured something in Japanese — he'd long ago ceased to speak any English. My aunt and I cried a little, and we left him.

I remember walking out on the black asphalt of the parking lot of the nursing home. It was heat-cracked and eroded already, and grass had veined itself into the interstices. There were coconut trees around, a cane field I could see across the street, and the ocean I knew was pitching a surf just beyond it. The green Ko'olaus came up behind us. Somewhere nearby, alongside the beach, there was an abandoned airfield in the middle of the canes. As a child, I'd come upon it playing one day, and my friends and I kept returning to it, day after day, playing war or sprinting games or coming to fly kites. I recognize it even now when I see it on TV — it's used as a site for action scenes in the detective shows Hollywood always sets in the islands: a helicopter chasing the hero racing away in a Ferrari, or gun dealers making a clandestine rendezvous on the abandoned runway. It was the old airfield strafed by Japanese planes the day the major flight attacked Pearl Harbor. It was the airfield the FBI thought my grandfather had targeted in his night fishing and signaling with the long surf poles he'd stuck in the sandy bays near Kahuku Point.

Kubota died a short while after I visited him, but not, I thought, without giving me a final message. I was on the mainland, in California studying for Ph.D. exams, when my grandmother called me with the news. It was a relief. He'd suffered from his debilitation a long time and I was grateful he'd gone. I went home for the funeral and gave the eulogy. My grandmother and I took his ashes home in a small, heavy metal box wrapped in a black *furoshiki*, a large silk scarf. She showed me the name the priest had given to him on his death, scripted with a calligraphy brush on a long, narrow talent of plain wood. Buddhist commoners, at death, are given priestly names, received symbolically into the clergy. The idea is that, in their next life, one of scholarship and leisure, they might meditate and attain the enlightenment the religion is aimed at. *"Shaku Shūchi,"* the ideograms read. It was Kubota's Buddhist name, incorporating characters from his family and given names. It meant "Shining Wisdom of the Law." He died on Pearl Harbor Day, December 7, 1983.

After years, after I'd finally come back to live in Hawaii again, only once did I dream of Kubota, my grandfather. It was the same night I'd heard HR 442, the redress bill for Japanese Americans, had been signed into law. In my dream that night Kubota was "torching," and he sang a Japanese song, a querulous and wavery folk ballad, as he hung paper lanterns on bamboo poles stuck into the sand in the shallow water of the lagoon behind the reef near Kahuku Point. Then he was at a work table, smoking a hand-rolled cigarette, letting it dangle from his lips Bogart-style as he drew, daintily and skillfully, with a narrow trim brush, ideogram after ideogram on a score of paper lanterns he had hung in a dark shed to dry. He had painted a talismanic mantra onto each lantern, the ideogram for the word "red" in Japanese, a bit of art blended with some superstition, a piece of sympathetic magic appealing to the magenta coloring on the rough skins of the schooling, night-feeding fish he wanted to attract to his baited hooks. He strung them from pole to pole in the dream then, hiking up his khaki worker's pants so his white ankles showed and wading through the shimmering black waters of the sand flats and then the reef. "The moon is leaving, leaving," he sang in Japanese. "Take me deeper in the savage sea." He turned and crouched like an ice racer then, leaning forward so that his unshaven face almost touched the light film of water. I could see the light stubble of beard like a fine, gray ash covering the lower half of his face. I could see his gold-rimmed spectacles. He held a small wooden boat in his cupped hands and placed it lightly on the sea and pushed it away. One of his lanterns was on it and, written in small neat rows like a sutra scroll, it had been decorated with the silvery names of all our dead.

NAOMI SHIHAB NYE

# *Maintenance*

FROM THE GEORGIA REVIEW

THE ONLY MAID I ever had left messages throughout our house: *Lady as I was cleaning your room I heard a mouse and all the clothes in your closet fell down to the floor there is too many dresses in there take a few off. Your friend Marta Alejandro.* Sometimes I'd find notes stuck into the couch with straight pins. *I cannot do this room today bec. St. Jude came to me in a dream and say it is not safe.* Our darkroom was never safe because the devil liked dark places and also the enlarger had an eye that picked up light and threw it on Marta. She got sick and had to go to a doctor who gave her green medicine that tasted like leaves.

Sometimes I'd come home to find her lounging in the bamboo chair on the back porch, eating melon, or lying on the couch with a bowl of half-melted ice cream balanced on her chest. She seemed depressed by my house. She didn't like the noise the vacuum made. Once she waxed the bathtub with floor wax. I think she was experimenting.

Each Wednesday I paid Marta ten dollars — that's what she asked for. When I raised it to eleven, then thirteen, she held the single dollars away from the ten as if they might contaminate it. She did not seem happy to get raises, and my friends (who paid her ten dollars each for the other days of the week) were clearly unhappy to hear about it. After a while I had less work of my own and less need for help, so I found her a position with two gay men who lived in the neighborhood. She called once to say she liked them very much because mostly what they wanted her to do was shine. Shine?

"You know, silver. They have a lot of bowls. They have real beautiful spoons not like your spoons. They have a big circle tray that shines like the moon."

My friend Kathy had no maid and wanted none. She ran ten miles a day and lived an organized life. Once I brought her a gift — a blue weaving from Guatemala, diagonal patterns of thread on sticks — and she looked at it dubiously. "Give it to someone else," she said. "I really appreciate your thinking of me, but I try not to keep things around here." Then I realized how bare her mantel was. Who among us would fail to place *something* on a mantel? A few shelves in her kitchen also stood empty, and not the highest ones either.

Kathy had very definite methods of housekeeping. When we'd eat dinner with her she'd rise quickly, before dessert, to scrape each plate and place it in one side of her sink to soak. She had Tupperware containers already lined up for leftovers and a soup pan with suds ready for the silverware. If I tried to help she'd slap at my hand. "Take care of your own kitchen," she'd say, not at all harshly. After dessert she'd fold up the card table we'd just eaten on and place it against the wall. Dining rooms needed to be swept after meals, and a stationary table just made sweeping more difficult.

Kathy could listen to any conversation and ask meaningful questions. She always seemed to remember what anybody said — maybe because she'd left space for it. One day she described having grown up in west Texas in a house of twelve children, the air jammed with voices, crosscurrents, the floors piled with grocery bags, mountains of tossed-off clothes, toys, blankets, the clutter of her sisters' shoes. That's when she decided to have only one pair of shoes at any time, running shoes, though she later revised this to include a pair of sandals.

Somehow I understood her better then, her tank tops and wiry arms . . . She ran to shake off dust. She ran to leave it all behind.

Another friend, Barbara, lived in an apartment but wanted to live in a house. Secretly I loved her spacious domain, perched high above the city with a wide sweep of view, but I could understand the wish to plant one's feet more firmly on the ground.

Barbara has the best taste of any person I've ever known — the best khaki-colored linen clothing, the best books, the name of the best masseuse. When I'm with her I feel uplifted, excited by life; there's so much to know about that I haven't heard of yet, and Barbara probably has. So I agreed to help her look.

We saw one house where walls and windows had been sheathed in various patterns of gloomy brocade. We visited another where the kitchen had been removed because the owners only ate in restaurants. They had a tiny office refrigerator next to their bed which I peeked into after they'd left the room: orange juice in a carton, coffee beans. A Krups coffee maker on the sink in their bathroom. They seemed unashamed, shrugging, "You could put a new kitchen wherever you like."

Then we entered a house that felt unusually vivid, airy, and hard-to-define until the realtor mentioned, "Have you noticed there's not a stick of wood anywhere in this place? No wood furniture, not even a wooden salad bowl, I'd bet. These people, very hip, you'd like them, want wood to stay in forests. The man says wood makes him feel heavy."

Barbara and her husband bought that house — complete with pear-shaped swimming pool, terraces of pansies, plum trees, white limestone rock gardens lush with succulents — but they brought wood into it. Never before had I been so conscious of things like wooden cutting boards. I helped them unpack and stroked the sanded ebony backs of African animals.

Then, after about a year and a half, Barbara called to tell me they were selling the house. "You won't believe this," she said, "but we've decided. It's the maintenance — the yardmen, little things always breaking — I'm so busy assigning chores I hardly have time for my own work anymore. A house really seems ridiculous to me now. If I want earth I can go walk in a park."

I had a new baby at the time and everything surprised me. My mouth dropped open, oh yes. I was living between a mound of fresh cloth diapers and a bucket of soiled ones, but I agreed to participate in the huge garage sale Barbara was having.

"That day," Barbara said later, "humanity sank to a new lowest level." We had made signs declaring the sale would start at 9 A.M., but by 8, middle-aged women and men were already ripping our boxes open, lunging into the back of my loaded pickup truck to see what I had. Two women argued in front of me over my stained dish drainer. I sold a kerosene heater which we'd never lit and a stack of my great-uncle's rumpled tablecloths, so large they completely engulfed an ironing board. One woman flashed a charm with my initial on it under my nose, saying, "I'd think twice about selling this, sweetheart — don't you realize it's ten carat?"

Afterwards we counted our wads of small bills and felt drained, diluted. We had spent the whole day bartering in a driveway, releasing ourselves from the burden of things we did not need. We even felt disgusted by the thought of eating — yet another means of accumulation — and would derive no pleasure from shopping, or catalogues, for at least a month.

While their new apartment was being refurbished, Barbara and her husband lived in a grand hotel downtown. She said it felt marvelous to use all the towels and have fresh ones appear on the racks within hours. Life seemed to regain its old recklessness. Soon they moved back to the same windswept apartment building they'd left, but to a higher floor. Sometimes I stood in their living room staring out at the horizon, which always seemed flawlessly clean.

My mother liked to sing along to records while she did housework — Mahalia Jackson, the Hallelujah Chorus. Sometimes we would sing duets, "Tell Me Why" and "Nobody Knows the Trouble I've Seen." I felt lucky my mother was such a clear soprano. We also sang while preparing for the big dinners my parents often gave, while folding the napkins or decorating little plates of hummus with olives and radishes.

I hungrily savored the tales told by the guests, the wild immigrant fables and metaphysical links. My mother's favorite friend, a rail-thin vegetarian who had once been secretary to Aldous Huxley, conversed passionately with a Syrian who was translating the Bible from Aramaic, then scolded me for leaving a mound of carrots on my plate.

"I'm not going to waste them!" I said. "I always save carrots for last because I love them best."

I thought this would please her, but she frowned. "Never save what you love, dear. You know what might happen? You may lose it while you are waiting."

It was difficult to imagine losing the carrots — what were they going to do, leap off my plate? — but she continued.

"Long ago I loved a man very much. He had gone on a far journey — our relationship had been delicate — and I waited anxiously for word from him. Finally a letter arrived and I stuffed it into my bag, trembling, thinking I would read it later on the train. Would rejoice in every word, was what I thought, but you know what happened? My purse was snatched away from me — stolen! — before I boarded the train. Things like that didn't even happen much in those days. I never saw the letter again — and I never saw my friend again either."

A pause swallowed the room. My mother rose to clear the dishes. Meaningful glances passed. I knew this woman had never married. When I asked why she hadn't written him to say she lost the letter, she said, "Don't you see, I also lost the only address I had for him."

I thought about this for days. Couldn't she have tracked him down? Didn't she know anyone else who might have known him and forwarded a message? I asked my mother, who replied that love was not easy.

Later my mother told me about a man who had carried a briefcase of important papers on a hike because he was afraid they might get stolen from the car. The trail wove high up the side of a mountain, between stands of majestic piñon. As he leaned over a rocky gorge to breathe the fragrant air, his fingers slipped and the briefcase dropped down into a narrow crevasse. They heard it far below, clunking into a deep underground pool. My mother said the man fell to the ground and sobbed.

The forest ranger whistled when they brought him up to the spot. "Hell of an aim!" He said there were some lost things you just had to say goodbye to, "like a wedding ring down a commode." My parents took the man to Western Union so he could telegraph about the lost papers, and the clerk said, "Don't feel bad, every woman drops an earring down a drain once in her life." The man glared. "This was not an earring — *I am not a woman!*"

I thought of the carrots, and the letter, when I heard his story. And of my American grandmother's vintage furniture, sold to indifferent buyers when I was still a child, too young even to think of antique wardrobes or bed frames. And I also thought of another friend of my parents, Peace Pilgrim, who walked across America for years, lecturing about inner peace and world peace. A single, broad pocket in her tunic contained all her worldly possessions: a toothbrush, a few postage stamps, a ballpoint pen. She had no bank account behind her and nothing in storage. Her motto was, "I walk till given shelter, I fast till given food." My father used to call her a freeloader behind her back, but my mother recognized a prophet when she saw one. I grappled with the details. How would it help humanity if I slept in a cardboard box under a bridge?

Peace Pilgrim told a story about a woman who worked hard so she could afford a certain style of furniture — French provincial, I think. She struggled to pay for insurance to protect it and rooms large enough to house it. She worked so much she hardly ever got to sit on it. "Then her life was over. And what kind of a life was that?"

Peace Pilgrim lived so deliberately she didn't even have colds. Shortly before her death in a car accident — for years she hadn't even ridden in cars — she sat on the fold-out bed in our living room, hugging her knees. I was grown by then, but all our furniture was still from thrift stores. She invited me to play the piano and sing for her, which I did, as she stared calmly around the room. "I loved to sing as a child," she said. "It is nice to have a piano."

In my grandmother's Palestinian village, the family has accumulated vast mounds and heaps of woolly comforters, stacking them in great wooden cupboards along the walls. The blankets smell pleasantly like sheep and wear coverings of cheerful gingham, but no family — not even our huge one on the coldest night — could possibly use that many blankets. My grandmother smiled when I asked her about them. She said people should have many blankets and head scarves to feel secure.

I took a photograph of her modern refrigerator, bought by one of the emigrant sons on a visit home from America, unplugged in a corner and stuffed with extra yardages of cloth and old magazines. I felt like one of those governmental watchdogs who asks how do you feel knowing your money is being used this way? My grandmother seemed nervous whenever we sat near the refrigerator, as if a stranger who refused to say his name had entered the room.

I never felt women were more doomed to housework than men; I thought women were lucky. Men had to maintain questionably pleasurable associations with less tangible elements — mortgage payments, fan belts and alternators, the IRS. I preferred sinks, and the way people who washed dishes immediately became exempt from after-dinner conversation. I loved to plunge my hands into tubs of scalding bubbles. Once my father reached in to retrieve something and reeled back, yelling, "Do you always make it this hot?" My parents got a dishwasher as soon as they could, but luckily I was out of college by then and never had to touch it. To me it only seemed to extend the task. You rinse, you bend and arrange, you measure soap — and it hasn't even started yet. How many other gratifications were as instant as the old method of washing dishes?

But it's hard to determine how much pleasure someone else gets from an addiction to a task. The neighbor woman who spends hours pinching off dead roses and browned lilies, wearing her housecoat and dragging a hose, may be as close as she comes to bliss, or she may be feeling utterly miserable. I weigh her sighs, her monosyllables about weather. Endlessly I compliment her yard. She shakes her head — "It's a lot of work." For more than a year she tries to get her husband to dig out an old stump at one corner but finally gives up and plants bougainvillea in it. The vibrant splash of pink seems to make her happier than anything else has in a long time.

Certain bylaws: If you have it, you will have to clean it. Nothing stays clean long. No one else notices your messy house as much as you do; they don't know where things are supposed to go anyway. It takes much longer to clean a house than to mess it up. Be suspicious of any cleaning agent (often designated with a single alphabetical letter, like *C* or *M*) that claims to clean everything from floors to dogs. Never install white floor tiles in the bathroom if your family members have brown hair. Cloth diapers eventually make the best rags — another reason beyond ecology. Other people's homes have charisma, charm, because you don't have to know them inside out. If you want high ceilings you may have to give up closets. (Still, as a neighbor once insisted to me, "high ceilings make you a better person.") Be wary of vacuums with headlights; they burn out in a month. A broom, as one of my starry-eyed newlywed sisters-in-law once said, *does a lot.* So does a dustpan. Whatever you haven't touched, worn, or eaten off of in a year should be passed on; something will pop up immediately to take its place.

I can't help thinking about these things — I live in the same town where Heloise lives. And down the street, in a shed behind his house, a man produces orange-scented wood moisturizer containing beeswax. You rub it on three times, let it sit, then buff it off. Your house smells like a hive in an orchard for twenty-four hours.

I'd like to say a word, just a short one, for the background hum of lesser, unexpected maintenances that can devour a day or days — or a life, if one is not careful. The scrubbing of the little ledge above the doorway belongs in this category, along with the thin lines of dust that quietly gather on bookshelves in front of the books. It took me an hour working with a bent wire to unplug the bird feeder, which had become clogged with fuzzy damp seed — no dove could get a beak in. And who would ever notice? The doves would notice. I am reminded of Buddhism whenever I undertake one of these invisible tasks: one acts, without any thought of reward or foolish notion of glory.

Perhaps all cleaning products should be labeled with additional warnings, as some natural-soap companies have taken to philosophizing right above the price tag. Bottles of guitar polish might read: "If you polish your guitar, it will not play any better. People who close their eyes to listen to your song will not see the gleaming wood. But you may feel more intimate with the instrument you are holding."

Sometimes I like the preparation for maintenance, the motions of preface, better than the developed story. I like to move all the chairs off the back porch many hours before I sweep it. I drag the mop and bucket into the house in the morning even if I don't intend to mop until dusk. This is related to addressing envelopes months before I write the letters to go inside.

Such extended prefacing drives my husband wild. He comes home and can read the house like a mystery story — small half-baked clues in every room. I get out the bowl for the birthday cake two days early. I like the sense of house as still life, on the road to becoming. Why rush to finish? You will only have to do it over again, sooner. I keep a proverb from Thailand above my towel rack: "Life is so short / we must move very slowly." I believe what it says.

My Palestinian father was furious with me when, as a teenager, I impulsively answered a newspaper ad and took a job as a maid. A woman, bedfast with a difficult pregnancy, ordered me to scrub, rearrange, and cook — for a dollar an hour. She sat propped on pillows, clicking her remote control, glaring suspiciously whenever I passed her doorway. She said her husband liked green Jell-O with fresh fruit. I was slicing peaches when the oven next to me exploded, filling the house with heavy black smoke. My meat loaf was only half baked. She shrieked and cried, blaming it on me, but how was I responsible for her oven?

It took me a long time to get over my negative feelings about pregnant women. I found a job scooping ice cream and had to wrap my swollen wrists in heavy elastic bands because they hurt so much. I had never considered what ice cream servers went through.

These days I wake up with good intentions. I pretend to be my own maid. I know the secret of travelers: each time you leave your home with a few suitcases, books, and note pads, your main-tenance shrinks to a lovely tiny size. All you need to take care of is your own body and a few changes of clothes. Now and then, if you're driving, you brush the pistachio shells off the seat. I love ice chests and miniature bottles of shampoo. Note the expansive breath veteran travelers take when they feel the road spinning open beneath them again.

Somewhere close behind me the outline of Thoreau's small cabin plods along, a ghost set on haunting. It even has the same rueful eyes Henry David had in the portrait in his book. A wealthy woman with a floral breakfast nook once told me I would "get over him" but I have not — documented here, I have not.

*

Marta Alejandro, my former maid, now lives in a green outbuilding at the corner of Beauregard and Madison. I saw her recently, walking a skinny wisp of a dog and wearing a bandanna twisted and tied around her waist. I called to her from my car. Maybe I only imagined she approached me reluctantly. Maybe she couldn't see who I was.

But then she started talking as if we had paused only a second ago. "Oh hi I was very sick were you? The doctor said it has to come to everybody. Don't think you can escape! Is your house still as big as it used to be?"

RICHARD RODRIGUEZ

# Late Victorians

FROM HARPER'S MAGAZINE

SAINT AUGUSTINE writes from his cope of dust that we are restless hearts, for earth is not our true home. Human unhappiness
is evidence of our immortality. Intuition tells us we are meant for
some other city.

Elizabeth Taylor, quoted in a magazine article of twenty years
ago, spoke of cerulean Richard Burton days on her yacht, days
that were nevertheless undermined by the elemental private re-
flection: This must end.

On a Sunday in summer, ten years ago, I was walking home from
the Latin mass at Saint Patrick's, the old Irish parish downtown,
when I saw thousands of people on Market Street. It was San
Francisco's Gay Freedom Day parade — not the first, but the
first I ever saw. Private lives were becoming public. There were
marching bands. There were floats. Banners blocked single lives
thematically into a processional mass, not unlike the consortiums
of the blessed in Renaissance paintings, each saint cherishing the
apparatus of his martyrdom: GAY DENTISTS. BLACK AND WHITE
LOVERS. GAYS FROM BAKERSFIELD. LATINA LESBIANS. From
the foot of Market Street they marched, east to west, following
the mythic American path toward optimism.

I followed the parade to Civic Center Plaza, where flags of routine nations yielded sovereignty to a multitude. Pastel billows
flowed over all.

Five years later, another parade. Politicians waved from white
convertibles. Dykes on Bikes revved up, thumbs upped. But now

banners bore the acronyms of death. AIDS. ARC. Drums were muffled as passing, plum-spotted young men slid by on motorized cable cars.

Though I am alive now, I do not believe that an old man's pessimism is truer than a young man's optimism simply because it comes after. There are things a young man knows that are true and are not yet in the old man's power to recollect. Spring has its sappy wisdom. Lonely teenagers still arrive in San Francisco aboard Greyhound buses. The city can still seem, I imagine, by comparison to where they came from, paradise.

Four years ago, on a Sunday in winter, a brilliant spring afternoon, I was jogging near Fort Point while overhead a young woman was, with difficulty, climbing over the railing of the Golden Gate Bridge. Holding down her skirt with one hand, with the other she waved to a startled spectator (the newspaper next day quoted a workman who was painting the bridge) before she stepped onto the sky.

To land like a spilled purse at my feet.

Serendipity has an eschatological tang here. Always has. Few American cities have had the experience, as we have had, of watching the civic body burn even as we stood, out of body, on a hillside, in a movie theater. Jeanette MacDonald's loony scatting of "San Francisco" has become our go-to-hell anthem. San Francisco has taken some heightened pleasure from the circus of final things. To Atlantis, to Pompeii, to the Pillar of Salt, we add the Golden Gate Bridge, not golden at all but rust red. San Francisco toys with the tragic conclusion.

For most of its brief life, San Francisco has entertained an idea of itself as heaven on earth, whether as Gold Town or City Beautiful or Treasure Island or Haight-Ashbury.

San Francisco can support both comic and tragic conclusions because the city is geographically *in extremis,* a metaphor for the farthest-flung possibility, a metaphor for the end of the line. Land's end.

To speak of San Francisco as land's end is to read the map from one direction only — as Europeans would read or as the East Coast has always read it. In my lifetime, San Francisco has become an Asian city. To speak, therefore, of San Francisco as land's end is to betray parochialism. Before my parents came to California from Mexico, they saw San Francisco as the North. The West was not west for them.

I cannot claim for myself the memory of a skyline such as the one César saw. César came to San Francisco in middle age; César came here as to some final place. He was born in South America; he had grown up in Paris; he had been everywhere, done everything; he assumed the world. Yet César was not condescending toward San Francisco, not at all. Here César saw revolution, and he embraced it.

Whereas I live here because I was born here. I grew up ninety miles away, in Sacramento. San Francisco was the nearest, the easiest, the inevitable city, since I needed a city. And yet I live here surrounded by people for whom San Francisco is a quest.

I have never looked for utopia on a map. Of course, I believe in human advancement. I believe in medicine, in astrophysics, in washing machines. But my compass takes its cardinal point from tragedy. If I respond to the metaphor of spring, I nevertheless learned, years ago, from my Mexican parents, from my Irish nuns, to count on winter. The point of Eden for me, for us, is not approach but expulsion.

After I met César in 1984, our friendly debate concerning the halcyon properties of San Francisco ranged from restaurant to restaurant. I spoke of limits. César boasted of freedoms.

It was César's conceit to add to the gates of Jerusalem, to add to the soccer fields of Tijuana, one other dreamscape hoped for the world over. It was the view from a hill, through a mesh of electrical tram wires, of an urban neighborhood in a valley. The vision took its name from the protruding wedge of a theater marquee. Here César raised his glass without discretion: To the Castro.

There were times, dear César, when you tried to switch sides if only to scorn American optimism, which, I remind you, had already become your own. At the high school where César taught, teachers and parents had organized a campaign to keep kids from driving themselves to the junior prom in an attempt to forestall liquor and death. Such a scheme momentarily reawakened César's Latin skepticism.

Didn't the Americans know? (His tone exaggerated incredulity.) Teenagers will crash into lampposts on their way home from proms, and there is nothing to be done about it. You cannot forbid tragedy.

By California standards I live in an old house. But not haunted. There are too many tall windows, there is too much salty light, especially in winter, though the windows rattle, rattle in summer when the fog lies overhead, and the house creaks and prowls at night. I feel myself immune to any confidence it seeks to tell.

To grow up homosexual is to live with secrets and within secrets. In no other place are those secrets more closely guarded than within the family home. The grammar of the gay city borrows metaphors from the nineteenth-century house. "Coming out of the closet" is predicated upon family laundry, dirty linen, skeletons.

I live in a tall Victorian house that has been converted to four apartments; four single men.

Neighborhood streets are named to honor nineteenth-century men of action, men of distant fame. Clay. Jackson. Scott. Pierce. Many Victorians in the neighborhood date from before the 1906 earthquake and fire.

Architectural historians credit the gay movement of the 1970s with the urban restoration of San Francisco. Twenty years ago this was a borderline neighborhood. This room, like all the rooms of the house, was painted headache green, apple green, boardinghouse green. In the 1970s homosexuals moved into black and working-class parts of the city, where they were perceived as pioneers or as blockbusters, depending.

Two decades ago some of the least expensive sections of San Francisco were wooden Victorian sections. It was thus a coincidence of the market that gay men found themselves living with the architectural metaphor for family. No other architecture in the American imagination is more evocative of family than the Victorian house. In those same years, the 1970s, and within those same Victorian houses, homosexuals were living rebellious lives to challenge the foundations of domesticity.

Was "queer bashing" as much a manifestation of homophobia as a reaction against gentrification? One heard the complaint often enough that gay men were as promiscuous with their capital as otherwise, buying, fixing up, then selling and moving on. Two incomes, no children, described an unfair advantage. No sooner would flower boxes begin to appear than an anonymous reply was smeared on the sidewalk out front: KILL FAGGOTS.

The three- or four-story Victorian house, like the Victorian novel, was built to contain several generations and several classes under one roof, behind a single oaken door. What strikes me is the confidence of Victorian architecture. Stairs, connecting one story with another, describe the confidence that bound generations together through time, confidence that the family would inherit the earth.

If Victorian houses exude a sturdy optimism by day, they are also associated in our imaginations with the Gothic — with shadows and cobwebby gimcrack, long corridors. The nineteenth century was remarkable for escalating optimism even as it excavated the back stairs, the descending architecture of nightmare — Freud's labor and Engels's.

I live on the second story, in rooms that have been rendered as empty as Yorick's skull — gutted, unrattled, in various ways unlocked, added skylights and new windows, new doors. The hallway remains the darkest part of the house.

This winter the hallway and lobby are being repainted to resemble an eighteenth-century French foyer. Of late we had walls and carpet of Sienese red; a baroque mirror hung in an alcove by the stairwell. Now we are to have enlightened austerity of an expensive sort — black-and-white marble floors and faux masonry. A man comes in the afternoons to texture the walls with a sponge and a rag and to paint white mortar lines that create an illusion of permanence, of stone.

The renovation of Victorian San Francisco into dollhouses for libertines may have seemed, in the 1970s, an evasion of what the city was actually becoming. San Francisco's rows of storied houses proclaimed a multigenerational orthodoxy, all the while masking the city's unconventional soul. Elsewhere, meanwhile, domestic America was coming undone.

Suburban Los Angeles, the prototype for a new America, was characterized by a more apparently radical residential architecture. There was, for example, the work of Frank Gehry. In the

1970s Gehry exploded the nuclear-family house, turning it inside out intellectually and in fact. Though, in a way, Gehry merely completed the logic of the postwar suburban tract house with its one story, its sliding glass doors, Formica kitchen, two-car garage. The tract house exchanged privacy for mobility. Heterosexuals opted for the one-lifetime house, the freeway, the birth-control pill, minimalist fiction.

The age-old description of homosexuality is of a sin against nature. Moralistic society has always judged emotion literally. The homosexual was sinful because he had no kosher place to stick it. In attempting to drape the architecture of sodomy with art, homosexuals have lived for thousands of years against the expectations of nature. Barren as Shakers and, interestingly, as concerned with the small effect, homosexuals have made a covenant against nature. Homosexual survival lay in artifice, in plumage, in lampshades, sonnets, musical comedy, couture, syntax, religious ceremony, opera, lacquer, irony.

I once asked Enrique, an interior decorator, if he had many homosexual clients. *"Mais non,"* said he, flexing his eyelids. "Queers don't need decorators. They were born knowing how. All this A.S.I.D. stuff — tests and regulations — as if you can confer a homosexual diploma on a suburban housewife by granting her a discount card."

A knack? The genius, we are beginning to fear in an age of AIDS, is irreplaceable — but does it exist? The question is whether the darling affinities are innate to homosexuality or whether they are compensatory. Why have so many homosexuals retired into the small effect, the ineffectual career, the stereotype, the card shop, the florist? *Be gentle with me?* Or do homosexuals know things others do not?

This way power lay: Once upon a time the homosexual appropriated to himself a mystical province, that of taste. Taste, which is, after all, the insecurity of the middle class, became the homosexual's licentiate to challenge the rule of nature. (The fairy in his blood, he intimated.)

Deciding how best to stick it may be only an architectural problem or a question of physics or of engineering or of cabinetry. Nevertheless, society's condemnation forced the homosexual to find his redemption outside nature. *We'll put a little skirt here.* The impulse is not to create but to re-create, to sham, to convert, to sauce, to rouge, to fragrance, to prettify. No effect is too small or too ephemeral to be snatched away from nature, to be ushered toward the perfection of artificiality. *We'll bring out the highlights there.* The homosexual has marshaled the architecture of the straight world to the very gates of Versailles — that great Vatican of fairyland — beyond which power is converted to leisure. In San Francisco in the 1980s the highest form of art became interior decoration. The glory hole was thus converted to an eighteenth-century French foyer.

I live away from the street, in a back apartment, in two rooms. I use my bedroom as a visitor's room — the sleigh bed tricked up with shams into a sofa — whereas I rarely invite anyone into my library, the public room, where I write, the public gesture.

I read in my bedroom in the afternoon because the light is good there, especially now, in winter, when the sun recedes from the earth.

There is a door in the south wall that leads to a balcony. The door was once a window. Inside the door, inside my bedroom, are twin green shutters. They are false shutters, of no function beyond wit. The shutters open into the room; they have the effect of turning my apartment inside out.

A few months ago I hired a man to paint the shutters green. I wanted the green shutters of Manet — you know the ones I mean — I wanted a weathered look, as of verdigris. For several days the painter labored, rubbing his paints into the wood and then wiping them off again. In this way he rehearsed for me decades of the ravages of weather. Yellow enough? Black?

The painter left one afternoon, saying he would return the next day, leaving behind his tubes, his brushes, his sponges and rags. He never returned. Someone told me he has AIDS.

Repainted façades extend now from Jackson Street south into what was once the heart of the black "Mo" — black Fillmore Street. Today there are watercress sandwiches at three o'clock where recently there had been loudmouthed kids, hole-in-the-wall bars, pimps. Now there are tweeds and perambulators, matrons and nannies. Yuppies. And gays.

The gay male revolution had greater influence on San Francisco in the 1970s than did the feminist revolution. Feminists, with whom I include lesbians — such was the inclusiveness of the feminist movement — were preoccupied with career, with escape from the house in order to create a sexually democratic city. Homosexual men sought to reclaim the house, the house that traditionally had been the reward for heterosexuality, with all its selfless tasks and burdens.

Leisure defined the gay male revolution. The gay political movement began, by most accounts, in 1969, with the Stonewall riots in New York City, whereby gay men fought to defend the nonconformity of their leisure.

It was no coincidence that homosexuals migrated to San Francisco in the 1970s, for the city was famed as a playful place, more Catholic than Protestant in its eschatological intuition. In 1975 the state of California legalized consensual homosexuality, and about that same time Castro Street, southwest of downtown, began to eclipse Polk Street as the homosexual address in San Francisco. Polk Street was a string of bars. The Castro was an entire district. The Castro had Victorian houses and churches, bookstores and restaurants, gyms, dry cleaners, supermarkets, and an elected member of the Board of Supervisors. The Castro supported baths and bars, but there was nothing furtive about them. On Castro Street the light of day penetrated gay life through clear plate-glass windows. The light of day discovered a new confidence, a new politics. Also a new look — a noncosmopolitan, Burt Reynolds, butch-kid style: beer, ball games, Levi's, short hair, muscles.

Gay men who lived elsewhere in the city, in Pacific Heights or in the Richmond, often spoke with derision of "Castro Street clones," describing the look, or scorned what they called the ghettoization of homosexuality. To an older generation of homosexuals, the blatancy of sexuality on Castro Street threatened the discreet compromise they had negotiated with a tolerant city.

As the Castro district thrived, Folsom Street, south of Market, also began to thrive, as if in counterdistinction to the utopian Castro. The Folsom Street area was a warehouse district of puddled alleys and deserted streets. Folsom Street offered an assortment of leather bars, an evening's regress to the outlaw sexuality of the fifties, the forties, the nineteenth century, and so on — an eroticism of the dark, of the Reeperbahn, or of the guardsman's barracks.

The Castro district implied that sexuality was more crucial, that homosexuality was the central fact of identity. The Castro district, with its ice cream parlors and hardware stores, was the revolutionary place.

Into which carloads of vacant-eyed teenagers from other districts or from middle-class suburbs would drive after dark, cruising the neighborhood for solitary victims.

The ultimate gay basher was a city supervisor named Dan White, ex-cop, ex-boxer, ex-fireman, ex–altar boy. Dan White had grown up in the Castro district; he recognized the Castro revolution for what it was. Gays had achieved power over him. He murdered the mayor and he murdered the homosexual member of the Board of Supervisors.

Katherine, a sophisticate if ever there was one, nevertheless dismisses the two men descending the aisle at the opera house: "All so sleek and smooth-jowled and silver-haired — they don't seem real, poor darlings. It must be because they don't have children."

Lodged within Katherine's complaint is the perennial heterosexual annoyance with the homosexual's freedom from child rearing, which places the homosexual not so much beyond the pale as it relegates the homosexual outside "responsible" life.

It was the glamour of gay life, after all, as much as it was the feminist call to career, that encouraged heterosexuals in the 1970s to excuse themselves from nature, to swallow the birth-control pill. Who needs children? The gay bar became the paradigm for the singles bar. The gay couple became the paradigm for the selfish couple — all dressed up and everywhere to go. And there was the example of the gay house in illustrated life-style magazines. At the same time that suburban housewives were looking outside the home for fulfillment, gay men were reintroducing a new generation in the city — heterosexual men and women — to the complacencies of the barren house.

Puritanical America dismissed gay camp followers as yuppies; the term means to suggest infantility. Yuppies were obsessive and awkward in their materialism. Whereas gays arranged a decorative life against a barren state, yuppies sought early returns, lives that were not to be all toil and spin. Yuppies, trained to careerism from the cradle, wavered in their pursuit of the northern European ethic — indeed, we might now call it the pan-Pacific ethic — in favor of the Mediterranean, the Latin, the Catholic, the Castro, the Gay .

The international architectural idioms of Skidmore, Owings & Merrill, which defined the city's skyline in the 1970s, betrayed no awareness of any street-level debate concerning the primacy of play in San Francisco nor of any human dramas resulting from urban redevelopment. The repellent office tower was a fortress raised against the sky, against the street, against the idea of a city. Offices were hives where money was made, and damn all.

In the 1970s San Francisco was divided between the interests of downtown and the pleasures of the neighborhoods. Neighborhoods asserted idiosyncrasy, human scale, light. San Francisco neighborhoods perceived downtown as working against their influence in determining what the city should be. Thus neighborhoods seceded from the idea of a city.

The gay movement rejected downtown as representing "straight" conformity. But was it possible that heterosexual Union Street was related to Castro Street? Was it possible that either was related to the Latino Mission district? Or to the Sino-Russian Richmond? San Francisco, though complimented worldwide for holding its center, was in fact without a vision of itself entire.

In the 1980s, in deference to the neighborhoods, City Hall would attempt a counterreformation of downtown, forbidding "Manhattanization." Shadows were legislated away from parks and playgrounds. Height restrictions were lowered beneath an existing skyline. Design, too, fell under the retrojurisdiction of the city planner's office. The Victorian house was presented to architects as a model of what the city wanted to uphold and to become. In heterosexual neighborhoods, one saw newly built Victorians. Downtown, postmodernist prescriptions for playfulness advised skyscrapers to wear party hats, buttons, comic mustaches. Philip Johnson yielded to the dollhouse impulse to perch angels atop one of his skyscrapers.

In the 1970s, like a lot of men and women in this city, I joined a gym. My club, I've even caught myself calling it.

In the gay city of the 1970s, bodybuilding became an architectural preoccupation of the upper middle class. Bodybuilding is a parody of labor, a useless accumulation of the laborer's bulk and strength. No useful task is accomplished. And yet there is something businesslike about the habitués, and the gym is filled with the punch-clock logic of the workplace. Machines clank and hum. Needles on gauges toll spent calories.

The gym is at once a closet of privacy and an exhibition gallery. All four walls are mirrored.

I study my body in the mirror. Physical revelation — nakedness — is no longer possible, cannot be desired, for the body is shrouded in meat and wears itself.

The intent is some merciless press of body against a standard, perfect mold. Bodies are "cut" or "pumped" or "buffed" as on an assembly line in Turin. A body becomes so many extrovert parts. Delts, pecs, lats.

I harness myself in a Nautilus cage.

Lats become wings. For the gym is nothing if not the occasion for transcendence. From homosexual to autosexual . . .

I lift weights over my head, baring my teeth like an animal with the strain.

. . . to nonsexual. The effect of the overdeveloped body is the miniaturization of the sexual organs — of no function beyond wit. Behold the ape become Blakean angel, revolving in an empyrean of mirrors.

The nineteenth-century mirror over the fireplace in my bedroom was purchased by a decorator from the estate of a man who died last year of AIDS. It is a top-heavy piece, confusing styles. Two ebony-painted columns support a frieze of painted glass above the mirror. The frieze depicts three bourgeois Graces and a couple of free-range cherubs. The lake of the mirror has formed a cataract, and at its edges it is beginning to corrode.

Thus the mirror that now draws upon my room owns some bright curse, maybe — some memory not mine.

As I regard this mirror, I imagine Saint Augustine's meditation slowly hardening into syllogism, passing down through centuries to confound us: Evil is the absence of good.

We have become accustomed to figures disappearing from our landscape. Does this not lead us to interrogate the landscape?

With reason do we invest mirrors with the superstition of

memory, for they, though glass, though liquid captured in a bay, are so often less fragile than we are. They — bright ovals or rectangles or rounds — bump down unscathed, unspilled through centuries, whereas we . . .

The man in the red baseball cap used to jog so religiously on Marina Green. By the time it occurs to me that I have not seen him for months, I realize he may be dead — not lapsed, not moved away. People come and go in the city, it's true. But in San Francisco in 1990, death has become as routine an explanation for disappearance as Allied Van Lines.

AIDS, it has been discovered, is a plague of absence. Absence opened in the blood. Absence condensed into the fluid of passing emotion. Absence shot through opalescent tugs of semen to deflower the city.

And then AIDS, it was discovered, is a nonmetaphorical disease, a disease like any other. Absence sprang from substance — a virus, a hairy bubble perched upon a needle, a platter of no intention served round: fever, blisters, a death sentence.

At first I heard only a few names, names connected, perhaps, with the right faces, perhaps not. People vaguely remembered, as through the cataract of this mirror, from dinner parties or from intermissions. A few articles in the press. The rumored celebrities. But within months the slow beating of the blood had found its bay.

One of San Francisco's gay newspapers, the *Bay Area Reporter*, began to accept advertisements from funeral parlors and casket makers, inserting them between the randy ads for leather bars and tanning salons. The *Reporter* invited homemade obituaries — lovers writing of lovers, friends remembering friends and the blessings of unexceptional life.

*Peter. Carlos. Gary. Asel. Perry. Nikos.*

Healthy snapshots accompany each annal. At the Russian River. By the Christmas tree. Lifting a beer. In uniform. A dinner jacket. A satin gown.

*He was born in Puerto La Libertad, El Salvador.*

*He attended Apple Valley High School, where he was their first male cheerleader.*

*From El Paso. From Medford. From Germany. From Long Island.*

I moved back to San Francisco in 1979. Oh, I had had some salad days elsewhere, but by 1979 I was a wintry man. I came here in order not to be distracted by the ambitions or, for that matter, the pleasures of others but to pursue my own ambition. Once here, though, I found the company of men who pursued an earthly paradise charming. Skepticism became my demeanor toward them — I was the dinner-party skeptic, a firm believer in Original Sin and in the limits of possibility.

Which charmed them.

*He was a dancer.*

*He settled into the interior-design department of Gump's, where he worked until his illness.*

*He was a teacher.*

César, for example.

César could shave the rind from any assertion to expose its pulp and jelly. But César was otherwise ruled by pulp. César loved everything that ripened in time. Freshmen. Bordeaux. César could fashion liturgy from an artichoke. Yesterday it was not ready (cocking his head, rotating the artichoke in his hand over a pot of cold water). Tomorrow will be too late (Yorick's skull). Today it is perfect (as he lit the fire beneath the pot). We will eat it now.

If he's lucky, he's got a year, a doctor told me. If not, he's got two.

The phone rang. AIDS had tagged a friend. And then the phone rang again. And then the phone rang again. Michael had tested positive. Adrian, well, what he had assumed were shingles . . . Paul was back in the hospital. And César, dammit, César, even César, especially César.

That winter before his death César traveled back to South America. On his return to San Francisco he described to me how he had walked with his mother in her garden — his mother chafing her hands as if she were cold. But it was not cold, he said. They moved slowly. Her summer garden was prolonging itself this year, she said. The cicadas will not stop singing.

When he lay on his deathbed, César said everyone else he knew might get AIDS and die. He said I would be the only one spared — "spared" was supposed to have been chased with irony, I knew, but his voice was too weak to do the job. "You are too circumspect," he said then, wagging his finger upon the coverlet.

So I was going to live to see that the garden of earthly delights was, after all, only wallpaper — was that it, César? Hadn't I always said so? It was then I saw that the greater sin against heaven was my unwillingness to embrace life.

It was not as in some Victorian novel — the curtains drawn, the pillows plumped, the streets strewn with sawdust. It was not to be a matter of custards in covered dishes, steaming possets, *Try a little of this, my dear.* Or gathering up the issues of *Architectural Digest* strewn about the bed. Closing the biography of Diana Cooper and marking its place. Or the unfolding of discretionary screens, morphine, parrots, pavilions.

César experienced agony.

Four of his high school students sawed through a Vivaldi quartet in the corridor outside his hospital room, prolonging the hideous garden.

*In the presence of his lover Gregory and friends, Scott passed from this life . . .*

*He died peacefully at home in his lover Ron's arms.*

*Immediately after a friend led a prayer for him to be taken home and while his dear mother was reciting the Twenty-third Psalm, Bill peacefully took his last breath.*

I stood aloof at César's memorial, the kind of party he would enjoy, everyone said. And so for a time César lay improperly buried, unconvincingly resurrected in the conditional: would enjoy. What else could they say? César had no religion beyond aesthetic bravery.

Sunlight remains. Traffic remains. Nocturnal chic attaches to some discovered restaurant. A new novel is reviewed in the *New York Times.* And the mirror rasps on its hook. The mirror is lifted down.

A priest friend, a good friend, who out of naïveté plays the cynic, tells me — this is on a bright, billowy day; we are standing outside — "It's not as sad as you may think. There is at least spectacle in the death of the young. Come to the funeral of an old lady sometime if you want to feel an empty church."

I will grant my priest friend this much: that it is easier, easier on me, to sit with gay men in hospitals than with the staring old. Young men talk as much as they are able.

But those who gather around the young man's bed do not see spectacle. This doll is Death. I have seen people caressing it, staring Death down. I have seen people wipe its tears, wipe its ass; I have seen people kiss Death on his lips, where once there were lips.

*Chris was inspired after his own diagnosis in July 1987 with the truth and reality of how such a terrible disease could bring out the love, warmth, and support of so many friends and family.*

Sometimes no family came. If there was family, it was usually mother. Mom. With her suitcase and with the torn flap of an envelope in her hand.

*Brenda. Pat. Connie. Toni. Soledad.*

Or parents came but then left without reconciliation, some preferring to say cancer.

But others came. Sissies were not, after all, afraid of Death. They walked his dog. They washed his dishes. They bought his groceries. They massaged his poor back. They changed his bandages. They emptied his bedpan.

Men who sought the aesthetic ordering of existence were recalled to nature. Men who aspired to the mock-angelic settled for the shirt of hair. The gay community of San Francisco, having found freedom, consented to necessity — to all that the proud world had for so long held up to them, withheld from them, as "real humanity."

And if gays took care of their own, they were not alone. AIDS was a disease of the entire city; its victims were as often black, Hispanic, straight. Neither were Charity and Mercy only white, only male, only gay. Others came. There were nurses and nuns and the couple from next door, co-workers, strangers, teenagers, corporations, pensioners. A community was forming over the city.

*Cary and Rick's friends and family wish to thank the many people who provided both small and great kindnesses.*

*He was attended to and lovingly cared for by the staff at Coming Home Hospice.*

And the saints of this city have names listed in the phone book, names I heard called through a microphone one cold Sunday in Advent as I sat in Most Holy Redeemer Church. It might have been any of the churches or community centers in the Castro district, but it happened at Most Holy Redeemer at a time in the history of the world when the Roman Catholic Church still pronounced the homosexual a sinner.

A woman at the microphone called upon volunteers from the AIDS Support Group to come forward. One by one, in twos and threes, throughout the church, people stood up, young men and women, and middle-aged and old, straight, gay, and all of them shy at being called. Yet they came forward and assembled in the sanctuary, facing the congregation, grinning self-consciously at one another, their hands hidden behind them.

I am preoccupied by the fussing of a man sitting in the pew directly in front of me — in his seventies, frail, his iodine-colored hair combed forward and pasted upon his forehead. Fingers of porcelain clutch the pearly beads of what must have been his mother's rosary. He is not the sort of man any gay man would have chosen to become in the 1970s. He is probably not what he himself expected to become. Something of the old dear about him, wizened butterfly, powdered old pouf. Certainly he is what I fear becoming. And then he rises, this old monkey, with the most beatific dignity, in answer to the microphone, and he strides into the sanctuary to take his place in the company of the Blessed.

So this is it — this, what looks like a Christmas party in an insurance office and not as in Renaissance paintings, and not as we had always thought, not some flower-strewn, some sequined curtain call of grease-painted heroes gesturing to the stalls. A lady with a plastic candy cane pinned to her lapel. A Castro clone with a red bandanna exploding from his hip pocket. A perfume-counter lady with an Hermès scarf mantled upon her left shoulder. A black man in a checkered sports coat. The pink-haired punkess with a jewel in her nose. Here, too, is the gay couple in middle age, wearing interchangeable plaid shirts and corduroy pants. Blood and shit and Mr. Happy Face. These know the weight of bodies.

*Bill died.*

*. . . Passed on to heaven.*

*. . . Turning over in his bed one night and then gone.*

These learned to love what is corruptible, while I, barren skeptic, reader of Saint Augustine, curator of the earthly paradise, inheritor of the empty mirror, I shift my tailbone upon the cold, hard pew.

DORIEN ROSS

# Seeking Home

FROM TIKKUN

YOU ARE beginning to succumb to the New York pressure to look
a certain way in order to feel a certain way. You are no closer to
understanding the mystery of style than you were in high school.
You remember a recent conversation with your longtime admired older friend Judith. You cannot deny that one of the reasons you admire Judith is the way she looks. At fifty years old she
looks younger than you: slender, groomed, and elegant. She tells
you the following story:

It seems that Calvin Klein sent spies to Ralph Lauren in an attempt to discover the secret of his ongoing and remarkable success. He discovers the secret: these clothes simulate the British
idea of *home*. Calvin Klein now seeks some idea of what American
home style would look like. Not an easy task. But he decides on
pioneer-mission style.

This, it seems, is what people are seeking. Seeking home.

You are writing this in an attempt to master your obsession,
but understanding has not halted the sense of danger. You know
you are in trouble because this is the second morning you have
awakened with a list of clothes in your mind that feel crucial to
your survival and sense of well-being on the street.

The List
1. sweater          $450
2. pants            $90
3. long coat        $500
4. one good dress   $200

You are actually considering spending over $1,000 on clothes. But what's money when we are talking well-being, security, belonging, and home? Spend $5,000 if that's what it will bring you!

Last night's meeting with Susan Hammerstein, a hot literary agent, was warm but disheartening. She basically told you that your writing is beautiful, literary, forceful, but totally unmarketable. Very personal writing she says.

You realize walking home that you are a stylistic outsider. There is too much of you showing through. The clothing list comes to mind. It is relentless. One good dress. One sweater. One long coat. Just like that one across from you on the bus. That's the one. Where did you get it? Pardon me, Miss, where did you get your coat? Bloomingdale's two years ago. And on sale. How fortunate. How smart of you. And your hair, if I may ask? Where was it cut? That's just the way I've always wanted mine to look. The side part just so. The way it falls over the shoulder.

You refrain from asking. Because you would not know where to stop. The next woman getting on the bus has just the right shoes. And the next, the scarf. What about that necklace?

You are relieved to finally get off the bus and walk rapidly, looking at no store windows, to your basement apartment. You close the door behind you and you try to stop the imagery. You light candles. You make tea. You put on Mozart. The list begins to fade.

Later that night a nasty habit returns. In your sleep you walk to the kitchen, take a loaf of bread and bring it back into bed. You begin to stuff handfuls — ripped off — into your mouth. This finally wakes you up. You know this person. This subterranean self. Desperate and helpless. She's been with you a long time. Since your teenage years. She knows nothing of style.

Your brother had style. Your mother also. But alas, you were born without style. You are convinced of this. Last night, before the bread escapade, you actually stood in front of the mirror and held your nose turned up, to see what you would have looked like with the nose job you were destined to have but staunchly refused.

This was a motion that occurred often in your adolescence. Your mother standing behind you in the mirror holding your nose up. First the front view. Then the profile. "Slightly turned up and the bump out . . ."

You didn't buy it. You were insulted. Outraged. It hadn't occurred to you until then that there was anything essentially wrong with your face.

Your uncle was one of the "big two" plastic surgeons on Long Island and you know you heard over and over that we could get a wholesale job. Your grandparents offered to foot the bill and send you to Europe as a reward. Now you understand that they were desperate for you not to look Jewish. They had a hatred for the Semitic face. They brought that hatred over from the old country. From the pine forests of Lithuania.

Uncle Saul Golden will do it wholesale. Everyone in your family except your father and your brother; every cousin, uncle, and aunt had the same nose. Saul Golden's vision of the all-American nose. All over Long Island, in the five towns, this nose appears in markets, synagogues, streets, PTA meetings. Exactly the same. All of them.

You were frightened of Uncle Saul. Not only did he once stick his tongue in your twelve-year-old mouth. In addition, each time you went to that house, that mansion built with old-world nose money, he would show you a picture book of nose choices. You remember the album. Large and glossy pictures of miserable-looking Semitic faces on one side, with the redone versions on the other. He would turn the pages and look at you lustfully.

The other day on the phone, your father made an astonishing joke. He was describing a very ugly person whom a close friend of his married. What was so ugly? you asked, always fascinated by this distinction. Just that really ugly kind of Jewish face, he said. The kind you can't look at. The kind they had posters of in Germany. The kind with the word *Juden* written underneath. Both of you laughed.

MARK RUDMAN

# *Mosaic on Walking*

FROM BOULEVARD

IN THIS SEASON I am often sulky, sullen, restless, withdrawn. I feel transparent, as if inhabited by the weather.

Only while walking am I relieved from distress, only then, released from the burden of self, am I free to think. I wanted to say walking brings relief from tension without sadness and then I think it is not so — these walks bring their own form of *tristesse*. There is discomfort when movement stops.

Though not exceptionally tall (a shade under six feet), I am a rangy, rambly walker. I take up a lot of space!

I know when I emphasize strolling and walking that I am pointing to a crisis in leisure time, my own, everyone's. We know what Wordsworth and Whitman and James did with their afternoons: they walked, with and without direction, destination.

Raw wind bites my neck. I have lost three scarves in the past ten days and feel the cold season won't last long enough for me to buy another.

The sponge, not the shell, should be our model. The armor that protects us is prelude to our downfall.

I choose this surly, in-between season precisely because its inhospitability to walking provides a frame, limits possibility. I won't be tempted to overload. And a burden of work to be done makes me fantasize a more leisurely, unstressed pace.

This Sunday evening, walking by the street where my friend X no longer lives, it seems strangely flattened out, straight, sober, for all its literal ups and downs, and in spite of the unbroken downslope toward the Hudson. No longer a text, no longer tortured. Maybe the street took on the attributes of X's search, his complicated, conflicted grasp and apprehension, his sense that the world (as text) was riddled with meanings. And now that he has gone it has become — just a street! The streetlamps have withdrawn from their contortions.

This is the danger of walking in a familiar city. Our unconscious dogs us like a double. Associations will rise unbidden from their coffers and containers. I can't seem to walk anywhere of late without this happening to me. Each neighborhood conceals a repository of framed images, old lovers, old friends, framed, that is, until they begin to unravel. When I walk by the apartments in the Village where I used to live and glance through the black rusted railings into the underground window, I imagine that I will be there, in that room, as I was ten years ago, raving and pacing.

A look in the real window below brings me back to reality. The bedroom's been converted into an office. I fantasize a lot about travel but I may time travel here more than I would in any unfamiliar place because when I am transported back to that place and time I am also seeing it through a prism: who I was then through who I am now, then that double perspective on whoever I am remembering, then their perspective. That's a figure with at least six sides.

Talking in Manhattan, I feel as if my past were riding alongside me on an outrigger.

My horror of leaving New York is bound up with the loss of walking space.

The blocks grow longer as you move west. The streets are too wide. The places we lived in the Southwest when I was a boy, Salt Lake City, Colorado Springs, were always surrounded, hemmed in, by mountains. Suddenly, looking up and around I'd feel dwarfed by the immensity of the sky and squeezed by the sense of bound distances, enclosures. I began to see everything in terms of its distance from the sea. The only other people on the block were so far away they could have been in another county.

In Manhattan I am aware at every moment that the tall buildings are man-made structures. Even the shoddy scaffolding of a new hotel going up can be reassuring. We know we're being measured by our life's terms, finite pressures, mortality, not the blank eternal gaze of sea and sky and mountain.

When my mother and I lived in Las Vegas, during the time she was getting her divorce, the desert was still across the street, opposite the strip. After dinner I'd drag her toward my favorite destination, a gully about a quarter mile into the desert. It came after rows of cacti. I would submit to bed only after I returned in the dusk to test their prickliness; I would try to move my fingers around the spines and press through the pulp to the sticky water without drawing blood. She'd never say we had to go back because it was getting dark, only because it was getting cold — which it was. I loved these succulents, which managed to survive on what seemed to be so little water.

Walking to a midtown lunch, I go by the building where my grandfather lived, and my mother and I lived for a time when I was a child. Heading downtown, the same afternoon, I pass the building where my father worked. I feel both haunted and vacant. Within ten minutes, moving from the East Side, just shy of the park, to the West, I can walk past Hortense Court, the building my great-grandmother designed, and the building on the other side of town where my father lived. Only once, twice a year does it occur to me that I live within blocks of where I lived when I was an infant. Being driven inward even while I walk exhausts me. I find consolation in Pavese's idea that there's no one who has not sprung from the silence of origins.

My first recurring dream of walking occurred when I was five. My great-grandfather, Benno Levy, is walking down a long narrow dirt road with his back to me in a black suit. He's carry-

ing a suitcase. There's dust on his shoes. I want him to turn back.
His gait is sturdy, determined. I know he's on his way to his
death. At his back, the pond in Suffern where I fished for catfish
with a string wound around the rabbit ears of a two-pronged
wooden fork. The muddy pond seemed paradisal to me. I would
stay outside fishing and chasing the dachsund while the grown-
ups underwent lunch — double-yolked eggs purchased from a
nearby chicken farm. I am conscious, from the earliest age, of
the need to be outside, not as pure act, but as escape from the
tedium, the repetitiveness, of adult life — words exchanged when
no words would do.

My father and I talked only when we walked because we did
not have to face each other. I find it hard to remember my father's springy, relaxed step, his beachy stroll which — consonant
with age and terror — degenerated into a shuffle (to raise the
feet is to admit hope for the future). My own gait alongside my
father's was always constrained, squeezing myself into the smallest space while he let his elbows swing to and fro. My father was
unafraid, unintimidated, would not be squelched. His daytime
sobriety was arresting, barrister-like, detached from context. He
never erased the mischievous look of glee and anguish while my
features, like my mother's, are strangely stark, angular, and im-
mobile. (Physiognomy is fate.) Yet we could still hardly relate —
my father's blustery, dramatic surges occupied center stage and
made me imagine an upside-down world of monologists — Mal-
colm Lowry ordering a "treble gin" after he'd slugged an unwit-
ting dray horse or snapped the mascot rabbit's neck, demanding everyone's attention. I developed a potent weapon: conceal-
ment.

Once movement is restricted, the walker's view of the city
changes irrevocably. I know; I hurt my knee. That year, limping
up the subway steps below Lex and Seventy-seventh, gripping a
cane en route to get a surgeon's verdict, I saw a young woman, a
flesh-colored skeleton, Hispanic or Indian, jet black hair, blue
jeans, turquoise-blue-beaded belt, blue denim shirt, seated on a
bench inside the terminus, long fingers pressed flat against the
bench as if she were trying to lift herself up, head thrown as far
back as it could go, mouth jacked open wide around an echoing

scream, and as I moved on, shoved by the crowd, nervous about falling and further damage to the lining of the joint that had been worn away by the torn cartilage, I still wanted desperately to help her . . . She is frozen there, like a possum on railroad tracks. Her teeth ground down, ridges of white stumps. And then her stillness. I looked at her chest. No sign of breath. No movement.

It was never simple, this matter of my knee, and as I limped along, encaned, through the throngs, I had a vision of the future — which had already arrived for so many I now walked beside — a future unconditionally tremulous and dim, and I was amazed I had not seen it before.

The only other time I walked so slowly was when I accompanied my blind grandfather on his errands. He took as much pleasure in his two-block trip to Chemical Bank as he might have in an afternoon's walk in the country. Maybe his blindness didn't bother him as much as it does others because he had such an acute sense of smell. He'd been in the perfume business. Colleagues called him The Nose. And he was just as proud of his long wide thick beak as he was of its unseen sensory qualities. He claimed to have invented the deodorant, but he took his product (which merely combined his usual scents with hydroxychloride) off the market because it closed up the pores, interfered with the sweat glands. He was one of those people who, having grown up in the country, working with his hands, hunting, fishing, playing ball, brought a certain pristine vigilance to ecological issues long before they began to be aired in public. He was violently opposed to aerosol cans and detergents. On one of our long-on-time, short-on-space walks he railed that he'd been "talking the detergents for twenty years, but no one listened."

Often, in the late afternoons, I would wheel my son in his stroller to the Cathedral of Saint John to see the peacock who we first sighted strutting through the Biblical Herb Garden. (He was hard to see at first, with his leafy tail against the bushes.) Once, returning home, we paused by the cathedral's hybrid, baroque children's statue, its warlike images of severed heads dangling from claws in opposition to the homage to peace on the plaque. The early moon had risen above the tip of Pegasus's wings; my son reached up and "picked it," putting his hand to his mouth, pretending to chew. But when, a moment later, the moon went behind a cloud and stayed there for what seemed like an eternal instant, he burst into tears: "I want my moon back!"

He was inconsolable. In the mind of a two-year-old, what's gone is gone forever.

Like a psychoanalyst of cities, I try to reconstruct why I find significance in these spaces we traverse, as in a vast red-brick building behind an imposing fence on Amsterdam Avenue. It takes up several acres in a city that's always short of space, its sign reads "International Youth Hostelry," and it is the perfect image of our time, I think: an immense empty structure, promising repose and rest, and yet with no possible angle of entry, no real existence beyond its façade. Or, walking through Tompkins Square Park in the gray, eerie January rain and afternoon dark, for the first time since the early seventies, to be transported backward in time only to tumble out into another vacant lot strewn with the kind of day it is, the sky hanging its laundry over the yellow rubble. Some neighborhoods in New York look like the outskirts of other cities where everything, suddenly, breaks down. The roofs don't so much cave in as disappear. These inner-city outskirts are the parts of the city no one sees, except those who live there, who rarely leave; this is what the imagination needs to reclaim.

In transit for four days, walking, and thinking about the kind of illuminations that might be gathered on the way from here to there; how to make the best of the in-between time; about the chiaroscuro of avenues, that moment of iron darkness at dusk.

West Side, Upper West Side, West Village, East Village; I am there, off balance, favoring my left leg by tilting to the right, yet walking, and thinking that great poetry has always been about this — ambulatory movement — and how difficult it is to remember to project ourselves, the unreleased contents of our psyches, into, say, that Abandoned Youth Hostelry. What we choose to see, perceive, is also ourselves. What appears to be chaos is an order of variables. It is the chaos of cities which attracts me.

In the city, people are often unsettled by the harsh opposition of extreme wealth and poverty. There is no moment in which these contrasts and tensions do not exist — engendering a furious anomie. The human heart cannot keep pace with a city's changes (Baudelaire's insight, not mine).

Walking stirs the broth of the unconscious. A misty labyrinth extends out from our feet. Those terrors about to leap out at us, that free-floating libido: they precede what we perceive.

In the months before my son was born, walking had a special cast. Same season as this one: late winter. Plenty of light, little warmth. To get the baby moving my wife and I walked back and forth across Central Park, around the baseball diamonds and the pond below the castle, into and through museums (canvases of bodies embracing, rising and falling and floating at the same time above a Day-Glo desert further illuminated by the halos of swimming pools . . .), up Broadway to be stared at by many passersby, and then we happened on what looked like a peaceful spot, under some plane trees and away from the rattle of machinery, when a lovely woman with tears in her eyes reached into a yellow phone box to the direct-to-police phone and said, "Miracle! It works!" She wore burgundy cords and an orange cotton turtleneck and held one of her children on her right hip.

"There's a little boy lost here. And his mother only speaks Yugoslavian. And his grandmother only speaks Yugoslavian." The next day, retracing our steps to this haven, we run into the woman on Broadway. "The little boy found his way home alone, ten blocks from where he started. And only four years old!"

My interest in the physiology of writing may stem from asthma. As a child, unable to listen to the reason of adults, each asthmatic gasp felt like it would be my last. And so to write I felt like I needed a deep breath, and a tremendous head of steam, before I could begin, for fear I'd never get a second wind. To whatever degree asthma really is brought on by nerves, once you have it you really have something to worry about. The asthmatic lives, cringing inwardly, in fear of suffocation.

Osip Mandelstam and Marcel Proust were asthmatics. This may have made each give priority to breathing, to put breathing in the foreground of consciousness. For Mandelstam, the "rhythm of the human gait" could provide a counterpoint to breathlessness. Proust approached each sentence as if it might have contained his last breath.

Walking is one way I have of dealing with my restlessness, and my desire to be far away from here (but where?) right now. These weeks elongate themselves. Even the light grows heavy and leans toward a perpetual evening.

I am much in the mood to get back into a mode where I am again a walker in the city, where what's perceived with each footfall is new and not bound by the conventions of past perception, past connection. But it is difficult to renew oneself endlessly. And yet that is the challenge of poetry (of life!) — to ply contradictions. I am thinking about how some poems mean to teach us about deep physiological rhythms, rhythms that give a poem an almost classical form without strain or archness; stopping, and starting, turning this corner and not that, choosing, and yet not staking everything on each swerve, keeping the next step ahead of the thought, keeping thinking in the body, as an extension of the senses; writing and walking; idle alertness, receptiveness; the need to look outward (to try), to project fearlessly, to identify and empathize, to arrest the day's (the moment's) flux by writing it down, and drawing strength from that, to trust that what's inside will be implied by the eye-to-object perception, that my sense now as I write of the particulars that surround my life are sufficient to embody vision, that the precise rhythms of these notations are a graph of the spirit. I know that when I remember walking across Tompkins Square Park in the rain the contours of that memory are imbued by the quality of the experience; I was on my way with a friend, or someone congenial, or someone I love. It all shows up, like a watermark. The rain may hurt my head, it may give relief.

The walk becomes metaphorical of the rest of life. There is little that we love to do (or love or do) that is not "fostered *alike*," Wordsworth reminds me, "by beauty and by fear." Everyone we see becomes a potential *doppelgänger* (double-goer). The walker in the city becomes the city.

*

As a boy in Chicago I walked the streets in a manic frenzy, surrounded by the immense railroad yard, the military barracks, and — further away but still present to my mind — the stockyards. And everywhere — inescapable — was the prairie. It is possible that my sense of beauty was formed by those contraries. I loved Chicago's mixture of wilderness and civilization. Maybe it mirrored my own restlessness.

These bursts of winter light make me restless, uncomfortable with habit, routine, any fixed way of doing things. I'm keyed to a detour. I know that I will vary my daily round. I know that I will wander around the city and kick myself for not having seen so many things before that are right under my nose. And I know that in this state of mind this city (any city?) can become like a foreign country.

In this mood I am impatient with competence, with anything whose result can be in any way predicted. Maybe it's the same impulse that sent Descartes to the wharf in Amsterdam: only among merchants and foreign tongues, the clear give and take of commerce, could he begin to think.

My friend and I are walking down West End Avenue in the morning light when we see a man, an albino, standing rigidly upright at the edge of a building but not leaning against it, with his head craned toward the sun, holding a pale lizard in his outstretched palm. We walk past, exchange puzzled glances, and my friend goes back and asks the man what he was doing: "Is that a gekko?" The man responds with pleasure (apparently no one else on their busy way had thought to inquire) and the pride of a messenger whose chance it was to bear good news he had memorized and repeated to himself many times: "They told me to sun it for an hour. Three times a day every three days." He blinked, registering our interest, then began to improvise: "But upstairs . . . upstairs they've got an alligator . . . but he's in the bathtub . . . they don't let me bring him down."

I think that walking is the only thing that can cure me (but of what?), and only momentarily. I take it back. Walking is the only consuming distraction, in the body, from the body. This is what lures the flaneur to be swallowed up by the crowd.

The rhythm of the swinging swings is not that far removed from walking. The rhythm of walking is not that far removed from the rocking cradle.

Often, walking, I am, for as long as the movement lasts, happy. Walking is a source of immediate joy, life as it is being lived, not contemplated.

Walking, the head stays still, the body moves through space like a flywheel, casting off anything unnecessary. Movement is the key.

Walking, we keep our pact with the earth, more happily than anyone would ever care to admit. Arrested walking brings another kind of perception: static, frightened.

I can tell when the crowd experiences a sudden elevation of mood. I take the pulse of the street and can tell what kind of day it is in the life of our times.

Walking, a slight imbalance (presence of a cumbersome package in one's hand) can turn this heaven into hell.

Hell — a suburb in which no one walks.

Walking puts the eye's prominence back in perspective. It instantiates the self. By identifying changes apart from ourselves we begin to set up internal markers.

Walking needn't be mentioned explicitly. It is the movement of the mind that counts. Merely to think of movement brings happiness.

On Manhattan streets in the violent late January sun — my heart soars.

Walking as embrace. It sets a ground for intimacy, lets connections occur. We talk and we drift apart. Nothing is demanded. The remembered event provokes the poem, which commemorates the event, marks the passing time, enlivens it, carouses.

*

Walking tosses up trusted variables. We think we're crossing Central Park but what extends out from us at all sides is a vast empty field that no one else is crossing.

Walking is the lyric of the multitude.

Walking provides a counterpoint, a counterstress, to the solitude of writing. Rising from our reveries, we are loath to be reminded of reality, and walking is a gentle immersion.

All day I anticipate walking across town, across Central Park, and I know I can merge crossing it with an unimportant but necessary errand. I move erratically, first down Broadway, then swerve abruptly left in a fever to reach the green. This is not a city without havens. I pass a lovely inviting garden, empty in the midday heat, on a block of otherwise uniform, renovated brownstones.

There is nothing you can't walk away, Kierkegaard said, and yes, walking alleviates stress and induces thought — unless you set out on a walk for this purpose, as I did on a humid afternoon in May, beginning with springy step and great hopes, ending with exhaustion and despair.

I am walking east when I pass the Claremont Stables at Eighty-ninth and Columbus, where my father rode in the years after he'd given up the luxury of keeping a horse, and where he took me riding when I came to town. This was his central pleasure and luxury, riding every morning before work. In some sense, he never recovered from this loss. What Hildesheimer says of Mozart is also true of my father: "It has also been verified that Mozart went for a horseback ride every morning, beginning in 1787. Dr. Barisani had prescribed riding to compensate for his sedentary life — *probably the only sound advice Mozart ever received in his life*" (my emphasis).

I had no desire to find traces of my past on these streets; it went that way against my will: so much of the pleasure of walking is bound up with palpably entering the future, as if that tree moving toward me as I walk were an index of time-in-space. To walk is to feel we are not at the mercy of the instant, that past and present is not flowing through us but that we are flowing through it. I wonder if we might not consider the unconscious as a spatial construct and think of it as surrounding us.

The rain this May morning makes me want to take back everything I've been saying about the pleasure of walking in the city — in *weather*. Only the tops of trees knock about on Broadway, wildly flailing, while there's a stillness at the knees. Heads bowed to keep the rain out of their eyes, people go by, calmly carrying shopping bags, for at that height nothing much is happening, while just above them tree trunks bend, branches shake, signs rock. The disturbance is all above our heads yet somehow encompassing.

I take it back: this evening, walking along Central Park West in an infernal mist, the wind blows hard and steady against my chest, then it stops. Only a faint spray keeps blowing in my face. To my right, all's serene and quiet. The park looks abandoned but for joggers on the paths and streets that cut across it west to east. I see no one walking on the grass or climbing the sleek black granite rocks. To my left, ambulances, Hispanic workers clustered beneath umbrellas with signs around their necks (one reads "Our Mothers Deserve Better Than This"), silently protesting exploitation by the Tavern-on-the-Green. At this moment an amber Art Deco apartment house, with its striated surface, makes me think of a ruin, and of how this city — this street, Central Park West — might appear to a stranger's eye in a far-off time.

I am walking behind a couple, each carrying a briefcase and tucked umbrella. They're walking at a good clip, at a speed I usually walk, but tonight I'm late and must walk fast to relieve my wife (who has to go out at eight) and to give my son his bath and read him *What Do People Do All Day?* There are large puddles on either side of us and it's difficult to pass. As I make my move to cut ahead the man turns to look at me and for a second I'm sure it is my college friend, whose face is unmistakable — hard, carved features, shock of black hair and high cheekbones like Jack Palance — only this man's features are softer.

The last time I ran into him in the street we went to his loft in Chelsea. He had, in the two years since we'd finished school, taken up painting, and the white walls of his loft were strewn with his stark black-and-white geometric grid paintings. I saw him next some seven years later at a Christmas party (at which everyone seemed to be turning thirty) in a tropical SoHo loft. He was, in every outer sense, unrecognizable in white shirt, blue blazer, gray slacks, Gucci loafers. He had "gone back to school" to become a psychiatric social worker — and that's why, tonight, I think that he could have transformed himself again into the "responsible citizen" on the sidewalk. I would have liked to have seen him tonight, for we shared something, an era.

We wake in the dark, in pleasure, in the rain, and I anticipate walking later under the blowing trees. My son's silhouetted in the doorway, in his Tweety pajamas, rubbing his eyes, muttering in his gruff voice: "You go to sleep in the dark, and you wake up in the dark."

Greenwich Avenue/Peacock Café. It is always around noon when I reach Greenwich Avenue, walking east. I pass the schoolyard where it's always recess. I look up and see the children's paintings on the back of a building, lined up, framed, to look like windows. I can feel myself gather momentum, as if the wind were at my back. It's as if the day were turning on its axis, its axle, at this moment; the light is changing to darkness now even though it will be slow to arrive. I can use the morning; the afternoon uses me.

"Sometimes" (my son prefaces everything with that word) we exit the park and walk by the Dakota, Seventy-second and Central Park West. He's always taken with the urge to smite the fetching gargoyles whose faces are at his eye level along the railing. While he's absorbed in that drama I imagine that I am in a medieval town somewhere in Provence, surrounded by magpies and the stern, contorted faces of the gargoyles. From this imagined hilltop I can see mushrooming shapes and colors, pale olives, soft blues and grays. Wasps cluster at the honey jars on the stone tables on the terrace, but no one brushes them away. No one gets stung. "They're not gargoyles — they're monsters!" he shouts, and jolts me back to where I am.

I feel as if I'm most flaneur-like when we're walking at a turtle's pace he sets. It brings to mind Antony's marvelous address to Cleopatra:

> No Messenger but thine, and all alone to night
> We'll wander through the streets, and note
> The qualities of people.

He must sample every hawker's tray for cars and trucks and guns, must yank every stray cord out of the tarred dirt, walk every catwalk, jump on or over every grating, every manhole. I don't like to think of what could happen if one were loose. "Stop it," I say. "But I *like* to," he says. I tell him about the eight-year-old who stepped on a loose manhole cover, fell under the earth, got sucked down, drowned. "Where were his mommy and his daddy?" he asks, as if by their mere presence they could have saved him from harm. "Daddy." "What, Sam." "What's 'drowned'?"

Walking upper Broadway's dire grid in the raw February air after a late Friday afternoon movie *(Three Fugitives),* my son lurches to each corner, then comes to an abrupt stop, hops around to face me, and waits. Two blocks from our apartment he wants to know if this is "New York." His most constant refrain since he first formed words has been: "Where we go-ing?" Which is always germane. "Where's that man going?" Or where the clouds have gone, why the wind blew them away, or why they're hiding under the park bench.

There is a man sitting on a garbage can, strumming a three-stringed, half-gutted guitar. Lean and handsome, he wears heavy green woolen army pants. My son asks, "Can I strum? Why it's only got half a face?" The man laughs, gently, and hands it to him with one word of caution: "Be careful, it's very delicate."

There are no longer many places where walking delivers joy. Most people have a constant pattern, in which there are not enough variables. Rhythm imitates bodily contexts. Whitman's easy

gait is the mother of his prosody. Only by picturing him as part
of a multitude can we grasp how easily his "I" becomes mine, or
yours. Whitman's call to the open road has a formal component,
a structure.

Walking icy roads in Vermont, I was forced to shuffle and keep
my body on an even keel. Then, in a burst of bravado, I failed —
and fell. Only the streets of Manhattan are second nature to me.
There I can move at breakneck speed, never stopping, dancing
through traffic, never once stopping for a light. The entire pleasure of living in the city is tied up with walking.

No, days are not marked on the calendar, linear time can do
no more than corroborate effects, but there is a certain mustiness
like an illness that has to be overthrown before we can begin. And
so it is no accident that I write on this, the first clement day of the
year, to gain clemency. I could consider the mustiness my own,
but what light alleviates is no one's property.

Language describes a possibility and it is possible to be myself
once I give up the need for unity, consistency. The lights (they
were not desperate) on the river under the bridge are city lights,
and yet the moment seems pristine, almost pastoral. The word,
if it contained the world, would tell all.

We walk the jogging trail home through Riverside Park, my
son stumbling and falling as he tries to munch a bagel and carry
his bow and three arrows in the other hand. It's the kind of perfect hour in the light with the wind off the river that it is impossible to transcend. The vanishing instant cuts acutely across our
eyebrows. His sense of being at odds is entirely bound up with
objects: bagel, bow, arrow, quiver to be made at home, the hat
my wife fashioned out of newspaper, the tights she donated to
his costume (and miraculously fit him). It is we who are left
guessing, and come up short; we who must be content that knowing always remains at a distance, disappearing.

Walking, I watch the plastic baggie wafting on the wind, I follow its shadow on the avenue, I see it snagged by a branch and
released, I wonder from what height it has fallen, if it was thrown

out intentionally or was sucked out by the wind by an open window; I want to lie back, and drift and dream and listen to the spare Brazilian guitar; I want to lie with my head again on her lap in Kensington Square Park; I want to lie down on the lawn in Kankakee, under the maple tree, some spring afternoon after school, thinking of no before or after, and wait, anxiously or not anxiously, for the little band to come by and play Wiffle Ball; or to lie prone on the grass in Patterson, New York, after work, in the early spring sun, knowing I would be alone and free the rest of the day. In the late afternoons you can hide in broad daylight. I want concord, concordance, with what the self inside the self is trying to be, manifest energy, as in those times when no one was pulling me apart, when routines were suspended, and I was with friends who saw me as I wanted to be seen, and not — as my father saw me; or as when I knew almost no one in New York and walked the hundred blocks from my apartment to hers, drinking cheap Portuguese wine, and reeling.

Later, moving west alone across Central Park at Seventy-ninth, I walk out of the Vista Rock Tunnel into a burst of noonday light, not carrying anything, not going anywhere in particular, — a rush of radiance, a haze on bush and branch, — the rain stops falling and I walk the city in the sun; I breathe easy as the light presses against the stand of trees on the rise above old stone walls . . . Ready to begin again.

REG SANER

# The Ideal Particle
# and the Great Unconformity

FROM THE GEORGIA REVIEW

SLOWLY we accepted the curve of the earth. It dawned on us like
a great change of mind, after which, earth's size came easy. Not
its age. Evidence was everywhere underfoot, unmistakable. We
chose not to see it.

The canyons of the Southwest take one by surprise. A hundred
paces or so to the left a provocative cactus flower draws you toward
it, over a pocked table of stone that may grow nothing taller than
lichen and sand. Then, as if between one step and the next, a
canyon decides to make itself visible. The slabs we call northern
Arizona are riven by depths unseen from a few hundred yards'
distance. Nor does even the Grand Canyon give itself away slowly.
It's just all at once *there*.

   That fact makes entirely believable the story about a nineteenth-century cowhand who'd never heard of it or its alleged
grandeurs. He didn't know what a high river can do with nobody
to tell it how, nor had symphonic strings or kettledrums told *him*
how to feel. He just stumbled onto the thing, gaped dumbfounded,
and gave a yelp: "Something has happened here!"

   In contrast, photosaturation has deadened us to Grand Canyon vistas. If, however, we'd like to see for ourselves those mineral centuries we pass our lives walking and motoring around
upon, while ignoring them, we must descend. Invited into its own
past, then further and deeper, the inner eye becomes visionary.

Having seen that world the best way, for ourselves, when at last we reascend to the rim we'll be standing on a terrace opposite the universe.

Oddly, she carries no pack. "Oh, I'll make it," she says. She is tall, stout, with salt-and-pepper hair mannishly short. She looks fifty or so, and her walking staff lends a kind of seniority, except for her dogged, almost apprehensive step — though the trail along this stretch is easy going compared to what lies ahead. But a mere mile and three quarters into her morning, she isn't. Not making it at all.

Only 1,600 vertical feet above her, above this stretch of sun-thumbed cliffs whose red detritus give the trail its brick-dust complexion, motorized tourists intending to whiz on by are, even now, suddenly slowing at one or another scenic vista, getting out and putting cameras to their faces. From up there the trails are mostly hidden by buttes, and hikers all but invisible. The attraction is photo opportunities.

But to the grim-visaged woman poking along behind the tip of her walking staff, what had been, on the rim, expanses of unpeopled gorgeousness is now red shale made of heat waves. Her step is a trudge. "All kinds," I say to myself. "All kinds want to be here, do their own seeing."

Downtrail a quarter mile or so I meet the husband. He too is tall, grayer than his wife, but lean. He wears a bright blue frame pack and carries by its top bar another just like it. Seeing me, he sets the second pack aside in the shade of an outcrop, then takes off his own. It handles heavy. "Where you headed?" I ask.

"We're spending our first night at Hermit Creek," he says. Clearly he believes it. Or is trying to?

"Um-m-m," I think. Ahead are the so-called Cathedral Stairs down through the Redwall — *very* steep — then miles more of mounting heat over rock trash and switchbacks down through the Supai formation onto the Tonto — which by the time they get there is going to be torrid. The woman is already whipped.

"My wife's still acclimating," the man says without my asking. "We're from Virginia, just getting used to the altitude. We're shuttling the packs downtrail."

The "we" is him. First his pack, for two hundred yards or so, then, having shucked it, the return uptrail for hers — and so on to Hermit Creek. Lean though he is, doing a strenuous seven miles that way would mean twenty-one miles, packs and all. "No way," I say to myself.

Among hikers into this canyon's desert realities, his brand of magical thinking is far from rare. Heading off again, I wince inwardly as he adds, "We've got food for a week."

As words go, "astronomy" and "physics" have been in use for millennia, whereas "geology" in its present sense dates back only a few hundred years. Till then the earth sciences lacked focus enough to warrant a name. But why? Why should the study of light-at-a-distance, astronomy, have produced notable results almost two thousand years before anything like geology got started? Lack of equipment? Hardly. A world of geology has been learned by just looking; not even a hammer is needed. And the laboratory everywhere.

True, the ancients didn't lack occasional bright ideas we'd call geological, "the ancients" being, when it comes to ideas that have reached us, not the Hittites or Chaldeans but almost invariably the Greeks. Yet nobody went around systematically looking to see how the earth is made, or what forces cause earth events to happen as they do. So why that indifference? Given the accurate scrutiny of sky effects, what explains such long disregard of activity within the earth's crust?

The answer may be simple as Up and Down. Things in the sky, we "look up to." Perhaps they ordain, control. Even foretell? Whereas Venus and Mars were sky fire, Earth was just dirt. Unlike Babylonian stars, ours don't portend anymore, but we still "look down on" things underfoot. Our sci-fi mania for leaving Earth far below to journey up into the heavens is an ancient ambition. Persons knowing little of the history of science will feel that claiming Up and Down as values, not just directions, is childish. Precisely. Which is why our sense of them as values is ageless. And why geology became really possible in the century of Galileo and Newton, when for the first time in the Christian era our everyday terra firma found itself part of the sky. Like a star or any other heavenly object, once Earth's status was promoted to that of a planet, it became considerable. In short, a proper object of study.

Few backpackers I've met bother much with geological labels. It's all rock, the various kinds have names — which one *could* learn. But what, beyond syllables, would you know if you did? Anyhow, enjoyment may be the best form of knowing this canyon.

Further downtrail I pass a slow-moving, hefty type who couldn't care less what these depths are made of. He simply wants them to take the measure of his character. Gabby in a big-city way, self-conscious about his slow pace and his flab, he blurts his reasons for putting himself through what, in his shape and limping on already awesome blisters, must be purgatorial. As apparently in some sense he intends it to be.

"I do this every few years," he says. "To test the spirit, find out if I'm up to it."

Odd, hearing in his Detroit accent that he's a salesman of business forms, order pads. His limp stalls; I halt with him. "I'm a pretty fair doctor," he says, shucking his pack and pulling from it a pint of whiskey. Unlacing a boot, he says, "This may take a while." To lance the worst of the blisters, then sterilize it with bourbon? "You go on ahead. And have a good one."

Five minutes later the trail's switchbacking has put me no more than a hundred feet below his wild, animal yowl. I look up startled. His face contorted, he holds his bourboned foot while rocking to and fro in exquisite pain — but nonetheless calls down to reassure me. "I thought I was ready for that," he says, "but I guess I wasn't."

What's it matter how old the earth is? These days not much, but in former ages it mattered. Earth's age, implicit in the Book of Genesis, wasn't open to question; therefore, incredible as it may seem now, you once could have been put to death for saying "millions of years." In times near as our great-grandfathers' you could have been suspected of heterodoxy merely by being a geologist. Right up to our own century, "millions of years" could give rise to imputations of atheism.

But poor James Ussher, Archbishop of Dublin! One literal-minded gesture now outweighs his seventeenth-century fame as a most learned man. Amused geologists never tire of celebrating his naïveté in dating the Creation overprecisely: 4004 B.C. But how? Well, to figure biblical chronology for his *Annales Veteris et Novi Testamenti* he simply assigned a year-value to the span of a human generation, then counted Old Testament generations up to his own times. At Cambridge University, Ussher's estimate didn't cut it fine enough for one John Lightfoot, a Hebrew scholar deeply read in rabbinical literature. Like a mathematician adding a few decimal places to the value of pi, Lightfoot worked it down to the very hour. The Holy Trinity had created Earth in 4004 B.C. on October 26 at nine o'clock in the morning!

Lifted from their historical moment, Ussher and Lightfoot do seem paragons of fatuity, but less so when we recall that the bygone enterprise of wringing chronological precision from Holy Writ occupied Isaac Newton obsessively for over a decade.

Northwest of Yuma Point there's a vest-pocket plateau of Wescogame sandstone far below the rim, but so aloof from terrain far below *it* that it seems to float. A campsite in the sky. And this evening, mine.

Backed to the east by a sheer, straw-yellow cliff of Coconino sandstone looming asteroidally huge, this tiny plateau-prominence begins as a steep talus slope footing that cliff, then as its steepness eases, it flattens, ending abruptly as butte. Like a ship's prow it sails into Grand Canyon space and seems to cruise there, high above another plateau, the Tonto, 1,400 feet down. Many trail-hours below, I see glimpses of what I've come a long way to look at firsthand, the Great Unconformity.

The canyon's stacked layers include a baker's dozen of gaps called unconformities, whose missing rock adds up to far more depth than what's here, but my personal aim on this outing is the big one. It's the one that John Wesley Powell first saw, then named the Great Unconformity. Though I've passed by it on previous trips, that was before I quite knew what it was. Maybe no human mind can know. Nonetheless, I want another look, a close-up. Having seen Denali, the Pacific, Etna, Mount Fuji, Vesuvius, the Alps — and having flown in one long admiration over the blue/white snow fields of Greenland — I suspect the Great Unconformity may be the most astonishing physical thing I'll ever lay eyes on.

Not in the sense of scenic magnificence; rather, a rift in geological time deeper than human thinking can go, a wound in the world's body whose absence I can put my hand on — the better to feel what happens. As a sort of erosional Sphinx, the Great Unconformity seems to promise carnal knowledge of time. I want my flesh-and-blood hand to touch exactly that.

After supper I poke around along the cliff rim to find a slab just right for a back rest. Months ago I'd planned to use these sundown hours for traipsing among limestone hunks fallen from the Kaibab formation 2,400 feet above, and the Toroweap just below it, their surface aboil with fossil brachiopods and sea worms. Instead I laze, doing nothing, while light shifts among canyon ridgelines in rags, among multitiered amphitheaters, terra-cotta buttes too proud to be human, and miles of haze, blue with purple at the end of them.

The seethe of invertebrates over great slabs fascinates me. My ignorance of their petrified lives is flawed by so few facts that when, traipsing along the Boucher Trail, I stop at a hulk toppled from high above, I'm too blank to be analytical. All I really know is what the clear light of morning tells me: that this canyon's stacked sea floors were once densely, dramatically aswarm with such creatures.

They squirmed, slithered, died, and were buried under precipitates of calcium carbonate sifting down fine as time; were fossilized and resurrected as limestone, covered in turn by strata of sandstone, shale, what have you; were uplifted, as our continent rose above sea level, and felt immemorial winds wear away all strata between them and the sun; whereupon their particular chunk, undermined by rains beyond counting, at last broke off and plunged them crashing down here to take up a new existence as surface attractions on boulders. And attract me they do, partly because their chert nodules resist weathering so much better than their encasing matrix of limestone.

I know their dim lives once included — *in potentia* — this one I'm living, yet filial piety doesn't keep me from wanting to pick up a rock and bash at the bulgiest specimen to see what his insides are like. But that would vandalize him, so I don't. Besides, from fossil hunting in Utah I know the first whack would get nowhere. My brachiopod avatar, silicified now, is harder than any rock I'd find hereabouts to smash him open with. Chips would fly, the brachiopod's rain-weathered bulge would receive only powdered dints, whereas my hammerstones would soon go to pieces and I'd end not much the wiser.

If I were determined enough to try various kinds of hammerstone, I would reenact the invention of geology. The earliest geologist, as Henry Faul tersely surmises him, would've been that person who held a stone in his hand, picked up another, then tossed the first stone aside because his second choice seemed likelier. Nothing controversial there. But when geology began asking where stones come from, what forces act on them, how one kind of "stone" (the kind now called fossils) came to be found inside another stone, and — most important — how *old* stones or fossils might conceivably be, then the bishops and ministers began harrumphing. Fossils became controversial inklings.

What a weariness it is to realize how slowly we humans open our eyes! The absurdities which organized religion led itself into while denying that Earth moves around the sun were lessons still unlearned when, at roughly the same time as the Copernican revolution, geology began asking why the relics of sea creatures occurred far inland, high up on mountains, began therefore asking, "This world, how old is it? What is its history?" Not even the voices raising such questions foresaw what an adventure they would become. In the Grand Canyon alone, fossilized life forms outnumber me and my whole species. Yet for a shamefully long run of centuries we didn't want to know what fossils were.

In ancient times a fossil was anything dug out of the ground — animal, mineral, artifact, it didn't matter. As usual, the first person to have understood the marine origin of fossils seems to have been Greek, one Xenophanes of Colophon, at around 500 B.C. Like any culture, Hellenic societies had their follies and taboos, but an apparatus of thought police wasn't among them. Thus neither Xenophanes nor Herodotus nor, much later, Aristotle felt constrained in pondering fossils, or forbidden to consider how wide time might be.

Our own culture's protoscientists have had to tread far more carefully when it came to such questions. The Book of Genesis saw to that — or, more accurately, Christianity's reading of Genesis as a literal description of how the world got made. Will anything else in the annals of credulity ever match that absurdity? Probably. Fear is often the threshold of knowledge, but the rate at which our species dares to know itself seems brachiopodally slow.

Yesterday evening, the evening before hiking down to my sky island, I watched a most jovial woman turn away from a guard-rail on the South Rim and, laughing at herself, admit to friends, "Ah cain't hep thankin' all this should be *Egypt!*" Moments later another woman leaned forward over that same rail on the South Rim. In a European accent of mild surprise, as if to herself, she said, "It is a hole." That too.

Now, an afternoon later, I dawdle away the light falling on terrain those women saw so differently, and notice that however firmly I pull my look elsewhere, the eyes drift back to a trail wisping across the broad Tonto Plateau. From an air mile away and 1,400 feet down, the trail is thread-thin, but the eyes see it clearly enough to discover nobody. I *pull* my eyes elsewhere. Almost without my permission, the eyes return, scanning, reporting again and again, "Nobody." Just cliff repetitions, sandstone harmonics.

Meanwhile, the Colorado River's blue-green continues to be equally mesmeric, with its roar arriving in waves — clear, then faint, then clear again. Between troughs of near silence its crests break like the rise and collapse of one ongoing sigh that always reminds me of a distant stadium's crowd noise, the hurrahs and applause of all throngs: the Roman Forum, the Colosseum, Athenian audiences, Persian armies, Assyrian ones. Except that the river is a dozen or twenty times older than anything human.

My eyes vary their routine by also scanning for river rafts. I tell them I don't mind being alone, the views are stupendous, the evening serene. Who needs *Homo sapiens*? For that matter, the ravens and swifts are company, aren't they? And my little plateau's piñon pines, the claret-cup cacti, the broad-leafed and narrow-leafed yuccas, the low, half-diaphanous clumps of rabbit brush. Shadow engulfs the Colorado, but crag lines east of it still bounce gold off its waters, with the eyes trying to see rafts in minuscule flecks the miles make nearly microscopic. "Is that one?" the eyes ask themselves. "Un-unh . . . just a riffle." And the boat which has pulled ashore onto a sandbar turns out to be plausible rock. Though we speak of the mind's eye, the eyes have a mind of their own.

In fact, they turn far-off motes into people often enough to finally learn by heart each man-shaped trail form that, stared at hard, doesn't budge. In their compulsive scanning for signs of life, however, the eyes won't take no. They insist on finding me some. And they want it human. "Dear bipedal creatures," they seem to feel, "how avid we are to take you in at this distance."

In evening's marvelous dilapidations, the lower buttes are now an enshadowed blue, while the loftier ones grow rustier by the minute, but still lift sunstruck pinnacles proud of their resistances. All of it high above the river's running whisper.

Turning westward to check the sun's remaining minutes, I notice a raven gliding in as if to alight. It skims along about twelve inches above the dust-puddled slab of this narrow plateau, then — as it continues out over suddenly nothing — I'm shot with adrenaline. Unconsciously, I'd become that raven, and when its level glide sailed out over the cliff edge, my safe inches of altitude turned to deep air — with me plummeting through it. An eight-hundred-foot drop isn't bottomless but my surprise makes it so.

Twenty minutes later, watching the daredevil feeding of swifts, I notice a variant; how a smaller, incomparably nimbler empathy causes me to fall a long way through one microsecond of panic. You can become a swift, I discover, wholly unaware you've done so. Any number of times, without thinking, just blurting and wheeling, blithely feeding on gnats or what have you, my aerobatic gaze drops from the swift I've become down through the space between me and the Tonto Plateau: "But I can't fly!"

Anywhere else, even in mountains, birds passing nearby at eye level have at least a slope under them. Here the sheer drops from this floating platform of butte create an illusion that fools me with as little as a yucca moth, flying two inches above a pool of brown sand. The moment its cabbage-white flutter takes it out past the cliff edge, I startle.

For many years, certainly ever since my first Inner Canyon trip and initial glances at the Great Unconformity, one of my large admirations has dwelt on a grain of quartz sand so tiny that ten laid edge to edge would span only a millimeter. Through a pocket lens I have often marveled at the gemlike purity and luster of such granules among the pink ridgelines and valleys of my fingerprint.

In fact, a sand grain one tenth of a millimeter is the size most easily airborne in wind, thus likeliest to begin a surface effect known as saltation: the chain reaction of granules knocked into the air by other wind-blown granules which, as they land, then strike yet more sand grains a microblow, lifting them just enough for wind to get at them. Hence the term "ideal particle." Hence too, Utah, for instance — whose water- and wind-carved forms owe much to the ideal particle's love of flight and changes of scenery. Around Mexican Hat, Utah, they say, "Nothing here but a lot of rocks and sand, and more rocks and more sand, and enough wind to blow every bit of it away." They know.

Allied with water, of course, there isn't anything in the entire Southwest that the ideal particle can't erase and start en route to the sea. It and its kin — silt, pebble, gravel, or boulder — created the Grand Canyon. Long, long, long before that, though mountains more than two miles high once rose where the canyon now is, the ideal particle abducted them.

Like water, sand is a wheel. Round and round its silicon goes, grain on grain, cycle on cycle. With its auxiliaries, ice and snow, sand has already leveled Colorado. Not once. Often. Quartz granules are made of pure patience. Delicately, translucently, the ideal particle's tenth of a millimeter encapsulates so many Tetons and Rockies and Appalachians brought low, it can afford to seem humble, agree to eat anything. Wherever we walk at the seashore, it nibbles dead skin off our footsoles.

Among Inner Canyon hikers "water" is the most spoken word, focusing talk like a bond, while most reasons for being on these trails go unsaid: buttes risen up from red epochs nobody was there to lay eyes on, monoliths astonished to see us — all shaped by rain and gravel and sand. If all that water, now nowhere to be seen, isn't far from our thoughts, it must be an obsession to flora on the Tonto Plateau. The verdigris slopes of Bright Angel shale afford barely enough moisture for omnipresent blackbrush and cacti — each guarding its water with thorns, or with needles thick as rain.

Then there's the Utah agave's wild efflorescence. Its moist yellow blossoms begin head-high, on a single fibrous stalk twice taller than a man. How much pollen they offer or nectar they ooze I can't say, but it's enough to allure the biggest, blackest bees I've ever seen. "Grumble bees" I call them, flying so sluggishly it seems they'd rather not be flying at all. I half drowse just watching one back out of a bloom, then sag heavily down onto a fresh set of petals. The agave's flowering — gaudy as Hollywood's idea of Persia — is, on its truculent side, armored water. Its base is a sword-burst of rigid blades that are reputed to have ripped up the guts of many a Spaniard fallen from his saddle while questing for gold and souls. So the Utah agave has to bide its time, taking maybe a dozen to fifteen to as much as twenty-five years to ejaculate that one opulent splurge of water-costly blossoms — then topples. Its husks litter the canyon like famished cattle.

Understandably, backpackers are warned to carry at least a gallon per day per person. I remember a puffy guy girdled with fat who came downtrail into the big campsite at Hermit Creek, shirtless, red-faced and gimpy from unaccustomed exertion. He slumped down, groaning, moaning. Half to himself, half to anyone within earshot, he said, "There was a moment up there," nodding up toward the Tonto, "when I just didn't know." Long pause. "I mean, I just didn't know." Another pause. Then softly, and more than half to himself, "Oh, I knew." Again pausing. "But I knew I was going to have to take my time."

"Did you have enough water?" I asked.

"Drank six quarts coming down," he said. "And only peed twice."

Earth centered the stars. In the cosmos, only Earth had a destiny. It had been expressly created for us. Every celestial body, however superior, revolved around us. Here Eden had been, and here the Fall; thus Earth was both center and sewer, the cynosure of all creation and its sink of iniquity. In that moral universe, "up there" was linked with "down here" by analogies abounding. Divine light was to the cosmos as the sun's was to Earth, and as the human mind to its body. After the Edenic apple got eaten, however, all below the moon had been corrupted. As one Thomas Burnet, a seventeenth-century divine, put it in his *Sacred Theory of the Earth,* our planet in its days of innocence before the Fall had been smooth, entirely; but postlapsarian Earth was "a ruin" whose "faults" were at once geological and a judgment of God. Though Burnet was a theologian, his views seemed to orthodox critics more mechanistic than scriptural. He held matter to be eternal, held that the world machine needed no Divine Machinist. Time and the properties of matter would of themselves give birth to this world we inhabit. Yet his was a *sacred* theory, a Creator behind it, which made his science too theological for freethinkers and too heretical for their opposites.

Among the latter, Edward Stillingfleet wrung his hands. If the world is eternal, he complained, then "the whole Religion of Moses is overthrown, all his Miracles are but Impostures, all the Hopes which are grounded on the Promises of God, are vain and fruitless."

Tongue clacking over religion's meddling with or in science is immensely satisfying, of course, and very bad for our characters. In relishing images of churchmen making museum pieces of themselves, even as today's "creationists" do now, we indulge in the sweet illusion of superiority — a particularly insidious form of self-abuse. Be that as it may, seventeenth-century controversy slowly yielded to the incontrovertible, and geology became possible. But the analogical universe faded slowly; for example, sunspots suggested a correspondence with earthly volcanoes. Ingeniously false, but error too can be fruitful. The fake correlation led to observations which took on a life of their own as what we now call the earth sciences. Thus Earth received a sort of promotion via the stars.

Still, medieval figments waned slowly, especially on geology's central question: How old is the earth? What theo-geological dust that kicked up! Lots of highly educated people tried hard *not* to let the planet's growth rings tell their own story.

Inches from my left ear a white-throated swift hustles past as if showing how close he can come — the aggressive, sibilant hiss I imagine of arrows. One swift blurts suicidally straight at a crag, misses by a handsbreadth of veer and plunges into its next audacity with a swerve equally implausible. Their changes of direction dazzle me! At high velocity they spin on a wing tip. And as always, watching them feed and aware they've been clocked at over seventy miles an hour (with unconfirmed reports of more

than double that), I think, "These are the hottest pilots going."
They, in turn, watching me sit quietly on an outcrop, content to
let them fire into blue canyon shadows and out again, may be
asking each other, "How can he live like that?"

They might well wonder, these birds that never hold still. I've
seen them nearly alight at a puddle, but mostly they drink on the
wing. In love with speed, they can mate while in flight, gather
nesting materials, and apparently, in certain instances anyhow,
even sleep flying. What energy they pour out hustling and
plunging and rolling away on the air!

Mornings and evenings make this, their canyon home, one maze
of flight corridors. And of stillness, stirred by just enough wind
to set up a hushaby soughing of piñon pines nearby. Much as I
want to hit the trail tomorrow long before sun does, I won't get
into my sleeping bag till a first two or three stars come through
the twilight, as if walking toward Earth.

Where great walls do the talking, where a gibbous moon becomes visible as desert silences happen, those walls, their depths,
their great river with tiny birds hurtling under and above them,
become so real as to stay that way, untranslatable. And swifts, incomparably more so. Yet what do such creatures amount to? A
pinch of white and dark fluff, hollow bone. A mature swift weighs
only a couple of ounces, but is anything else in creation so entirely, so audaciously alive? "No," I think, "not possible." So for
me the swift is not "a lower form," is instead a perfection.

That's a long flight from archaeopteryx, the world's first bird,
of about 150 million years back, whose leathery membranes were
"wings" fit only for gliding. Lacking muscle enough to flap them,
and thus having to climb any tree it launched from, the archaeopteryx looks comic enough to us; nonetheless, like the failed
ignition of some defunct star, its clumsy hope of colonizing the
air reaches me now, serialized through intervening species, by
way of these swifts. They are indeed the definitive bird. Leaving
this canyon, I'll top out on a rim that was still ocean floor 100
million years before the appearance of archaeopteryx. Reptilian
as its skin flap and tendon contraption may have been, from such
cumbersome glides this very sky's first flying animal was born.

As an English observer put it in the early nineteenth century, "It
was a mooted question whether geology and Christianity were

compatible." To fervid literalists of the Bible it seemed that those men going round the British countryside tapping at rocks with their odd little hammers were bent on chipping away at Genesis.

For one thing, long before the nineteenth century, a strictly literal reading of Genesis made it risky to say too much about fossils. On the third day the Lord separated land and sea. On the fifth day he created fishes and fowl. On the sixth terrestrial creatures. So how could shells found far inland possibly be marine in origin? Relics of Noah's Flood? Some believers invoked that possibility, but doing so was particularly awkward in the case of fossilized species now nowhere alive. Literally interpreted, Genesis doesn't mention animal extinctions — which in any case the Ark was built to prevent.

Sixteenth-century writers on fossils sometimes stepped very gingerly. A common ploy for avoiding imputations of heresy was to discuss fossils and Earth's age in safely hypothetical terms, as the Copernicans had learned to do; that is, to affirm nothing as fact. Even so, when protogeologists began realizing that fossils might prove the calculus stones with which to date various strata, enormously unbiblical time spans with their unbiblical extinctions and sudden appearances of new species began to dawn.

Meanwhile, orthodox thinkers argued that fossils weren't living animals, ever. Couldn't have been. A medieval view held that they were *lusus naturae*, "sports of nature," possibly conceived by Satan to confuse people. A sixteenth-century savant cataloguing the Vatican's mineral collection suggested that fossils were neither extinct creatures nor anything else but just odd things God just happened to have made. Da Vinci, of course, had known exactly what they were, but confided only in the mirror script of his notebooks. Geologically minded others in the sixteenth century knew too, even while orthodoxy kept trying to explain them away.

Little did humble crinoids and three-inch trilobites crawling over the Paleozoic ooze dream of one day becoming Gorgons or Medusas, too terrible for gazing on directly. Theirs was a past we didn't want to believe was inside us.

At 7:30 in the morning, the trail down and across Travertine Canyon remains mostly shaded; a sort of glade, so cool and leafy and fragrant — what with the blossoming shrubs of mock orange, the mountain maple, fendlerbush, serviceberry — that rattlers are quite out of mind. Watching the wing blur of humming-birds as they float and dart among blooms on a shrub of mock orange, I forget to be wary. By mere chance, turning to photo-graph a ledge I've just descended, I see it there, tucked in a niche at shoulder height, where I just now passed within inches. Classic.

If this one's typical, maybe I can't hear them. From its tail vi-bration, surely it must be buzzing; must've buzzed as I passed it. The lower body coiled, its upper portion cocked in an *S* curve, it flicks a black tongue, tasting the air, but often putting the forked tip on the ledge before it. To know where its ledge ends? Pick up vibrations? The final few inches of tail twitch, then blur. I hear nothing. Odd to think of its rattling as I walked by, gazing at hummingbirds.

Usually I keep snakes well in mind, scorpions too. I'd have said I keep serpents at the level of a phobia, except that this one, my first canyon rattler, despite fangs and venom, is beautiful. Very. It disquiets me that my hearing, a bit the worse for loud noises in war, may be unable to warn me. It's further bad news to see that the evolution of this subspecies, Grand Canyon rattler, has matched the beige sandstone with its beige underbelly and sides. I'm fascinated by the delicate tongue, a glistening flicker, black as obsidian, liquid as oil.

But shoulder height is too near the heart. If it had struck, I'd have tried to smash it to pulp. Since it didn't, I'm free to see time's intricate beauty in even a rattler.

On an Earth only six thousand years old there would still be sand enough in any hourglass to bury us all. And if the cosmos re-tained only nineteenth-century dimensions, Earth would still be almost infinitely small within it.

Even the medieval cosmos would do. In Dante's universe, if you traveled at what we know is the speed of light, you'd reach the nearest star in five minutes. In ours, you wouldn't quite have arrived four years later! By the seventeenth century, cosmic scale hadn't grown much. France's polymath savant Father Mersenne held the universe to be about 55 million miles across, which in our world gets you little more than halfway to the sun. So despite Mersenne's being a Copernican and a booster of Galileo, his cosmos was still surprisingly medieval, only about five light-minutes wide. The same Father Mersenne, a formidable mathematician, calculated that in 1634 the earth was exactly 5,954 years old. By comparison, in eastern Nevada lives a bristlecone pine whose growth rings span 75 percent of Mersenne's estimate for the age of the earth. When it came to the scale of this actual universe, our forefathers had no idea.

Or chose not to, like everyone. No sooner are certain realities admitted to the brain than something within us secretly dissolves them, just as, by day, the mind takes back what it dreamed.

During my scrambling descent through Mississippian limestone of the early Carboniferous down into Temple Butte limestone, I'm vexed to see that my $3.99 watch, bought expressly for this rough terrain, is again useless. After half an hour on the trail its crystal is once more opaqued with sweat beads glistening inside it like mercury. So much for "Waterproof to thirty meters." Back in Boulder my friend Ron would say, "Three ninety-nine? You didn't pay enough." On the contrary, too much. Well, whatever the o'clock, it's between 350 million and 400 million years ago, local time.

The leather headband of my wide-brimmed straw rides on a film of salt water, and wiping it off with a bandanna is token resistance. For five hundred feet down through Redwall limestone, however, the microclimate isn't desert but shaded oasis, and that helps. Apparently runoff takes the same trail, because green sprays of skunkbush and bricklebush alternate with tufts of long-bladed grasses kept alive by their memories of rain. Which doesn't keep my sweat from finding channels of its own.

What a comic figure I make, slithering, clinging to carnal hunks of Toroweap limestone fallen all the way here, lurching deeper into erosions the European woman called "a hole." To do what? To see for myself. If a judge sentenced criminals to this trail, he'd be removed from the bench, prosecuted, and convicted. Sweat dribbles onto the lens of my sunglasses, yet looking up at the sun-lit ocher of cliff walls without them makes the eyes wince.

Except for my presence, no sign of *Homo sapiens*; and maybe not even then. Aside from the chink of rock chips scattered by my boots, all I hear is an animal's breathing and the creaking of his pack. After millennia of practice, I suppose our highest flight within that webworks called the mind has been to realize that's who we are: animals. Till lately, we were too backward to make the discovery, thus closer to being what we feared to be, by that very refusal. Like a kid in a retention home, we fantasized stories we truly seemed to believe — about what a big shot our dad was, and how much he loved us, and how he was one day going to take us out of this place, to live in a fancy house and have everything. Childlike too was our refusal to share the ancestry of mammals. The ruckus we kicked up over being blood cousins to apes was the strident denial of a six-year-old whose playmates have just told him how babies are *really* made.

With each knee-jolt downward a last quart sloshes inside its canteen to remind me I'm an erstwhile sea creature crawled ashore; the salinity of that amniotic fluid has come along inside my cells, whose survival requires me to tote the anciently mothering element in bottles, jars, bags, what have you — a fish who preferred terra firma while taking his sea with him.

"The total destruction of the land is an idea not easily grasped, though we are the daily witness of its process." This audacious concept in the style of James Hutton marks a decisive breakthrough in dating the age of the earth. An eighteenth-century Scot with a genius both for the invisible obvious and for good fellowship, Hutton has been called "the founder of modern geology," as well as "the man who invented time." His French contemporary Georges-Louis Leclerc, Comte de Buffon, espoused similar views about everyday causes, and was incomparably the better stylist; Lamarck was better known outside his own country; Charles Lyell — born the year Hutton died, and following Hutton's lead — was the enabling eye behind Darwin. Still, the explorers of stone time included no one who uttered thunderbolts so blandly as Hutton. His facts were few as his insights, but those few were profound. And seminal.

Had I accompanied Hutton on one of his outings — for instance to Jedborough, when he spoke of inland stone having once been ocean floor — I'd have boggled mightily. There, some fifty miles south of Edinburgh, where the younger "Old Red" sandstone lies horizontally across nearly vertical "schistus" of far greater

age, was a big time gap. For us today the idea of strata once present and now missing isn't fantastic. Hutton's close friend John
Playfair, however, would've seen the gap as an "abyss of time."
An abyss many thousands of times older than the entire earth
was then believed to be? I'd have boggled plenty at that.

Hutton would've tried to explain. The layers of "schistus," being
enormously older than the sandstone on top of it, revealed — if
you knew how to read rock's chronicles — the drowning, the
metamorphosis, and the resurrection of continents. All of which
required, according to Hutton, epochs too vast for human vision
to see very far into. Summing up his view of stone's endless cycles, Hutton chose words more shocking, then, and more frequently quoted both then and now, than any in the history of
geology: "The result, therefore, of our present enquiry is, that
we find no vestige of a beginning — no prospect of an end."

"Hindu nonsense," I'd have thought, "and downright heretical!" Not all his zesty high spirits, nor the charm of his Scots burr,
would have got me past the impossibility of rain showers and grit
dismantling entire continents. In his own day he knew well that
his *Theory of the Earth* would meet minds conventionally, biblically
closed. Anybody looking at mountains, fault lines, or chasms could
*see* that apocalyptic events must have caused them. Thus whether
you inclined to "catastrophism" and its doctrine of grand, once-
and-for-all upheavals in a past that wouldn't happen again, or to
"diluvialism" and its image of a global ocean precipitating, forever, the world's supply of stone — granite included — you sub-
scribed to the idea that it takes big causes to make big effects.
That was common sense, bolstered by the ageless appeal of fire
and flood in myth; as if it would be a godless world indeed without cataclysms.

Hutton's *Theory*, on the other hand, was neither apocalyptic nor
Wagnerian. Geologically speaking, he argued, nothing happened in the past that hasn't always happened and that isn't happening right now. Past causes are ongoing and uniform. Hence
the label by which his view came to be known: "uniformitarian-
ism." Though he allowed for leaps and upheavals, he empha-
sized everyday forces. Eminently sensible now, in hindsight, but
nonsensical then.

If that's so, why can't we see them? "We can and do," his answer would have come, "but don't realize what we're witness to, because the earth is so much older than we've supposed." That was it in a nutshell: so much older than we've supposed. Rather than invoke a past in which remote catastrophes gave Earth its present continents and their appearance, Hutton urged people to consider forces daily seen and felt; in short, to consider "little causes, long continued." These, operating over a sort of temporal eternity, were powerful enough to destroy whole continents. "What more can we require?" he asked, then answered, "Nothing but time." Surely that wasn't asking worlds.

Of me it would have been. Back then, where the age of the world was involved, it would've put me on an Earth wholly alien to my vision. It would have changed who and where and what I thought I was. Hutton anticipated my reaction: "It is not any part of the process that will be disputed; but after allowing all the parts, the whole will be denied; and for what? — only because we are not disposed to allow that quantity of time which the ablution of so much wasted mountain might require."

He was right. Like all the top-flight geological minds of Hutton's day, I'd have been a catastrophist, with maybe a splash of diluvialism.

Surely it's no coincidence that, long before Copernicus, Aristarchus of Samos said, "Earth circles the sun," and was ignored for two thousand years. Space and time do tend to interpenetrate each other. As for time, Aristotle hadn't minced words. Earth and the world were eternal. In the beginning, there was no beginning. There would be no end. Christian Europe referred to and deferred to Aristotle on any subject but that. The eternity of matter was pagan: heretical, insidious, atheistical.

Time-timidity prevailed till the era of Galileo and Newton. In eighteenth-century France, for example, Benoit de Maillet actually dared write of millions and billions of years. And of the eternity of matter. Even of life arisen spontaneously from "seeds" and marine creatures. But his curious compilation, *Telliamed* (de Maillet backwards), lay unpublished. Then, in 1748, two decades after his death, de Maillet's timorous editor fudged his original numbers downward by replacing big figures with vague phrases, or simply moving de Maillet's decimal points a few or more digits to the left!

Symptomatic, too, was the case of one of de Maillet's clever countrymen, Buffon. No editorial tampering undercut his estimates; he did it himself. After devising a series of quite intelligent experiments with the cooling of molten spheres, Buffon arrived at three million years as Earth's real age. But because even in the closing decades of the Age of Reason, he felt, readers wouldn't stand for "millions," he downscaled his own estimate to seventy-five thousand years. Then, having it both ways, he admitted to his readers what he had done. Inevitably, France's theologians roused themselves.

His compatriot Lamarck, a generation younger and a celebrated precursor of Darwin, found time-timidity infuriating. The threshold of the nineteenth century was, he felt, no place to keep nattering over the purblind vistas of what came to be called Mosaic geology — and the world's paltry six thousand years, as inferred from Genesis. Impatient with persons who want to go on counting Earth's years on their fingers and toes, he said, snappishly, "For Nature, these time-spans that stagger the mind are but instants."

"Which is," one can imagine him feeling, "simply how things stand. End of discussion." The nineteenth century had dawned, but of course it wasn't the end at all. Scriptural orthodoxy had become a sort of loyalty oath which custodians of the status quo required its members to sign. The young Darwin, hopeful of a country parsonage, professed faith in "the strict and literal truth of every word in the Bible." Then, only a few years later, weighing animal differences such as those between archaeopteryx and pigeons, he could say, "It leads you to believe the world older than geologists think."

Breathing infinite distances can enervate the soul. Once more readjusting my heavy pack's hip belt, I look out now over the Tonto Plateau. Amid its Sonoran expanses footing cliff lines abysmally old, and side canyons filled with departures, a hot gust of wind empties me. "What am I doing here? What point? Why go or be anywhere?"

Dry slabs, dry shale flakes, dry detritus, dry buttes, dry gullies. Dust, dryness. Parched air, terra-cotta rock. My weather bob reads 113 degrees Fahrenheit. Hearing water slosh inside my canteen, I know it's as much there to be abstained from as drunk, know my sips must be few and miserly. Soon I've drifted into trail trance, aware only of rubble meeting each footfall. It crunches under hot bootsoles like slag, my bare legs pass among hostilities in the shape of beavertail cactus, but neither heat nor the dryness account for my being instantly emptied in midstride, as if between the world's body and mine a void had opened.

Like stepping into a local warping of Earth's magnetic field, all my thought-atoms realign so that I feel "how it really is." Not a trick heat plays on the mind. Instead, the truth: nature as one self-sufficient machine where anything that can die is called "life," and ourselves the losses we agree to live out. It's as if the atmosphere suddenly vanished. Without a vapor of illusion to absorb its lethal radiations, the sun pours down a ruthless clarity denying everything I'd like to be true.

Then, perhaps because any truth is only half its story, the moment passes. What the canyon tells us is, yes, its truth, inhuman, not ours. Our truth is a small mortality centering a labyrinthine strangeness. Is it a strangeness worth the price of existence to know? We can't know, can't even suppose, can only answer, "Well, yes, certainly it's worth it. Except when it isn't." Meanwhile we feel the size of creational powers implacable, astonishing. But "lethal"? Only so to us mortals, and even then only if we're afraid to die. I am. I can also imagine *hoping* to become slightly less so. I might do it by agreeing to be fully within whatever this is, instead of resisting, withholding.

Easy to say. Yet whatever the "really" may be in "How it really is," that's surely what I'm also hoping to glimpse at least distantly in this canyon. On the other hand, if evolution has wired us to keep moving by keeping at least some illusions alive, how close can anyone come to whatever "really" is?

To my right, and a hundred feet up where the sloping of Bright Angel shale breaks downward from Muav limestone, three blossoming agave plants flaunt their pollen-yellow banners among tumbled boulders — Coconino hunks, hunks fallen from the Supai group, oddments of Redwall limestone that carried Temple Butte limestone along as it smashed its way down. How placidly their tons lie around, as if permanent residents, not transients just passing through. As they really are. As it all is, all on its way to the Gulf of California. Meanwhile, above Redwall boulders teeming with fossil crinoids, corals, bryozoans, my big black "grumble bees" drowsily carry on lives of social insects, gathering pollen over trilobites whose habits, unknowable, survive only in seas of limestone.

Wind whispers lightly through miles of blackbrush — knee-high, waist-high. What with that, and a midafternoon sun too hot for unshaded rattlers, and the steady boot crunch of shale almost finer than cinders, the mind quietly drifts into itself. Then a stretch of prickly pear cactus thickens till there's more cactus than room to avoid it, and I waken, picking my steps over their needles, and detritus more like industrial waste than geology.

I look closer. "Mosaic floor!" I blurt out loud. Indeed it is. Part geology, part meteorology, "mosaic floor" has nothing to do with the biblical Moses, but instead describes desert leveled by wind and virtually paved with more or less flat rock bits, like chips in mosaics. The Sahara contains oceans of mosaic floor, all the stones "ventifacts," meaning wind-carved and polished. These Tonto *tesserae* are much smaller than those African ones, nor are they so evidently wind-worked; but inlaid by canyon winds they most certainly are, and neatly. Rust-red shale the size of half dollars, verdigris shale, bits small and dark as coffee beans, edges still crisp, unrounded as yet by the ideal particle. It delights me to find Saharan ventifacts by the mile here in Arizona — a veritable floor indeed; cunningly, fastidiously wind-paved, broken only by the ubiquitous blackbrush and cactus.

If continental drifting and lifting ever stops — as, with the inevitable cooling down of Earth's core and mantle, we're told it must — this flatness is what all terrain will come to. A peneplain. Land's highest elevations will be worn down to, say, a few bare tens of meters above the world's oceans. Weather and the ideal particle will see to it.

The eighteenth-century French woman who called Copernicus's theory "a slander on mankind" might as well have been speaking of Buffon, Lamarck, and Hutton. The Copernican revolution and the discovery of geological time were aspects of the same thing. Ultimately their space/time would redefine us.

Orthodoxy couldn't let that happen. It had already done the defining. To hard-shell devotees of what came to be called "scriptural geology," as one observer put it, "science might be true, but Holy Writ *was* true." After all, said Thomas Chalmers in 1813, by way of reviewing Cuvier's definitive book on fossils, Moses was an eyewitness to creation; that fact made him far more reliable than any amount of conjecture based on bits and scraps of creatures dug up long after. So orthodoxy dodged and paltered and resorted to hypotheses like "special creation": species might come or go if God had handled each appearance or extinction as a special case. Which, as need arose, it was found He had. Often.

It was in southern Colorado where I first really saw, felt, and wandered barefoot over a lot of mountain ridgelines now ground into powder. There, on a June morning like a festival, I began suspecting that the oldest, most irresistible of immortals was the ideal particle.

The Great Sand Dunes National Monument sits eight thousand feet above sea level, at the westward foot of the Sangre de Cristo range. As usual in the San Luis Valley's high desert, the June sky was an intense blue set off by a few small cloud blossoms. Their brightnesses drifted, freely distorting in the usual westerly breeze blowing almost constantly, the same breeze which, for several dozen millions of years, has been granulating blue skylines of the San Juan Mountains, haze-blue in the distance, and tumbling their sands fifty miles east over that valley floor, already thick with the alluvium of glacier leavings.

What with that moving air and Colorado sun on the skin, the desert morning was cool/hot. At first the dunes themselves weren't impressive. Nothing on their smooth surfaces gave scale — till flyspecks way up on them kept turning out to be clusters of people. Across ankle-deep Medano Creek I waded, carrying my shoes, to begin the climb up sand ridges toward the crest of the monument's officially highest dune, seven hundred feet above the valley floor it sits on.

Legging it steeply uphill in fine sand at that altitude promotes heavy breathing. So because two thirds of each step forward went nowhere, I paused now and again, panting, enjoying the phenomenon of gusts curling a tan haze off dune summits above me, like snow smoking from mountain ridges. Stone snow. By 11 A.M. the surface granules had grown painfully hot after only a few steps. Quickly digging the feet just under the crust allows the cool, moist sand there to quench footsoles — exactly like dousing a fire — but before long, those feet may rebel. Short of the highest dune's crest, mine certainly did, insisting I put on shoes again.

Sometimes a gust would sweep over that crest just inches above its surface, with hordes of minute grains biting my ankles like static. A bit eerie, not just to see but to feel in their prickle on my own skin those "little causes, long continued" which will one day wear all mountains and their continents down to a virtual slab. Grains considerably less than a millimeter wide are harmless as gnats, but given their own sweet time, Huttonian time, they're piranha. Lightly they nibbled at me, tasting my possibilities.

And that is where I first *felt* myself completely inside geological time, on a gala morning when I and the clusters of people like me were never more alive. Those dunes were luminosities of beige — blond, tan, ecru, fawn, dove brown — as their silicon grains took in the sun's photons and gave them back in a luster minutely diffracted. By the trillions.

Then too, over the nuances of beige, summer tourists were spattered like a grand beach party or a flags-of-all-nations display. Sand's luminosity made white slacks, shorts, and T-shirts dazzling, just as it saturated the firecracker reds, the bright greens and citrons. Meanwhile, in the kind of day memory builds on, a high desert sky and its fast-scudding cloud puffs presided over everything, including fir and spruce forestation of the Sangre de Cristo, the unkempt cottonwoods lining Medano Creek, and higher up on evergreen slopes, pale columns of aspen newly leafing out. So the blaze blue of that sky was omni-temporal: a June of 35 million years ago, and another June 35 million summers up ahead, with my own "now" in between.

It was there, too, that I first saw sands in the act of crossbedding. "Big deal," I'd have said to myself before hiking inside the Grand Canyon, where I saw that crossbedding is really a sort of voiceprint left by winds which blew here long, long before anything human stood up in them. Paleowinds, the geologists call them. That enthralled me.

In such fossil dunes those flowlines show abrupt changes of angle where wind piled new dunes over old ones. The crossbedding I was seeing at the Great Sand Dunes was, instead, that of winds alive, lively, unfossilized; my winds, ours, our weather unhardened, unburied beneath thousands of feet under yet other deposits. Yet because I had seen the crossbedding of 270 million years ago in Coconino stone of the Grand Canyon, I was therefore seeing two June mornings in one. That Coconino stuff had been desert sand identical to what I was standing on, rounded by endless saltation in the very same wind. But those Grand Canyon paleowinds had sent dunes piling over each other when "here" was Pangaea, the globe's one and only continent. Now "here" is North America, and Pangaea has broken up, drifted off as shards we call Eurasia, Australia, Antarctica, Africa, South America. "How it really is" can be dizzying.

So atop that highest dune I felt a pre-paleowind gusting sand's migrations straight at my ankles. Under intense sun drenching our summer colors, amid the laughter and sand frolicking of children, we were flesh-events, happy to owe what we could only repay by enjoying it, cavorting or struggling or strolling on grains fated to sink beneath the sea again, and, solidified, to reemerge with an untrodden continent.

While I was what had become of some sea lily's or ammonite's future, I was also ancestral to an eventual something-or-other. So between the twin blacknesses of Before and After, being alive was the open and close of a camera's tripped shutter. My prints in hot sand were already posthumous.

At the popular Hermit Creek campsite, a nexus of Inner Canyon trails, I meet some of everybody. On my way to jump into a plunge-pool of the creek itself I notice Sunfoot under a catclaw tree. Shirtless, he sits on a square of blue-flannel blanket, trying to pull a dirty sock over his severely sunburned instep. The other foot looks equally angry. Though his lean physique and bearded face imply a workingman who knows his way around, I'm surprised any hiker would let his feet get that badly burned. As he eases another half inch of sock onto his right foot I ask, "How'd it happen?"

"Fell asleep over at Granite Rapids," he says, deadpan, changing to sardonic grin when he adds, "for maybe three hours."

Just watching him work that grungy sock over skin needing

burn cream and bandages makes me cringe. Both insteps are so
scarlet I wonder how he'll get boots on. "Can you walk?"

"I'll be all right once I get going," he says, then tells me he'd
planned on another four days in the canyon. "But with this . . ."
He gestures at the feet. We stare at epidermal tissue already beginning to weep and blister. "I figure maybe second degree," he
says. I nod a bit squeamishly and wish him luck, trying not to
guess what the miles up to the rim will do, and glad I won't be
around when he peels those socks off.

After my dip in the creek, refreshed with sopping clothes that'll
dry only too soon, I decide to stroll the mile and a half down
Hermit Canyon to the river. For ten or twelve minutes of wetness
my dunked shirt and shorts air-condition me. Soon, in a deep
narrows of surreal erosions, I come upon the Two Jollies, a pair
of women relishing their late lunch like schoolgirls. Plump and
middle-aged, they admit their descent was quite tiring, but don't
go *on* about it. They are so visibly pleased with that shady spot in
those narrows that I head off again delighted as they.

Because the mile and a half of creekbed down to the Colorado
is in places a lush tangle of willow limbs, of tamarisk, of rushes
thick and tall and green, my lunging and thrashing along the creek
feels African as the Congo. While in a phase of that daydream I
encounter Lord Tarzan, heading back up to Hermit Creek
campsite from the river. He's an Englishman living in Canada,
medium tall and, for a man of fifty, very well muscled. Though
he flew jets for the RAF — in Africa, oddly enough — it was as a
twelve-year-old in Australia that he saw the documentary on the
Grand Canyon which left him "very much wanting to see it."

Naturally I wonder what he thinks now that he has. His voice
is mellifluous yet deep. "I've been on the Zambeze," he says, "and
on the Amazon. The Colorado is by far the most . . . romantic."
Like his athletic body, the voice is also muscular. That and its
British vowels lend his slightest remark a sort of stage presence.
Though he's a librarian, he's frank to add, "But you won't find
many librarians in Toronto like me, I'm afraid." He hikes the
canyon annually, and is by consensus the informal leader of several other Canadians still recovering from heat at their campsite.
"Coming down," he says, "that sun off those walls . . . well, it hit
us rather hard, I can tell you. Felt a bit woozy myself — as if I'd

had, you know, one beer more than I needed." Then with energy, "Two of our lads got thoroughly hammered by it."

When in 1794 a geo-theologian named Richard Kirwan fired off a critical blast at James Hutton's *Theory of the Earth,* he charged that it belied Mosaic history, and — almost worse — hurls the reader into a view of time "from which human reason recoils." How true. Hutton himself predicted as much. Indeed we do recoil. We come from Japan, Hungary, England, Switzerland, France, and so forth, to the Grand Canyon to do just that, gaze into the very abysses that make us tremble. In the canyon's "abyss of time" we find ourselves missing from our own planet.

Here too we see ourselves as transitional creatures: body hair once pelt; toenails once claws; vertebral column adapted from our days as quadrupeds; hands that used to be forepaws; brain on its way to being, perhaps, something better than a reservoir of reptilian and mammalian cunning. Had the Grand Canyon been formed in Europe instead of the American West, these awarenesses might've dawned on us several hundred years before human reason stopped recoiling from them quite so convulsively.

"Recoil? How very naïve!" says every Grand Canyon pebble. Yes, egoism is indeed a form of naïveté.

To come from another direction at what the canyon says, we may reflect on Charles Darwin's debt to Lyell's 1830 classic *Principles of Geology*: "I always feel as if my books came half out of Lyell's brain," Darwin very generously admitted, and went on to add that Lyell's work "altered the whole tone of one's mind." Yes. Earth's age — or a pebble's age, as far as that goes — once known, changes the mind forever.

Some minds. For many, what was being deciphered in Earth's palimpsest was too much like being told, "You're a foundling."

About two hours down from the rim they had met a man lying flat on his back in the middle of the trail. "It wasn't a place to lie down," says the young Swiss woman. "It was very filled with . . . roughness. You wouldn't imagine lying down there." Her brown eyes widen. So the man had lain outstretched, no pack, just a white plastic canteen.

"He said he had left his pack lower down," the Swiss male tells me, "left it at the top of those Cathedral Stairs. He talked as if believing he really might die."

What a contrast with themselves: she in her white bikini, whom I first sighted poking around among the river's massive, stream-polished boulders; he, lounging under a sandbank's lacy tamarisk grove. They've spent much of the day just watching the river pour past, on its way to put long slow movements in the backs of Mexican farmers.

"I have been to your country four times," she says, "but always New York. This trip I wanted to see more." Her black hair, cut boyishly short, makes them almost brother and sister. First L.A., then Yosemite, Joshua Tree, now the Grand Canyon. "But Death Valley," she says, "forty-four degrees!"

Since that's only about 110 degrees Fahrenheit, no hotter than the river beach we're standing on, her retrospective dismay seems odd. Maybe the Colorado's roar cools by suggestion. Or maybe the pair hit Death Valley too soon out of Zug, Switzerland, a small lakefront town lying at about the same latitude as Duluth, Minnesota. Culture shock, stricken people — if I'm confused, they seem to be too.

The prostrate man had apparently started up toward the rim from Monument Creek. As if thinking he might be a goner, he had kept asking these tourist-hikers to look after his wife. "He would say it many times," the young woman insisted, "'my wife has stopped moving, my wife has stopped moving.' But then he would say he had to go for help."

The Swiss couple shrug, as if still baffled. A fishy breeze whiffing off the loud river stirs among nearby tamarisk fronds. "He kept asking us to take the compass out of his pack," she says, puzzled, shading her eyes the better to look at me. "He kept repeating it. The compass had been his father's. When we asked what we should do with it . . . he didn't tell us."

Having left him at his own insistence, they had found his wife further downtrail. She had got into the shade of a boulder, had even rallied. Thus able to continue uptrail? They thought maybe yes. "Maybe" seems odd. Are they now embarrassed at having left the Virginia woman to shift for herself?

Then I put myself in the Swiss couple's boots. On reaching that stricken man's wife and finding she's not only alive but has rallied, is apparently able to move, and has water — am I really going to shepherd her back up toward the rim?

Does a thirst for longevity explain the blithe way we deal in many hundreds of millions of years? To be enlarged, augmented, if only vicariously? And do our heady references to "the local galaxy cluster" participate in that grandeur? I suspect so. As if we sensed in them our chance, our only chance, to be immortal. The Grand Canyon's Redwall, five hundred feet of time precipitated as limestone, does indeed claim I never existed; but my over-hearing oceans long lost in its fossils fills me with all the 350 million years their waves and precipitates invested here for safe-keeping.

Perhaps our quasi-godlike habit of tossing around the big figures of space/time is snobbery of scale; but simultaneously, our eon dealing, like the gallows humor of combat veterans, may also camouflage chagrin at our simply enormous loss of prestige. As if in an expanding universe our egos implode to match the expansion.

Though all this may seem a strictly recent dilemma, the paradox of disastrous discovery is anciently evident in Lucretius, whose *De Rerum Natura* was written expressly to announce a sort of liberating good news: that our world is not controlled by gods. Nature and everything in it derives instead, Lucretius claimed, from chance collisions of atoms; thus fear and trembling before the gods was childish. The only "immortals" in our world, said Lucretius, were atoms. Earth and sun had a beginning, would have an end, but their atoms would not. They alone were eternal. For Lucretius, however, the price of that liberated but evacuated universe was a sort of brave desolation, expressed on almost every page.

Atop the highest of the Great Sand Dunes, with windblown saltations of ideal particles prickling my bare ankles, I had actually thought of Lucretius and his atom-immortals. Much of that blowing sand I knew to be pure quartz, and such a grain is nearly indestructible. Other mineral grains making up sand tend to dissolve, lose their identities, or be powdered to those finenesses we know as silt or clay. Along the valley south of Lauterbrunnen,

Switzerland, with snows of the Jungfrau, the Eiger, the Gross-horn, and the Schilthorn feeding its gravity-fattened waters, I've watched the silt of powdered granite go rampaging down the Lütschine River as "glacial milk," in a branch appropriately called "Weisse," or white. But a grain of quartz sand has other and longer journeys to go.

In Colorado's San Luis Valley there are now a few particular grains long eroded from their parent granite, long tumbled by water and wind, which — after thousands of centuries — finally arrived at my ankle. But when the dunes eventually sink beneath other, more recent deposits millions of years from now, those few grains will by chemical action and pressure get cemented to fellow grains as sandstone.

*Not* the end of the story — far from it! Hence the beginning of my fascination that my ankle had been kissed by some of Lucretius's eternal atoms. Or, as this world goes, by one at least halfway eternal — because every grain at the Dunes is incomparably more ancient than the name of any god, known or forgotten. The least grain among them may well be circulating here undiminished long after the last god is gone.

Provided the sandstone that captured it sinks no deeper than six miles below the earth's surface, thus escaping the heat and pressure of greater depths which would transform its silicon dioxide, each quartz speck hitting my ankle will remain nearly indestructible. And in all probability will rise again, as further crustal upheavals thrust each once more into the sun. The San Juans they came from, the Sangre de Cristo range, the San Luis Valley — these will long since have vanished from the face of the earth. But ice, rain, and sun-driven winds, the old reliables, will be there to get at those particles. Thus resurrected and set again on their travels each will tumble and swim till recemented as one of the countless trillions making up yet another sandstone. That new layer will in turn be overlaid by sedimentation, will sink from view, will be again thrust into the light, and with it my ideal particles will again be granulated, set on yet further travels. "Yes, everything goes," says the wind, "nothing is final."

Ad infinitum? Not quite. But for such a quartz grain to have its angularities tumbled away, softened toward roundness, does take a very long time. In fact, the degree of rounding is a good measure of such a particle's age. Oddly enough, the finer the grain, the slower the rounding. Particles that bounced off my skin could conceivably be washed along hundreds of miles of beach and remain little altered. A study of grains along the Mississippi between Cairo, Illinois, and New Orleans showed slight change in them, though they had been sifted, shifted, and nudged a thousand miles! Laboratory agitation mimicking that swash and roll in streams or ocean waves shows that it takes many thousands of miles to produce "even moderate rounding." So Lucretius's "eternal" atoms and my ideal particle seem at least cousins.

Certainly an actual, individual quartz grain can be blown away, buried, resurrected, and re-eroded good as new through unimaginable chunks of time. The Harvard geologist Raymond Siever offers his "rough guess" of about 200 million years per cycle. And how many cycles might an actual sand grain undergo? Siever thinks a Devonian sand grain, for example, laid down maybe 380 million years back, could conceivably have circled through burial and resurrection *ten times* since first being nicked off its parent granite some 2.4 billion years ago. As Siever points out, "That is a history that encompasses more than half the age of the earth."

If so, out of tennis shoes worn at the Dunes, I'm still shaking grains older than Lord Kelvin's 1897 estimate for the entire planet. Older by sixty times! That's why I've come to think of a tiny quartz granule as the littlest cause, and longest continued. Though its minute translucence may contain only half of all the time in the world, my skin thinks that's plenty immortal, and all the more eerie to be kissed by.

In canyon country, the only thing left of Noah's Flood is a rainbow. Not long ago I stood on a nine-thousand-foot summit of Utah's Aquarius Plateau and surveyed distant blue buttes, ten-mile-long, blue-forested mesas. Had an eighteenth-century "Neptunist" stood beside me, he would have explained those erosional terraces as sediment of one global ocean, forms later scarred and carved by the Universal Deluge. At the Grand Canyon, however, my "Neptunist" would have seen that his theory didn't hold water — because it held too much. Instead of relics from catastrophic inundation, he would have begun seeing "fluvialism," the slow, daily, prosaic stripping away of a continent by the rains and winds of common weather. Southwestern Utah is an odd place to think of Edinburgh. I kept remembering the ebullience of James Hutton, and thinking what panoramic satisfaction the Aquarius Plateau would have given him and his theories.

In the latter nineteenth century the brilliant American geologist Clarence Dutton did stand there, and — in contradistinction to "inundation" — coined a phrase fitting what he saw: the Great Denudation.

Not long ago, atop a "lithified" dune near Hite's Crossing, Utah, I watched an attractive young German woman scan part of that denudation's sun-drenched landscape. Hundreds of feet below us, Lake Powell's blue waters, alive with wind warps, made those sandstone erosions all the more brilliantly "other." She was tall, slender, dark-haired, and seemed timid. Her husband stroked her hair, held her hand, murmured reassurances. Evidently she needed coaxing to stand at that overlook. I chatted with them briefly. They were from heavily industrial Stuttgart.

Because in Europe even the Alps have been domesticated for centuries, the Germans, Dutch, French, and Italians flocking to our high Southwest see, in its sensualities of extreme destitution, a world wholly "other." In coral dunes, painted deserts of pinked blues and red mesas, they tour through spaces that throw the mind wide open. A world away from Europe's hand-crafted landscapes, they steer rental cars or campers among Paiute spirits of many distances: past Bryce Canyon's Pink Cliffs, past the Gray Cliffs to Zion's White Cliffs and eastward from there past the Vermilion Cliffs along the road to Lake Powell. Under the amplitude of southwestern skies, they spend whole days driving through red epochs laid naked.

Certainly my Stuttgart couple were doing that, even as they stood looking out over an expanse where seven thousand feet of stone had been eaten away before the Grand Canyon was begun. Did they know those details? Highly unlikely. I gestured out toward the mist-free, unmuted miles with their hallucinatory clarities of rock and asked the shy young woman, "What do you think of it? What's your reaction?"

In a quiet voice she said, "It gives me fear. Oh, it is of course . . . very beautiful. But it makes me frightened."

*

As geology accrued fact and coherence, many intelligent Christians felt the absurdity of setting Earth's age at six thousand years. Nature's design, they conceded, was simply of more ancient date than had been supposed. But design there was. On all sides that axiom went unexamined. Behind his "little causes, long continued" even Hutton saw a "wise and beneficent design." Agreement on a moral nature, a nature with aims, a nature swayed by providential guidance — which is to say, a nature made expressly for us — that was bedrock.

Charles Darwin's guardian grudgingly approved his ward's intent to voyage on the *Beagle*, because, as he said, "Natural History . . . is very suitable to a clergyman." Aboard ship, young Darwin was shocked to hear a shipmate admit disbelief in the Flood.

Meanwhile geologists went right on tapping at the world, which provoked John Ruskin's petulance: "If only the geologists would let me alone, I could do very well, but those dreadful hammers! I hear the clink of them at the end of every cadence of the Bible verses."

Soon the vogue of "natural theology" began collapsing under the growing weight of enormous fossil deposits. Evolution, from ancient times a perennial guess, became more and more self-evident. Not only that. As the millennially slow growth of languages became better documented, and archaeological digs went deeper into our human past, Earth aged implicitly in them; aged too by inference drawn from the known speed of light and star distances. Scriptural geology began seeming odd as, say, Baptist meteorology or statutory mathematics or Mormon physics.

A pair of ravens are grooming themselves near pools in the rock. A third, apart, perches quietly on a slab. Wind ruffles its throat feathers, which show a surprise whiteness under their black, as if its ancestry were that of a dove whose surface plumage got sunblackened.

This afternoon, once more hiking the Tonto Plateau, my mind had shrunk to only a couple of thoughts: water and shade. What an oasis is made of. Small wonder, I thought, that Arab cultures devised almost an art form of water. For the past hour now I've wanted the sun to sink behind Tapeats sandstone ledges shading this part of Slate Creek's canyon. Finally it does.

I had felt too hot for paying much mind to blackbrush, spat-
ters of agave, or cushion cacti in their fat clouds of thorn; or
acres of shale giving off heat ripples bright as the onslaught of
migraine. My thought had been water: "How much have I got?
Is Slate Creek still running?" For the first time in my life I had
seen pools and water ripples I knew weren't real — but not mi-
rage. Sane hallucinations instead, wishful ones, the kind that
often precede seeing and create it. When, via switchbacks off the
plateau, I at last began descending into Slate Creek's side canyon, its trickle glinted salvation.

Resupplied, I had followed its broad but mostly dry streambed
down to Crystal Rapids and the river, past pools full of tadpoles,
past spadefoot toads that hopped into fronds of arroyo willow.
Often when my oots scattered gravel, a gaudy collared lizard or
sleek whiptail had flicked from sight. Soon the creek's rivulet disappeared into its own sandy bed. Threading a shortcut through
mesquite trees so sparse and twisted you couldn't use such wood
for anything, not even admiration, I had passed colonies of beavertail cactus as my descent took me below the level of Tapeats
sandstone into steep, fire-struck walls of black Vishnu schist, rising higher the further I descended. From that creekbed, dry as
chalk dust, but well before it came into view, I had caught faintly
audible hints of the river's long power. Its whisper quickened my
stride, rising closer to a roar the nearer I drew.

I'd known Crystal Rapids to be among the wildest runs on the
Colorado. Soon its wavetrain, white-capped and crested, was
pouring by me in one muscular surge that explained the Grand
Canyon as nothing else could.

It was not some sort of god. It was no more than gravity's way
with water — and water's way with rain. Loaded with silt, sand,
gravel, it pulled tons of the continent past me by the minute. I
could *think* of the Colorado as a sort of band saw, but couldn't
feel it was. Not that only. In the river's roaring lament of descending joy, in its mountains, mesas, and buttes going back to
be sea floor, I had felt a strangeness whose force we call "nature."
It had left nothing to say, nothing to feel but awe.

By 8:00 P.M., back at my campsite a mile and a half up from
the river, air has finally cooled from the afternoon high of 113
degrees to 85. Meanwhile the Tapeats ledges above me have
dimmed from blond to cinnamon to burnt sienna to umber . . .

then twilight. Bats low overhead flitter between me and first stars. All around me, Cambrian stone laid down when the moon was much closer to Earth; a paleo-moon, huge and luminouis and unseen by anyone. From nearby Slate Creek, toad song.

Desert canyons by night are anything but voiceless. Yet peaceful, supremely. In such canyons your own presence can feel like the human race down to one person — which is to exist more actually than any other way I know. Often I've wondered if all the trail sweat and exertion might not be aimed, unconsciously, at sitting quietly while dusk rises and at feeling lost alive in glimpses that add up to the momentary creature called "me." A someone, in a something. A one.

Borrowing the old idea of the human body as "a little world made cunningly," we can use it as a microcosm of time. Any woman or man, for example, standing five feet ten can be seen in proportion to Earth's 4,500 million years, with the planet's birth beginning at the footsoles. Up high as the kneecaps would be equivalent to 3,200 million years ago: anaerobic bacteria form in Earth's Archaeozoic oceans. Three inches higher would mark 3,000 million years back, and the development of photosynthesis in anaerobic bacteria. With photosynthesis the planet's conversion of carbon dioxide gases to oxygen begins. A billion years go by, during which oxygen is poison, unless you can breathe it. As yet nothing can. Then, at the level of the abdomen, oxygen-using bacteria first appear. At the naval, Vishnu schist and gneiss are metamorphosed from sedimentary rock of unknowable antiquity. Thus far, obviously, time has risen waist-high without raising life much taller than germs.

Heart-high, 1,150 million years ago, multicellular plants and animals finally form. Another half-billion years go by.

Then at the collarbone, around the time Tapeats sandstone begins to be deposited, invertebrates develop shells. Voilà! Onto the world stage leaps, or slithers, the brachiopod. Trilobites appear, and with them life acquires the first high-definition eyes. Earth's seas still contain nothing much livelier than they, and sea worms, naked or shelled. Dry land is still one supercontinent, Pangaea. 750,000 centuries go by, without creatures yet leaving the sea. Nor will they for a longish while.

By the level of the mouth, fish have evolved. The tip of the nose marks maximum dispersal of Pangaea's fragments, our present continents. Then at the cheek bones, conifers and reptiles come on the scene. Yet at the eyebrows — in Permian time — a setback occurs, "the great dying" of almost everything alive. Only 5 percent of living species escape. And when we've risen to a level one inch from the top of the head, death strikes again in the famous extinction of dinosaurs, along with three fourths of all living creatures. Humans still nowhere.

When does dawn become day? There can be no fixed point at which we modulated from *Homo erectus* to *Homo sapiens,* but 500,000 years ago is a widely accepted figure. An "ago" that recent leaves us, on the scale we've been using, invisible. On that scale a man's overnight growth of whisker more than equals humankind's stay on this planet. Our presence as a species gets effaced with his morning shave.

We may scratch our heads in disbelief. If in doing so, however, we find there a single windblown speck of sand as little as two tenths of a millimeter in diameter, one just visible to the naked eye, its width will equal — compared to a person standing five-ten — the time spanned by our species. We've been human no longer than that granule is wide.

Up in bright morning and once more out on that broad Tonto plateau which hikers must travel to get from one side canyon to the next, I'm heading for Marsh Butte, and from there to my appointment with the Great Unconformity, when I spy, five hundred yards off, a pair of lounging figures. They turn out to be Tom and Nettie.

Their frame packs propped as back rests, they are taking their ease in late morning sun, sitting on litters of Bright Angel shale, catching rays my skin prefers to avoid. Tom's a lean and grizzled fifty, while bottle-blond Nettie's not much over half that. In swapping the usual oddments of trail chat, I learn they're from L. A., and have been in the canyon sixteen days. "Ye gods!" I gasp. "How much weight does that come to?"

"What's left doesn't weigh much. Enough for dinner tonight," Tom says.

"We're going out tomorrow," says Nettie.

All that food, plus gear! "But seriously, how much does sixteen days of food weigh?"

"Too much," she says, and her smile winces. Plain-pretty, neat figure in shorts and red halter, strong-looking thighs and calves, Nettie can't be much more than five-two or five-three, and maybe 120 pounds.

"We didn't weigh it," Tom says.

I nod agreement. "Best not to know."

"Yeah," she says, nodding back.

"Where are you headed?" Tom asks.

"Oh, a butte — near the Tapeats ledge between Slate Creek and Topaz. There's a spot I've wanted to get a good look at."

"It's nice down there in Slate," he says, "a lot of water."

"Lots of water," she agrees.

But I'm still thinking weight. "Sixteen days of food!"

"Aw, you'd be surprised," Tom says, implying I could do likewise.

"Obviously you had to really plan. Take the lightest stuff possible." I expect to hear freeze-dried this, powdered that.

Nettie seems abashed. "Well, we ate, uh . . . rice and beans."

"Pretty much," Tom says, "for protein." Meaning, I presume, the beans. And "pretty much," it turns out, means rice and beans only.

"Yes," he says, "we talk about food quite a bit."

"But beans take forever to cook," I say. "Doesn't that mean fuel?"

"Well," she says of the rice, "we've got some, uh . . . quick. And we soak the beans overnight. And then you have to simmer 'em about . . . twenty minutes. We brought *small* beans."

"That's still a lot of fuel."

"Yeah," Nettie says. "We brought a lot."

Well, I think but don't say, if you're happy I am. And since this is Tom's fifth year of backpacking the canyon, they knew what they were doing.

No sooner have I headed off again than I turn around, grabbing my shirt-pocket camera for a souvenir snapshot. At once Nettie pulls from her pack an old-time Nikon — big, heavy as a paving brick — and asks me to take one of them with it. "We've got five shots left," she says.

"Do you have any sisters?" I ask, hefting the killer Nikon as if ready to marry into genes that can handle such tonnages.

"Two," she says, not getting my joke, "but I'm the only one who does, uh . . . major backpacking."

"Yes," I say, focusing. "I'd call it that. Definitely major."

"Fatal" was Richard Kirwan's word when in 1797 he published his strident attack on James Hutton's *Theory of the Earth*. Because Kirwan held that the Bible gives a literal account of creation, it followed that encouraging Hutton's view would be fatal not only "to the credit of the Mosaic history," but fatal as well "to religion and morality." Though Kirwan seems two hundred years out of date, he was right. Gazing through sun-ripened stone into the back of forever can be dangerous.

Is that an unconscious element in my seeing gneiss and schist walls of the river gorge as hyper-ugly? Could it be I've even sought them out to defy? Maybe they're what I think time without light or us or anything living looked like. Other canyon rock has color, linearity, legible order. Vishnu schist and gneiss is a lot of molten crumples, rock vomit, hot messes riven here and there — and thus relieved in its darkness — by intrusions of pink Zoroaster granite. But otherwise Vishnu (which in Sanskrit means "to pervade") is bleak to the point, almost, of malignancy. Often eight hundred feet high, its faces say, "Nature is anything that can happen." So Kirwan was right. Religion and morality aren't the only things that schist nearly 2 billion years old can imperil. Scrutinizing Vishnu walls can put a sag in one's shoulders at thinking how much one has mistaken for real.

Kirwan was wrong too, of course. Everybody who reads his attack on Hutton takes a smack at him — which he deserved. In his petty, literal-minded way, however, he reacted as most of us do when the chill of infinity blows through us: "Close that universe, I'm freezing!" Rejecting Hutton's endless ages of hammer-deciphered stones, Kirwan wanted a world that made sense. Who doesn't? We take a smack at him for wanting it to make *his* sense, and only his. An impulse far older than Genesis.

We too peep into the inhuman vastitudes that surround us, begot us, feed us, scare us, allure us into sighing "magnificent!" even as they grind our bones to powder; and our hearts insist on evoking some shadow figure behind the whole show. Which is to say, an invisible It ever so remotely like us. With whom — this sovereign Invisibility, this It — we sense some murky relation, some accord so vague we say "the Creator," a sort of here-there-and-everywhere that does all we know and don't know. An impulse old as mythology: blood taking thought, answering itself with a god. And our greatest poverty — would it be to discover that reality is what it seems? That what we see is all there is? Would that be destitution?

"There are two things the human eye cannot look at for very long," said La Rochefoucauld, "the sun, and death." Vishnu schist is like that, with its nearly 2 billion years. A sort of black sun.

Not believing for a moment in shadow figures, however, I usually find "all there is" so unfathomable — however sweaty and occasionally tedious, however occasionally starved and bare — that, when my senses return from deep boredom, I'm convinced nothing more hyper-surreal than being alive inside "all there is" can ever possibly happen. As for that, boredom itself is a mercy, and its illusory longevities, priceless. Through them we can imagine we really do live here.

"Seeing with one's own eyes." Yet it's the mind's eye doing the seeing, or failing to. I now laugh to realize that by dipping into side canyons several times during the last two days I've passed right through the Great Unconformity without noticing. What with reacting to glare, mesquite trees, flamboyant lizards, extraterrestrial cactus forms, while roving this shambled terrain that Thomas Burnet's *Sacred Theory of the Earth* would have explained as the wages of sin, I had eyes for everything else.

Which shows that the Great Unconformity isn't a thing. It's something you know about what you see. Like erosion itself, it's what's missing. As for eyes, any tourist told what to look for can easily see the Unconformity from the rim.

And yet I had wanted a close-up, wanted if possible to put my hand exactly there where the 550-million-year-old Tapeats sandstone, which runs up and down the canyon, sits atop the Vishnu schist "unconformably." Thus the name. And "Great" because where sandstone and schist meet, 1,200 million years of stone once here now isn't. One-point-two billion. Swept away.

\*

Gingerly, I step out onto a slab that looks okay, but when with a crockery grind it teeters slightly, I freeze. "Forget it!" For the moment, anyhow.

Downclimbing stacked slabs of Tapeats to reach its interface with the Vishnu could be trickier than I thought. Less well cemented than, say, Wescogame or Coconino, its mocha- or cream- or cinnamon-colored layers vary from solid to rotten. Weathering undercuts many of the protrusions. Eventually each will give way, crashing down toward the river like everything here, just as eight hundred feet higher up, chunks of Redwall feel Temple Butte limestone melt from under them, feel themselves come to an edge there's no denying, no holding on to. That's gravity's simple plan: one by one.

Under the shade of a narrow overhang I wriggle very cautiously out of my pack, carefully set it down away from the edge, then rest awhile and consider.

Opposite my skimpy perch, raven shadows ripple across uneven layers and ledges of Tapeats. High cirrus veils the sun ever so slightly. The rippling of those wing shadows entrances me. All the same, I remind myself of being scrunched onto an edge where downward glances send mild electroscares through the neural system. Like an undermusic to canyon silence comes the surge and fade of Crystal Rapids' attenuated roar, as if wind through pines. For a long while I'm content simply to let the canyon happen. As bonus, I spot a much safer route through the Tapeats opposite, less like rock climbing than stepping downstairs.

Finally, by edging out onto a safely sizable ledge of Vishnu, I can actually reach up, put my hand on pebbly stuff underlying the Tapeats. Where that conglomerate meets hard black schist, I touch the Great Unconformity. My extended index finger and thumb grasp 1.2 billion years of absentee rock.

Eons, eras, periods, epochs, ages — it's as if rock time were the size of this canyon, and all life the size of my hand.

The dark Vishnu stuff my thumb touches was the foundation of mountains taking 100 million years to stand up. Among little causes, long continued, sandblasting by my ideal particle nibbled their altitudes till the mountains were blown clean away, flattened to a peneplain. Longs Peak in Colorado rises 14,255 feet, but if it were seven times that lofty, and eroded merely an inch every thousand years, the time spanned by my finger and thumb would grind it to sea level.

Like everything born of fire, our planet is cooling. But this "secular cooling" will eventually bring continental drift to a standstill. As convected heat within Earth's mantle and outer core loses its radioactive enthusiasm, the lithosphere under sea and land will thicken. Once continental plates lock in place, volcanoes won't erupt nor will new mountains thrust up to replace old mountains worn down. Thus our planet's flat future: its alps will be molehills low as a hundred feet or so above sea level.

With mountains — which sand comes from — leveled once and for all, sand will find nothing to abrade but itself. Can only tumble itself to silicon dust. If nothing lay on top of Vishnu schist, concealing its upper surfaces, what I'd see would be a thrice-ancient peneplain. Earth's future, sand's end.

Why should a vast desolation inhabit that prospect? It does — as if the planet's two faces, one back in Vishnu time and the other far up ahead, had fused to an unbroken loneliness. But this is mere sentimentalism. Creatureless planets can't "feel." Besides, those 1.2 billion years of absentee rock were all Precambrian, gone long before the planet was ours. Nothing lived then but anaerobic bacteria, and maybe a lot of blue-green algae, cyanophytes. Still, a world where feelings have no place to go fills me with the very emptiness it denies.

To approach that sort of tremendous absence inhabiting the Great Unconformity's fathomless rift, I've fumbled my way here. And touched it — as if the stuff it's made of were some sort of power: steadfastly evanescent, without judgment, wanting nothing, holy. Which doesn't mean "good." Nor does it need our belief. It's just that, since neither logic nor physics offers ways to think about it, we've no rational way to ask what or why. It's all we do ask. On sandstone right above me, under Arizona sun, the fine quartz grains glint and sparkle.

In Greek, "seeing for one's self" is "autopsy."

Crosswinds on U.S. 180 rock my car and stampede herds of tumbleweed over the road in flumes of copper dust. Later, midafternoon on Arizona 160, I reach Cow Springs just as two Navajo males are running around battening hatches of a big souvenir stand. The frayed edges of its gala banners crackle and burn in gusts that have bent many of the metal flagstaffs.

Winds wobbling my steering for hours now hurl dust devils three hundred feet into the air. After spiraling apart they blow across the sky's intense blue like pink cannon smoke. I approach a valley so hazed I at first assume it's industrial, then find it's just desert weather filling the air with sand tumbled almost to the fineness of silt. Its delicate pinks derive from ancestral Rockies brought down while our southwestern horizons were taking up a new life as permanent desert — in "just a few" million years. Erstwhile summits now sifting around as coral-tinted particles are actively eating at the ruddier hues of eroded mesas, which are indeed all the colors of Egypt. Before my eyes the Great Denudation goes on. I'm driving in it!

Just as I'm supposing only ravens or crows could make a living here, amid mile on unbroken mile famished for vegetation, I whip past a "town": one building, three burros. Plus an intelligent dog, barking sheep across the road and down a slight gully. The old Navajo woman following after them wears a loose purple gown bathed by the same wind.

Toward evening the gusts have died to light breeze tousling rabbit brush, ruffling sage. Nine miles off the main road I pull into a favorite campsite among juniper and piñon just above Tsegi Canyon. By now the sun is low. I read awhile. In a brand new book, never opened before, I'm puzzled at finding sand, all but too small to see, between any pages I turn to. How? Beats me. With my pocket lens I make out several particles and smile at their tireless ubiquity. Later, to follow what the last of the light is doing, I climb an overlook of Navajo sandstone. The whole place is crossbedded dunes now petrified.

For more than an hour I enjoy the living wind on my face, just dawdling; watching the henna ravens of sunset, looking miles up Tsegi Canyon, deciphering on crossbedded formations what that wind's paleoflow has written. Is writing. On me, on canyon walls, on everywhere. I give up trying to think what cannot be thought: time's great pressure and strength. The littlest causes, their long continuance. Their cool, patient luster inside each blowing grain.

AMY TAN

# Mother Tongue

I AM NOT a scholar of English or literature. I cannot give you much more than personal opinions on the English language and its variations in this country or others,

I am a writer. And by that definition, I am someone who has always loved language. I am fascinated by language in daily life. I spend a great deal of my time thinking about the power of language — the way it can evoke an emotion, a visual image, a complex idea, or a simple truth. Language is the tool of my trade. And I use them all — all the Englishes I grew up with.

Recently, I was made keenly aware of the different Englishes I do use. I was giving a talk to a large group of people, the same talk I had already given to half a dozen other groups. The nature of the talk was about my writing, my life, and my book, *The Joy Luck Club*. The talk was going along well enough, until I remembered one major difference that made the whole talk sound wrong. My mother was in the room. And it was perhaps the first time she had heard me give a lengthy speech, using the kind of English I have never used with her. I was saying things like, "The intersection of memory upon imagination" and "There is an aspect of my fiction that relates to thus-and-thus" — a speech filled with carefully wrought grammatical phrases, burdened, it suddenly seemed to me, with nominalized forms, past perfect tenses, conditional phrases, all the forms of standard English that I had learned in school and through books, the forms of English I did not use at home with my mother.

Just last week, I was walking down the street with my mother, and I again found myself conscious of the English I was using, the English I do use with her. We were talking about the price of new and used furniture and I heard myself saying this: "Not waste money that way." My husband was with us as well, and he didn't notice any switch in my English. And then I realized why. It's because over the twenty years we've been together I've often used that same kind of English with him, and sometimes he even uses it with me. It has become our language of intimacy, a different sort of English that relates to family talk, the language I grew up with.

So you'll have some idea of what this family talk I heard sounds like, I'll quote what my mother said during a recent conversation which I videotaped and then transcribed. During this conversation, my mother was talking about a political gangster in Shanghai who had the same last name as her family's, Du, and how the gangster in his early years wanted to be adopted by her family, which was rich by comparison. Later, the gangster became more powerful, far richer than my mother's family, and one day showed up at my mother's wedding to pay his respects. Here's what she said in part:

"Du Yusong having business like fruit stand. Like off the street kind. He is Du like Du Zong — but not Tsung-ming Island people. The local people call putong, the river east side, he belong to that side local people. That man want to ask Du Zong father take him in like become own family. Du Zong father wasn't look down on him, but didn't take seriously, until that man big like become a mafia. Now important person, very hard to inviting him. Chinese way, came only to show respect, don't stay for dinner. Respect for making big celebration, he shows up. Mean gives lots of respect. Chinese custom. Chinese social life that way. If too important won't have to stay too long. He come to my wedding. I didn't see, I heard it. I gone to boy's side, they have YMCA dinner. Chinese age I was nineteen."

You should know that my mother's expressive command of English belies how much she actually understands. She reads the *Forbes* report, listens to *Wall Street Week*, converses daily with her stockbroker, reads all of Shirley MacLaine's books with ease — all kinds of things I can't begin to understand. Yet some of my friends tell me they understand 50 percent of what my mother says. Some say they understand 80 to 90 percent. Some say they understand none of it, as if she were speaking pure Chinese. But to me, my mother's English is perfectly clear, perfectly natural. It's my mother tongue. Her language, as I hear it, is vivid, direct, full of observation and imagery. That was the language that helped shape the way I saw things, expressed things, made sense of the world.

Lately, I've been giving more thought to the kind of English my mother speaks. Like others, I have described it to people as "broken" or "fractured" English. But I wince when I say that. It has always bothered me that I can think of no way to describe it other than "broken," as if it were damaged and needed to be fixed, as if it lacked a certain wholeness and soundness. I've heard other terms used, "limited English," for example. But they seem just as bad, as if everything is limited, including people's perceptions of the limited English speaker.

I know this for a fact, because when I was growing up, my mother's "limited" English limited *my* perception of her. I was ashamed of her English. I believed that her English reflected the quality of what she had to say. That is, because she expressed them imperfectly her thoughts were imperfect. And I had plenty of empirical evidence to support me: the fact that people in department stores, at banks, and at restaurants did not take her seriously, did not give her good service, pretended not to understand her, or even acted as if they did not hear her.

My mother has long realized the limitations of her English as well. When I was fifteen, she used to have me call people on the phone to pretend I was she. In this guise, I was forced to ask for information or even to complain and yell at people who had been rude to her. One time it was a call to her stockbroker in New York. She had cashed out her small portfolio and it just so happened we were going to go to New York the next week, our very first trip outside California. I had to get on the phone and say in an adolescent voice that was not very convincing, "This is Mrs. Tan."

And my mother was standing in the back whispering loudly, "Why he don't send me check, already two weeks late. So mad he lie to me, losing me money."

And then I said in perfect English, "Yes, I'm getting rather concerned. You had agreed to send the check two weeks ago, but it hasn't arrived."

Then she began to talk more loudly. "What he want, I come to New York tell him front of his boss, you cheating me?" And I was trying to calm her down, make her be quiet, while telling the stockbroker, "I can't tolerate any more excuses. If I don't receive the check immediately, I am going to have to speak to your manager when I'm in New York next week." And sure enough, the following week there we were in front of this astonished stockbroker, and I was sitting there red-faced and quiet, and my mother, the real Mrs. Tan, was shouting at his boss in her impeccable broken English.

We used a similar routine just five days ago, for a situation that was far less humorous. My mother had gone to the hospital for an appointment, to find out about a benign brain tumor a CAT scan had revealed a month ago. She said she had spoken very good English, her best English, no mistakes. Still, she said, the hospital did not apologize when they said they had lost the CAT scan and she had come for nothing. She said they did not seem to have any sympathy when she told them she was anxious to know the exact diagnosis, since her husband and son had both died of brain tumors. She said they would not give her any more information until the next time and she would have to make another appointment for that. So she said she would not leave until the doctor called her daughter. She wouldn't budge. And when the doctor finally called her daughter, me, who spoke in perfect English — lo and behold — we had assurances the CAT scan would be found, promises that a conference call on Monday would be held, and apologies for any suffering my mother had gone through for a most regrettable mistake.

I think my mother's English almost had an effect on limiting my possibilities in life as well. Sociologists and linguists probably will tell you that a person's developing language skills are more influenced by peers. But I do think that the language spoken in the family, especially in immigrant families which are more insular, plays a large role in shaping the language of the child. And I believe that it affected my results on achievement tests, IQ tests, and the SAT. While my English skills were never judged as

poor, compared to math, English could not be considered my
strong suit. In grade school I did moderately well, getting perhaps B's, sometimes B-pluses, in English and scoring perhaps in
the sixtieth or seventieth percentile on achievement tests. But those
scores were not good enough to override the opinion that my
true abilities lay in math and science, because in those areas I
achieved A's and scored in the ninetieth percentile or higher.

This was understandable. Math is precise; there is only one
correct answer. Whereas, for me at least, the answers on English
tests were always a judgment call, a matter of opinion and personal experience. Those tests were constructed around items like
fill-in-the-blank sentence completion, such as, "Even though Tom
was _____, Mary thought he was _____." And the correct answer always seemed to be the most bland combinations of thoughts,
for example, "Even though Tom was shy, Mary thought he was
charming," with the grammatical structure "even though " limiting the correct answer to some sort of semantic opposites, so you
wouldn't get answers like, "Even though Tom was foolish, Mary
thought he was ridiculous." Well, according to my mother, there
were very few limitations as to what Tom could have been and
what Mary might have thought of him. So I never did well on
tests like that.

The same was true with word analogies, pairs of words in which
you were supposed to find some sort of logical, semantic relationship — for example, "*Sunset* is to *nightfall* as _____ is to
_____." And here you would be presented with a list of four
possible pairs, one of which showed the same kind of relation-
ship: *red* is to *stoplight, bus* is to *arrival, chills* is to *fever, yawn* is to
*boring.* Well, I could never think that way. I knew what the tests
were asking, but I could not block out of my mind the images
already created by the first pair, "*sunset* is to *nightfall*" — and I
would see a burst of colors against a darkening sky, the moon
rising, the lowering of a curtain of stars. And all the other pairs
of words — red, bus, stoplight, boring — just threw up a mass of
confusing images, making it impossible for me to sort out something as logical as saying: "A sunset precedes nightfall" is the same
as "a chill precedes a fever." The only way I would have gotten
that answer right would have been to imagine an associative situation, for example, my being disobedient and staying out past

sunset, catching a chill at night, which turns into feverish pneumonia as punishment, which indeed did happen to me.

I have been thinking about all this lately, about my mother's English, about achievement tests. Because lately I've been asked, as a writer, why there are not more Asian Americans represented in American literature. Why are there few Asian Americans enrolled in creative writing programs? Why do so many Chinese students go into engineering? Well, these are broad sociological questions I can't begin to answer. But I have noticed in surveys — in fact, just last week — that Asian students, as a whole, always do significantly better on math achievement tests than in English. And this makes me think that there are other Asian-American students whose English spoken in the home might also be described as "broken" or "limited." And perhaps they also have teachers who are steering them away from writing and into math and science, which is what happened to me.

Fortunately, I happen to be rebellious in nature and enjoy the challenge of disproving assumptions made about me. I became an English major my first year in college, after being enrolled as pre-med. I started writing nonfiction as a freelancer the week after I was told by my former boss that writing was my worst skill and I should hone my talents toward account management.

But it wasn't until 1985 that I finally began to write fiction. And at first I wrote using what I thought to be wittily crafted sentences, sentences that would finally prove I had mastery over the English language. Here's an example from the first draft of a story that later made its way into *The Joy Luck Club,* but without this line: "That was my mental quandary in its nascent state." A terrible line, which I can barely pronounce.

Fortunately, for reasons I won't get into today, I later decided I should envision a reader for the stories I would write. And the reader I decided upon was my mother, because these were stories about mothers. So with this reader in mind — and in fact she did read my early drafts — I began to write stories using all the Englishes I grew up with: the English I spoke to my mother, which for lack of a better term might be described as "simple"; the English she used with me, which for lack of a better term might be described as "broken"; my translation of her Chinese, which could certainly be described as "watered down"; and what I imagined to be her translation of her Chinese if she could speak in perfect English, her internal language, and for that I sought to preserve the essence, but neither an English nor a Chinese structure. I wanted to capture what language ability tests can never reveal: her intent, her passion, her imagery, the rhythms of her speech and the nature of her thoughts.

Apart from what any critic had to say about my writing, I knew I had succeeded where it counted when my mother finished reading my book and gave me her verdict: "So easy to read."

JANE TOMPKINS

# At the Buffalo Bill Museum —
# June 1988

FROM THE SOUTH ATLANTIC QUARTERLY

THE VIDEO at the entrance to the Buffalo Bill Historical Center
tells us that Buffalo Bill was the most famous American of his
time, that by 1900 over a billion words had been written about
him, and that he had a progressive vision of the West. Buffalo
Bill had worked as a cattle driver, a wagoneer, a Pony Express
rider, a buffalo hunter for the railroad, a hunting guide, an army
scout and sometime Indian fighter; he wrote dime novels about
himself and an autobiography at the age of thirty-three, by which
time he was already famous; and then he began another set of
careers — first he became an actor, performing on the urban stage
in wintertime melodramatic representations of what he actually
earned a living at in the summer (scouting and leading hunting
expeditions), and finally he became the impresario of the Wild
West show, a form of entertainment which he invented and carried on as actor, director, and all-round idea man for thirty years.
Toward the end of his life he founded the town of Cody, Wyoming, to which he gave, among other things, $200,000. Strangely
enough, it was as a progressive civic leader that Bill Cody wanted
to be remembered. "I don't want to die," the video at the entrance tells us he said, "and have people say — oh, there goes another old showman. . . . I would like people to say — this is the
man who opened Wyoming to the best of civilization."

The best of civilization. This was the phrase that rang in my
head as I moved through the museum, which is one of the most

disturbing places I have ever visited. It is also a wonderful place. It is four museums in one: the Whitney Gallery of Western Art, which houses art works on western subjects; the Buffalo Bill Museum proper, which memorializes Cody's life; the Plains Indian Museum, which exhibits artifacts of American Indian civilization; and the Winchester Arms Museum, a collection of firearms, historically considered.

The whole operation is extremely well designed and well run, from the video program at the entrance that gives an overview of all four museums, to the fresh-faced young attendants wearing badges that say "Ask Me," to the museum shop stacked with books on western Americana, to the ladies' room — a haven of satiny marble, shining mirrors, and flattering light. Among other things, the museum is admirable for its effort to combat prevailing stereotypes about the so-called "winning of the West," a phrase it self-consciously places in quotation marks. There are placards declaring that all history is a matter of interpretation, and that the American West is a source of "myth." Everywhere except, perhaps, in the Winchester Arms Museum, where the rhetoric is different, you feel the effort of the museum staff to reach out to the public, to be clear, to be accurate, to be fair, not to condescend, in short, to educate in the best sense of the term.

On the day I went, the museum was featuring an exhibition of Frederic Remington's works. There are two facts about these productions that make them different from those of artists one is used to encountering in museums. The first is that Remington's paintings and statues function as a historical record. Their chief attraction has always been that they transcribe scenes and events that have vanished from the earth. The second fact, related to this, is the brutality of their subject matter. Remington's work makes you pay attention to *what is happening* in the painting or the piece of statuary. When you look at his work you cannot escape from its subject.

Consequently, as I moved through the exhibit, the wild contortions of the bucking broncos, the sinister expression invariably worn by the Indians, and the killing of animals and men made the placards discussing Remington's use of the "lost wax" process seem strangely disconnected. In the face of unusual violence, or implied violence, their message was: what is important here is technique. Except in the case of paintings showing the battle of

San Juan Hill, where white Americans were being killed, the material accompanying Remington's works did not refer to the subject matter of the paintings and statues. Nevertheless, an undertone of disquiet ran beneath the explanations; at least I thought I detected one. Someone had taken the trouble to ferret out Remington's statement of horror at the slaughter on San Juan Hill; someone had also excerpted the judgment of art critics commending Remington for the lyricism, interiority, and mystery of his later canvases — pointing obliquely to the fascination with bloodshed that preoccupied his earlier work.

The uneasiness of the commentary, and my uneasiness with it, were nothing compared to the blatant contradictions in the paintings themselves. A pastel palette, a sunlit stop-action haze, murderous movement arrested under a lazy sky, flattened onto canvas and fixed in azure and ocher — two opposed impulses nestle here momentarily; the tension that keeps them from splitting apart is what holds the viewer's gaze.

The most excruciating example of what I mean occurs in the first painting in the exhibit. Entitled *His First Lesson,* it shows a horse standing saddled but riderless while a man pierces it just below the shoulder with a sharp instrument. The white of the horse's eye signals his pain. The man who is doing the piercing is simultaneously backing away from the reaction he clearly anticipates, and the man who holds the horse's halter is doing the same. But what can they be afraid of? For the horse's right rear leg is tied a foot off the ground by a rope that is also tied around his neck. He can't move. That is the whole point.

"His First Lesson." Whose? And what lesson, exactly? How to stay still and stand pain? How not to break away when they come at you with sharp instruments? How to be obedient? How to behave? It is impossible not to imagine that Remington's obsession with physical cruelty had roots somewhere in his own experience. Why else, in statue after statue, is the horse rebelling? The bucking bronco — symbol of the state of Wyoming, on every license plate, on every sign for every bar, on every belt buckle, mug, and decal — this image Remington cast in bronze over and over again. There is a wild diabolism in the bronzes; the horse and rider seem one thing, not so much rider and ridden as a single bolt of energy gone crazy and caught somehow, complicatedly, in a piece of metal.

In the paintings it is different, more subtle and bizarre. The cavalry on its way to a massacre, sweetly limned, softly tinted, poetically seized in midcareer, and gently laid on the two-dimensional surface. There is about these paintings of military men in the course of their deadly duty an almost maternal tenderness. The idealization of the cavalrymen in their dusty uniforms on their gallant horses has nothing to do with patriotism; it is pure love.

Remington's paintings and statues, as shown in this exhibition, embody everything that was objectionable about his era in American history. They are imperialist and racist; they glorify war and the torture and killing of animals; there are no women in them anywhere. Never the West as garden, never as pastoral, never as home. But in their aestheticizing of violent life Remington's pictures speak (to me at least) of some other desire. The maternal tenderness is not an accident, nor the beauty of the afternoons, nor the warmth of the desert sun. In these paintings Remington plays the part of the preserver, as if by catching the figures in color and line he could save their lives, and absorb some of that life into himself.

In one painting that particularly repulsed and drew me, a moose is outlined against the evening sky at the brink of a lake. He looks expectantly into the distance. Behind him and to one side, hidden from his view, and only just revealed to ours, for it is dark there, is a hunter poised in the back of a canoe, rifle perfectly aimed. We look closer; the title of the picture is *Coming to the Call*. Ah, now we see. This is a sadistic scene. The hunter has lured the moose to his death. But wait a moment. Isn't the sadism really directed at us? First we see the glory of the animal; Remington has made it as noble as he knows how. Then we see what is going to happen. The hunter is one up on the moose but Remington is one up on us. He makes us feel the pain of the anticipated killing, and makes us want to hold it off, to preserve the moose, just as he has done. Which way does the painting cut? Does it go against the hunter — who represents us, after all — or does it go against the moose, who came to the call? Who came, to what call? Did Remington come to the West in response to it — to whatever the moose represents, or to whatever the desire to kill the moose represents? But he hasn't killed it; he has only preserved an image of a white man about to kill it. And what call do we answer when we look at this painting? Who is calling whom? What is being preserved here? That is the question that for me hung over the whole museum.

The Whitney Gallery is an art museum: its allegiance is to "art" as our academic tradition has defined it. In this tradition, we come to understand a painting by having in our possession various bits of information. Something about the technical process used to produce it (pastels, watercolors, woodblock prints, etc.); something about the elements of composition — line and color and movement; something about the artist's life (where born, how educated, by whom influenced, which school belonged to or revolted against); something about his relation to this particular subject, such as how many times he painted it, or whether it contains his favorite model. Occasionally there will be some philosophizing about the themes or ideas the paintings are said to represent.

The problem is, when you're faced with a painter like Remington, these bits of information, while nice to have, don't explain what is there in front of you. They don't begin to give you an account of why a person should have depicted such things. The experience of a lack of fit between the explanatory material and what is there on the wall is one I've had before in museums, when, standing in front of a painting or a piece of statuary, I've felt a huge gap between the information on the little placard and what it is I'm seeing. I realize that "works of art," so-called, all have a subject matter, are all engaged with life, with some piece of life no less significant, no less compelling than Remington's subjects are, if we could only see its force. The idea that art is somehow separate from history, that it somehow occupies a space that is not the same as the space of life, seems out of whack here.

I wander through the gallery thinking these things because right next to it, indeed all around it, in the Buffalo Bill Museum and in the Plains Indian Museum, are artifacts that stand not for someone's expertise or skill in manipulating the elements of an artistic medium, but for life itself; they are the residue of life.

The Buffalo Bill Museum envelops you in an array of textures, colors, shapes, sizes, forms. The fuzzy brown bulk of a buffalo's hump, the sparkling diamonds in a stickpin, the brilliant colors of the posters — there's something about the cacophonous mixture that makes you want to walk in and be surrounded by it, as if you were going into a child's adventure story. It all appeals to the desire to be transported, to pretend for a little while that we're cowboys or cowgirls; it's a museum where fantasy can take over. In this respect, it is true to the character of Buffalo Bill's life.

As I moved through the exhibition, "the best of civilization" was the phrase that rang through my head, and particularly I thought of it as I looked at certain objects on display in a section of the museum that re-creates rooms from Cody's house. Ostrich and peacock feather fans, a chair and a table made entirely of antlers, a bearskin rug. Most of all, I thought of the phrase as I looked at the heads on the wall: Alaska Yukon moose, Wapiti American elk, musk-ox (the "Whitney," the "DeRham"), mountain caribou (the "Hyland"), Quebec Labrador caribou (the "Elbow"), Rocky Mountain goat (the "Haase," the "Kilto"), woodland caribou (world's record, "DeRham"), the "Rogers" freak Wapiti, the "Whitney" bison, the "Lord Rundlesham" bison. The names that appear after the animals are the names of the men who killed them. Each of the animals is scored according to measurements devised by the Boone and Crockett Club, a big-game hunters' organization. The Lord Rundlesham bison, for example, scores 124⅝, making it number 25 in the world for bison trophies. The "Reed" Alaska Yukon moose scores 247. The "Witherbee" Canada moose holds the world's record.

Next to the wall of trophies is a small enclosure where jewelry is displayed: a buffalo-head stickpin and two buffalo-head rings, the heads made entirely of diamonds, with ruby eyes, the gifts of the Russian Crown Prince; a gold and diamond stickpin from Edward VII; a gold, diamond, and garnet locket from Queen Victoria. The two kinds of trophies — animals and jewels — form an incongruous set, the relationship between them compelling but obscure.

If the rest of the items in the museum — the dime novels with their outrageous covers, the marvelous posters, the furniture, Cody's wife's dress, his daughter's oil painting — if these have faded in my mind, it is because I cannot forget the heads of the animals as they stared down, each with an individual expression

on its face. When I think about it I realize that I don't know why
these animals' heads are there. Buffalo Bill didn't kill them; perhaps they were gifts from the famous people he took on hunts.
A different kind of jewelry.

After the heads, I began to notice something about the whole
exhibition. In one display, doghide chaps, calfskin chaps, An-
gora goatskin chaps, and horsehide chaps. Next to these a rawhide lariat and a horsehair quirt. Behind me, boots and saddles,
all of leather. Everywhere I looked there was tooth or bone, skin
or fur, hide or hair, or the animal itself entire — two full-size
buffaloes (a main feature of the exhibition) and a magnificent
stone sheep (a mountain sheep with beautiful curving horns). This
one was another world's record. The best of civilization.

In the literature about Buffalo Bill you read that he was a conservationist, that if it were not for the buffaloes in his Wild West
shows, the species might have become extinct. (In the seventeenth century, 40 million wild buffalo roamed North America;
by 1900 all the wild buffalo had been killed except for one herd
in northern Alberta.) That the man who gained fame first as a
buffalo hunter should have been an advocate for conservation
of the buffalo is not an anomaly but typical of the period. The
men who did the most to preserve America's natural wilderness
and its wildlife were big-game hunters. The Boone and Crockett
Club, founded by Theodore Roosevelt, George Bird Grinnell, and
Owen Wister, turns out to have been one of the earliest organi-
zations to devote itself to environmental protection in the United
States. The Readers' Encyclopaedia of the American West says that
the club "supported the national park and forest reserve movement, helped create a system of national wildlife refuges, and
lobbied for the protection of threatened species, such as the buffalo and antelope." At the same time, the prerequisites for mem-
bership in the club were "the highest caliber of sportsmanship
and the achievement of killing 'in fair chase' trophy specimens
[which had to be adult males] from several species of North
American big game."

The combination big-game hunter/conservationist suggests that
these men had no interest in preserving the animals for the animals' sake but simply wanted to ensure the chance to exercise
their sporting pleasure. But I think this view is too simple; some-

thing further is involved here. The men who hunted game had a kind of love for game and a kind of love for nature which led them to want to preserve the animals which they also desired to kill. That is, the desire to kill the animals was in some way related to a desire to see them live. It is not an accident, in this connection, that Theodore Roosevelt, Owen Wister, and Frederic Remington all originally went west for reasons of health. Their devotion to the West, their connection to it, their love for it, is rooted in their need to reanimate their own lives. The preservation of nature, in other words, becomes for them symbolic of their own survival.

In a sense, then, there is a relationship between the Remington exhibition in the Whitney Gallery and the animal memorabilia in the Buffalo Bill Museum. The moose in *Coming to the Call* and the moose heads on the wall are not so different as they might apppear. The heads on the wall serve an aesthetic purpose; they are decorative objects, pleasing to the eye, which call forth certain associations. In this sense they are like visual works of art. The painting, on the other hand, has something of the trophy about it. The moose as Remington painted it is about to *become* a trophy, yet in another sense it already is one. Remington has simply captured thee moose in another form. In both cases the subject matter, the life of a wild animal, symbolizes the life of the observer. It is the preservation of that life which both the painting and the taxidermy serve.

What are museums keeping safe for us, after all? What is it that we wish so much to preserve? The things that we put in safekeeping, that we put in our safe-deposit boxes and keep under lock and key, are always in some way intended finally as safeguards of our own existence. The money and jewelry and stock certificates are meant for a time when we can no longer earn a living. Similarly, the objects in museums preserve for us a source of life from which we need to nourish ourselves when the resources that would normally supply us have run dry.

The Buffalo Bill Historical Center, full as it is of dead bones, lets us see more clearly than we normally can what it is that museums are for. It is a kind of charnel house that houses images of living things that have passed away but whose life force still lingers around their remains and so passes itself on to us. We go and look at the objects in the glass cases and at the paintings on the wall, as if by standing there we could absorb into ourselves some of the energy that flowed once through the bodies of the live things represented. A museum, rather than being, as we normally think of it, the most civilized of places, a place most distant from our savage selves, actually caters to the urge to absorb the life of another into one's own life.

To give the idea its most extreme form, museums are a form of cannibalism made safe for polite society. If we see the Buffalo Bill Museum in this way, it is no longer possible to separate ourselves from the hunters responsible for the trophies with their wondering eyes or from the curators who put them there. We are not, in essence, different from Teddy Roosevelt, or Frederic Remington, or Buffalo Bill, who killed animals when they were abundant in the Wild West of the 1880s. If, in doing so, those men were practicing the ancient art of absorbing the life of an animal into their own through the act of killing it, realizing themselves through the destruction of another life, then we are not so different from them as visitors to the museum. We stand beside the bones and skins and hooves of beings that were once alive, or stare fixedly at their painted images. Indeed our visit is only a safer form of the same enterprise.

So I did not get out of the Buffalo Bill Museum unscathed, unimplicated in the acts of rapine and carnage which these remains represent. And I did not get out without having had a good time, either, because however many dire thoughts I may have had, the exhibits were interesting and fun to see. I was even able to touch a piece of buffalo hide they have displayed especially for that purpose (it was coarse and springy). Everyone else had touched it, too. The hair was worn down, where people's hands had been, to a fraction of its original length.

After this, the Plains Indian Museum was a terrible letdown. I went from one exhibit to another expecting to become absorbed, but nothing worked. What was the matter? I thought I was interested in Indians, had read about them, taught some Indian literature, felt drawn to their religion. I had been prepared to enter this museum as if I were going into another children's story, only this time I would be an Indian instead of a cowboy or a cowgirl. But the objects on display, most of them behind glass, seemed paltry and insignificant. They lacked visual presence somehow. The bits of leather and sticks of wood triggered no fantasies in me. I couldn't make anything of them.

At the same time, I noticed with some discomfort that almost everything in those glass cases was made of feathers and claws and hide, just like the men's chaps and ladies' fans in the Buffalo Bill Museum, only there was no luxury here. Plains Indian culture, it seemed, was made entirely from animals. Their mode of life had been completely dependent on animals for food, clothing, shelter, equipment, everything. In the Buffalo Bill Museum I was able to say to myself: Well, if these men had been more sensitive, if they had had a right relation to their environment and to life itself, the atrocities that produced their trophies would never have occurred. They never would have exterminated the Indians and killed off the buffalo. But faced with the spectacle before me, it wasn't possible to say just what a right relation to the environment might be. I had expected that the Plains Indian Museum would show me how life in nature ought to be lived: not the wholesale destruction practiced by Euro-Americans, but an ideal form of communion with animals and the land. What the museum seemed to say, on the contrary, was that both colonizer and colonized had had their hands imbrued with blood. The Indians had lived off animals and had made war against each other. Violence was simply a necessary and inevitable part of life. There was no such thing as the life lived in non-violent harmony with nature. It was all bloodshed and killing, an unending cycle, over and over again, and no one could escape.

But perhaps there was a way to understand the violence that made it less terrible. Perhaps if violence was necessary, a part of nature, intended by the universe, then it could be seen as sacramental. Perhaps it was true what Calvin Martin had said in *Keepers of the Game:* that the Indians had a sacred contract with the animals they killed, that they respected them as equals and treated their remains with honor and punctilio. If so, the remains of animals in the Plains Indian Museum weren't the same as those left by Buffalo Bill and his friends. They certainly didn't look the same. All I knew for certain was that these artifacts, lifeless and shrunken, spoke to me of nothing I could understand. No more did the life-size models of Indians, with strange featureless faces, draped in costumes that didn't look like clothing. The figures, posed awkwardly in front of tepees too white to seem real, carried no sense of a life actually lived, any more than the objects in the glass cases had.

The more I read the placards on the wall, the more disaffected I became. Plains Indian life, apparently, had been not only bloody but exceedingly tedious. All those porcupine quills painstakingly softened, flattened, dyed, then appliquéd through even more laborious methods of stitching or weaving. Four methods of attaching porcupine quills, six design groups, population statistics, patterns of migration. There wasn't any glamour here at all. No glamour in the lives the placards told about, no glamour in the objects themselves, no glamour in the experience of looking at them. Just a lot of shriveled things accompanied by some even drier information.

Could it be, then, that the problem with the exhibitions was that Plains Indian culture, if representable at all, was simply not readable by someone like me? Their stick figures and abstract designs could, by definition, convey very little to a Euro-American eye trained to know what glamour is by slick magazines. One display in particular seemed to illustrate this. It was a piece of cloth, behind glass, depicting a buffalo skin with marks on it. The placard read: "Winter Count, Sioux ca. 1910, after Lone Dog's, Fort Peck, Montana, 1877." The hide with its markings, now copied onto cloth, had been a calendar, each year represented by one image, showing the most significant event in the life of the tribe. To one side of the glass case was a book-length pamphlet explaining each image, year by year: 1800–1801, the attack of the Uncapoo on a Crow Indian fort; 1802–1803, a total eclipse of the sun. The images, once you knew what they represented, made sense, and seemed poetic interpretations of the experiences they stood for. But without explanation they were incomprehensible, empty.

The Plains Indian Museum just stopped me in my tracks. It was written in a language I had never learned. I didn't have the key. Maybe someone did, but I wasn't too sure.

For it may not have been just cultural difference that made the text unreadable. I began to suspect that the text itself was corrupt. That the architects of this museum were going through motions whose purpose was, even to themselves, obscure. Knowing what event a figure stands for in the calendar doesn't mean you understand an Indian year. The deeper purpose of the museum began to puzzle me. What is an Indian museum for, anyway? Why should we be bothering to preserve the vestiges of a people whose culture we had effectively extinguished? Wasn't there an air of bad faith about this? Did the museum exist to assuage our guilt and not for any educational reason? I did not and do not have an answer to these questions. All I know is that I felt I was in the presence of something pious and a little insincere. It had the aura of a failed attempt at virtue, as though the curators were trying to present, as interesting, objects whose purpose and meaning even they could not fully imagine.

In a last-ditch attempt to salvage something, I went up to one of the guards and asked where the movie was showing that the video had advertised, the movie about Plains Indian life. "Oh, the slide show, you mean," he said. "It's been discontinued." When I asked why, he said he didn't know. It occurred to me then that that was the message the museum was sending, if I could read it — that that was the bottom line. Discontinued, no reason given.

The movie in the Winchester Arms Museum, "Lock, Stock, and Barrel," was going strong. The film began with the introduction of the cannon into European warfare in the Middle Ages, and was working its way slowly toward the nineteenth century when I left. I was in a hurry. Soon my husband would be waiting for me in the lobby. Trying to get a quick impression of the objects on display, I went from room to room, but the objects in this museum repelled me even more than the artifacts in the Indian museum had. They were all the same: guns, guns, and more guns. Some large drawings and photographs on the walls tried to give a sense of the context in which the arms had been used, but the effect was nil. It was case after case of rifles and pistols, repeating themselves over and over, and even when some slight variation caught my eye the differences meant nothing to me.

But the statistics that accompanied a display of commemorative rifles did mean something. I saw the Antlered Game Commemorative Carbine. Date of manufacture: 1978. Number produced: 19,999. How many antlered animals had each carbine killed? I saw the Canadian Centennial, 1962, 90,000; the Legendary Lawman, 1978, 19,999; the John Wayne, 1980–81, 51,600. Like the titles of the various sections of the museum, these names had a message. The message was: guns are patriotic. Associated with national celebrations, law enforcement, and cultural heroes, the firearms were made to seem inseparable from the march of American history: Firearms in Colonial America; Born in America: The Kentucky Rifle; The Era of Expansion and Invention; The Civil War: Firearms of the Conflict; The Golden Age of Hunting; Winning the West. The guns embodied phases of the history they had helped to make, and the fact that firearms had *had* a history seemed to consecrate them, to make them worth not only preserving but revering.

Awe and admiration are the attitudes the museum invites. You hear the ghostly march of military music in the background; you imagine flags waving and sense the implicit reference to feats of courage in battle and glorious death. The place had the air of an enormous reliquary, or of the room off the transept of a cathedral where the vestments are kept. These guns were not there merely to be seen or even studied; they were there to be venerated.

But I did not look closely. I did not try to appreciate the guns. Unconsciously, I said to myself, my ability to empathize, to extend myself toward the virtues of an alien craft, ends here. For here in the basement the instruments that had produced the hides and horns upstairs, and had massacred the Indians, were being lovingly displayed. And we were still making them. Fifty-one thousand six hundred John Waynes in 1980–81. Arms were going strong.

As I bought my books and postcards in the gift shop, I noticed a sign that read, "Rodeo Tickets Sold Here," and something clicked into place. So that was it. *Everything* was still going strong. The whole museum was just another rodeo, only with the riders and their props stuffed, painted, sculpted, immobilized, and put under glass. Like the rodeo, the museum witnessed a desire to bring back the United States of the 1880s and 1890s. The quotation marks around the phrase "the winning of the West," the statements about myth and interpretation, were only gestures in the direction of something that had nothing to do with the museum's real purpose. The American people did not want to let go of the winning of the West. They wanted to win it all over again, in imagination. It was the ecstasy of the kill, as much as the life of the hunted, that we fed off here. The Buffalo Bill Historical Center did not repudiate the carnage that had taken place in the nineteenth century. It celebrated it. With its gleaming restrooms, cute snack bar, opulent museum shop, wooden Indians, thousand rifles, and scores of animal trophies, it helped us all reenact the dream of excitement, adventure, and conquest that was what the Wild West meant to most people in this country.

This is where my visit ended. But it had a sequel. When I left the Buffalo Bill Historical Center I was full of moral outrage, an indignation so intense it made me almost sick, though it was pleasurable, too, as such emotions usually are. But the outrage was undermined by the knowledge that I knew nothing about Buffalo Bill, nothing of his life, nothing of the circumstances that led him to be involved in such violent events. And I began to wonder if my reaction wasn't in some way an image, however small, of the violence I had been objecting to. So I began to read about Buffalo Bill, and as I did, a whole new world opened up.

"I have seen him the very personification of grace and beauty . . . dashing over the free wild prairie and riding his horse as though he and the noble animal were bounding with one life and one motion." That is the sort of thing people wrote about Buffalo Bill. They said "he was the handsomest man I ever saw." They said there "was never another man lived as popular as he was." They said there "wasn't a man, woman or child that he knew or ever met that he didn't speak to." They said he "was handsome as a god, a good rider and a crack shot." They said he "gave lots of money away. Nobody ever went hungry around him." They said he "was way above the average, physically and every other way."

These are quotes from people who knew Cody, collected by one of his two most responsible biographers. She puts them in the last chapter, and by the time you get there they all ring true. Buffalo Bill was incredibly handsome. He was extremely brave and did things no other scout would do. He carried messages over rugged territory swarming with hostile Indians, riding all night in bad weather to get through, and then taking off again the next day to ride sixty miles through a blizzard. He was not a proud man. He didn't boast of his exploits. But he did do incredible things, not just once in a while but on a fairly regular basis. He had a great deal of courage; he believed in himself, in his abilities, in his strength and endurance and knowledge. He was very skilled at what he did — hunting and scouting — but he wasn't afraid to try other things. He wrote some dime novels; he wrote his autobiography at age thirty-three, without very much schooling. He wasn't afraid to try acting even though the stage terrified him and he knew so little about it that, according to his wife, he didn't even know you had to memorize lines.

Maybe it was because he grew up on the frontier, maybe it was just the kind of person he was, but he was constantly finding himself in situations that required resourcefulness and courage, quick decisions and decisive action and rising to the occasion. He wasn't afraid to improvise.

He liked people, drank a lot, gave big parties, gave lots of presents, and is reputed to have been a womanizer.[1] When people came to see him in his office tent on the show grounds, to shake his hand or have their picture taken with him, he never turned anyone away. "He kept a uniformed doorman at the tent opening to announce visitors," writes a biographer. "No matter who was outside, from a mayor to a shabby woman with a baby, the Colonel would smooth his mustache, stand tall and straight, and tell the doorman to 'show 'em in.' He greeted everyone the same." "He told the damnedest stories you ever heard," writes the son of an Indian who worked in the Wild West show, "entertaining his troupe of performers for hours with Old West blood and guts make-believe. He was admired by all, including the hundreds of Indians he took along on tour. Indians love a man who can tell good stories." They also admired him for fighting well, said his biographers. Though I looked for it, I could find no evidence that contradicts those claims.

As a showman, he was a genius. People don't say much about why he was so successful; mostly they describe the wonderful goings-on. But I get the feeling that Cody was one of those people who was connected to his time in an uncanny way. He knew what people wanted, he knew how to entertain them, because he *liked* them, was open to them, felt kinship with them, or was so much in touch with himself at some level that he was thereby in touch with almost everybody else.

He liked to dress up and had a great sense of costume (of humor, too, they say). Once he came to a fancy-dress ball, his first, in New York, wearing white tie and tails and a large Stetson. He knew what people wanted. He let his hair grow long and wore a mustache and beard because, he said, he wouldn't be believable as a scout otherwise. Hence his Indian name, Pahaska, meaning "long hair," which people loved to use. Another kind of costume. He invented the ten-gallon hat, which the Stetson company made to his specifications. Afterward, they made a fortune off of it. In the scores of pictures reproduced in the many books about him, he most often wears scout's clothes — usually generously fringed buckskin, sometimes a modified cavalryman's outfit — though of ten he's impeccably turned out in a natty-looking three-piece business suit (sometimes with overcoat, sometimes not). The photographs show him in a tuxedo, in something called a "Mexican suit," which looks like a cowboy outfit, and once he appears in Indian dress. In almost every case he is wearing a hat, usually the Stetson, at exactly the right angle. He poses deliberately, and with dignity, for the picture. Cody didn't take himself so seriously that he had to pretend to be less than he was. "Jesus / he was a handsome man," wrote e. e. cummings in "Buffalo Bill's defunct."

What made Buffalo Bill so irresistible? Why is he still so appealing, even now, when we've lost, supposedly, all the illusions that once supported his popularity? There's a poster for one of his shows when he was traveling in France that gives a clue to what it is that makes him so profoundly attractive. The poster consists of a huge buffalo galloping across the plains; in the center of the buffalo's hump is a cutout circle that shows the head of Buffalo Bill, white mustachioed and bearded now, in his famous hat, and beneath, in large red letters, are the words *"Je viens."*

*Je viens,* I am coming, are the words of a savior. The announcement is an annunciation. Buffalo Bill is a religious figure of a kind who makes sense, I think, within a specifically Christian tradition. That is, he comes in the guise of a redeemer, of someone who will save us, who will through his own actions do something for us that we cannot. He will lift us above our lives, out of the daily grind, into something larger than ourselves.

His appeal on the surface is to childish desires, the desire for glamour, fame, bigness, adventure, romance. But these desires

are also the sign of something more profound, and it is to something more profound in us that he also appeals. Buffalo Bill comes
to the child in us, understood not as that part of ourselves which
we have outgrown but the part that got left behind, of necessity,
a long time ago, having been starved, bound, punished, disciplined out of existence. He promises that that part of the self can
live again. He has the power to promise these things because he
represents the West, that geographical space of the globe which
was still the realm of exploration and discovery, which was still
open, which had not yet quite been tamed when he began to play
himself on the stage. He not only represented it, he *was* it. He
brought the West itself with him when he came: the very Indians,
the very buffaloes, the very cowboys, the very cattle, the very
stagecoach itself which had been memorialized in story. He performed in front of the audience the feats that had made him famous. He shot glass balls and clay pigeons out of the air with
amazing rapidity. He rode his "watersmooth-silver stallion" at
full gallop.

"I am coming." The appearance of Buffalo Bill, in the flesh,
was akin to the apparition of a saint or of the Virgin Mary to
believers. He was the incarnation of an ideal. He came to show
people that what they had only imagined was really true. The
West really did exist. There really were heroes who rode white
horses and performed amazing feats. e. e. cummings was right
to invoke the name of Jesus in his poem. Buffalo Bill was a secular messiah.

He was a messiah because people believed in him. When he
died, he is reputed to have said, "Let my show go on." But he had
no show at the time, so he probably didn't say that. Still, the words
are prophetic because the desire for what Buffalo Bill had done
had not only not died but would call forth the countless reenact-
ments of the Wild West, from the rodeo — a direct descendant
of his show — to the thousands of western novels, movies, and
television programs that comprise the western genre in the twentieth century, a genre that came into existence as a separate category right about the time that Bill Cody died. Don Russell main-
tains that the way the West exists in our minds today is largely
the result of the way Cody presented it in his show. That was
where people got their ideas of what the characters looked like.

Though many Indian tribes wore no feathers and fought on foot, you will never see a featherless, horseless Indian warrior in the movies because Bill employed only Sioux and other Plains tribes that had horses and traditionally wore feathered headdresses. "Similarly," he adds, "cowboys wear ten-gallon Stetsons, not because such a hat was worn in early range days, but because it was part of the costume adopted by Buffalo Bill for his show."[2]

But the deeper legacy is elsewhere. Buffalo Bill was a person who inspired other people. What they saw in him was an aspect of themselves. It really doesn't matter whether Cody was as great as people thought him or not, because what they were responding to when he rode into the arena, erect and resplendent on his charger, was something intangible, not the man himself but a possible way of being. William F. Cody and the Wild West triggered the emotions that had fueled the imaginative lives of people who flocked to see him, especially men and boys who made up the larger portion of the audience. He and his cowboys played to an inward territory: a Wild West of the psyche that hungered for exercise sprang into activity when the show appeared. *Je viens* was a promise to redeem that territory, momentarily at least, from exile and oblivion. The lost parts of the self symbolized by buffaloes and horses and wild men would live again for an hour while the show went on.

People adored it. Queen Victoria, who broke her custom by going to see it at all (she never went to the theater and on the rare occasions when she wanted to see a play, she had it brought to her), is supposed to have been lifted out of a twenty-five-year depression caused by the death of her husband after she saw Buffalo Bill. She liked the show so much that she saw it again, arranging for a command performance to be given at Windsor Castle the day before her Diamond Jubilee. This was the occasion when four kings rode in the Deadwood coach with the Prince of Wales on top next to Buffalo Bill, who drove. No one was proof against the appeal. Ralph Blumenfeld, the London correspondent for the *New York Herald,* wrote in his diary while the show was in London that he'd had two boyhood heroes,

> Robin Hood and Buffalo Bill, and delighted in Cody's stories of the Pony Express and Yellow Hand. Everything was done to make Cody conceited and unbearable, but he remained the simple, unassuming

child of the plains who thought lords and ladies belonged in the picture books and that the story of Little Red Riding Hood was true. I
rode in the Deadwood coach. It was a great evening in which I realized a good many of my boyhood dreams, for there was Buffalo Bill
on his white rocking horse charger, and Annie Oakley behind him.[3]

Victor Weybright and Henry Blackman Sell, from whose work
on the Wild West some of the foregoing information has come,
dedicated their book to Buffalo Bill. It was published in 1955.
Nellie Irene Snyder Yost, whose 1979 biography is one of the
two scholarly accounts of Cody's life, dedicates her book "to all
those good people, living or dead, who knew and liked Buffalo
Bill."[4] Don Russell's *Lives and Legends of Buffalo Bill* (1960), the
most fact-filled scholarly biography, does not have a dedication,
but in the final chapter where he steps back to assess Cody and
his influence, Russell ends by exclaiming: "What more could possibly be asked of a hero? If he was not one, who was?"[5]

Let me now pose a few questions of my own. Must we throw
out all the wonderful qualities that Cody had, the spirit of hope
and emulation that he aroused in millions of people, because of
the terrible judgment history has passed on the epoch of which
he was a part? The kinds of things he stands for — courage, dar-
ing, strength, endurance, generosity, openness to other people,
love of drama, love of life, the possibility of living a life that does
not deny the body and the desires of the body — are these to be
declared dangerous and delusional because he manifested some
of them while fighting Indians, and others while representing his
victories to the world? And the feelings he aroused in his audiences — the idealism, the enthusiasm, the excitement, the belief
that dreams could become real — must these be declared misguided or a sham because they are associated with the imperialis-
tic conquest of a continent, with the wholesale extermination of
animals and men?

It is not so much that we cannot learn from history as that we
cannot teach history how things should have been. When I set
out to discover how Cody had become involved in the killing of
Indians and the slaughter of buffalo, I found myself unable to
sustain the outrage I had felt on leaving the museum. From his
first job as an eleven-year-old herder for an army supply outfit,
sole wage earner for his ailing, widowed mother, who had a new
infant and other children to support, to his death in Colorado at

seventy-one, there was never a time when it was possible for me to say, There, there you went wrong, Buffalo Bill, you should not have killed that Indian. You should have held your fire and quit the army and gone to work in the nineteenth-century equivalent of the Peace Corps. You should have known how it would end. My reading made me see that you can't prescribe for someone in Buffalo Bill's position — what he should have done, how things should have been — and it made me reflect on the violence of my own reaction. I saw how eager I had been to get off on being angry at the museum. The thirst for moral outrage, for self-vindication, lay pretty close to the surface.

I cannot resolve the contradictions between my experience at the Buffalo Bill Museum, with its celebration of violent conquest, and my response to the shining figure of Buffalo Bill as it emerged from the pages of books. On the one hand, a history of shame; on the other, an image of the heart's desire. But I have reached one conclusion that for a while, at least, will have to serve.

Major historical events like genocide and major acts of destruction are not simply produced by impersonal historical processes or economic imperatives or ecological blunders; human intentionality is involved and human knowledge of the self. Therefore, if you're really interested in not having any more genocide or killing of animals, no matter what else you might do — condemning imperialism or shaking your finger at history — if you don't first, or also, come to recognize the violence in yourself and your own anger and your own destructiveness, whatever else you do won't work. It isn't that genocide doesn't matter. Genocide matters and it starts at home.

### NOTES

1. Iron Eyes Cody, as told to Collin Perry, *Iron Eyes: My Life as a Hollywood Indian* (New York, 1982), 16.
2. Don Russell, *The Lives and Legends of Buffalo Bill* (Norman, Okla., 1960), 470.
3. Victor Weybright and Henry Blackman Sell, *Buffalo Bill and the Wild West* (New York, 1955), 172.
4. Nellie Irene Snyder Yost, *Buffalo Bill, His Family, Friends, Fame, Failures, and Fortunes* (Chicago, 1979).
5. Russell, *Lives and Legends*, 480.

MARIANNA DE MARCO TORGOVNICK

# On Being White, Female, and Born in Bensonhurst

FROM PARTISAN REVIEW

THE MAFIA protects the neighborhood, our fathers say, with that peculiar satisfied pride with which law-abiding Italian Americans refer to the Mafia: the Mafia protects the neighborhood from "the coloreds." In the fifties and sixties, I heard that information repeated, in whispers, in neighborhood parks and in the yard at school in Bensonhurst. The same information probably passes today in the parks (the word now "blacks," not "coloreds") but perhaps no longer in the schoolyards. From buses each morning, from neighborhoods outside Bensonhurst, spill children of all colors and backgrounds — American black, West Indian black, Hispanic, and Asian. But the blacks are the only ones especially marked for notice. Bensonhurst is no longer entirely protected from "the coloreds." But in a deeper sense, at least for Italian Americans, Bensonhurst never changes.

Italian-American life continues pretty much as I remember it. Families with young children live side by side with older couples whose children are long gone to the suburbs. Many of those families live "down the block" from the last generation or, sometimes still, live together with parents or grandparents. When a young family leaves, as sometimes happens, for Long Island or New Jersey or (very common now) for Staten Island, another arrives, without any special effort being required, from Italy or a poorer neighborhood in New York. They fill the neat but anonymous houses that make up the mostly tree-lined streets: two-, three-, or four-family houses for the most part (this is a working, lower to middle-middle class area, and people need rents to pay mortgages), with a few single family or small apartment houses tossed in at random. Tomato plants, fig trees, and plaster madonnas often decorate small but well-tended yards which face out onto the street; the grassy front lawn, like the grassy back yard, is relatively uncommon.

Crisscrossing the neighborhood and marking out ethnic zones — Italian, Irish, and Jewish, for the most part, though there are some Asian Americans and some people (usually Protestants) called simply Americans — are the great shopping streets: Eighty-sixth Street, Kings Highway, Bay Parkway, Eighteenth Avenue, each with its own distinctive character. On Eighty-sixth Street, crowds bustle along sidewalks lined with ample, packed fruit stands. Women wheeling shopping carts or baby strollers check the fruit carefully, piece by piece, and often bargain with the dealer, cajoling for a better price or letting him know that the vegetables, this time, aren't up to snuff. A few blocks down, the fruit stands are gone and the streets are lined with clothing and record shops, mobbed by teenagers. Occasionally, the el rumbles overhead, a few stops out of Coney Island on its way to the city, a trip of around one hour.

On summer nights, neighbors congregate on stoops which during the day serve as play yards for children. Air conditioning exists everywhere in Bensonhurst, but people still sit outside in the summer — to supervise children, to gossip, to stare at strangers. *"Buona sera,"* I say, or *"Buona notte,"* as I am ritually presented to Sal and Lily and Louie, the neighbors sitting on the stoop. *"Grazie,"* I say when they praise my children or my appearance. It's the only time I use Italian, which I learned at high school, although my parents (both second-generation Italian Americans, my father Sicilian, my mother Calabrian) speak it at home to each other but never to me or my brother. My accent is the Tuscan accent taught at school, not the southern Italian accents of my parents and the neighbors.

It's important to greet and please the neighbors; any break in this decorum would seriously offend and aggrieve my parents. For the neighbors are the stern arbiters of conduct in Bensonhurst. Does Mary keep a clean house? Did Gina wear black long enough after her mother's death? Was the food good at Tony's wedding? The neighbors know and pass judgment. Any news of family scandal (my brother's divorce, for example) provokes from my mother the agonized words: "But what will I *tell* people?" I sometimes collaborate in devising a plausible script.

A large sign on the church I attended as a child sums up for me the ethos of Bensonhurst. The sign urges contributions to the church building fund with the message, in huge letters: "EACH YEAR ST. SIMON AND JUDE SAVES THIS NEIGHBOR-HOOD ONE MILLION DOLLARS IN TAXES." Passing the church on the way from largely Jewish and middle-class Sheepshead Bay (where my in-laws live) to Bensonhurst, year after year, my husband and I look for the sign and laugh at the crass level of its pitch, its utter lack of attention to things spiritual. But we also understand exactly the values it represents.

In the summer of 1989, my parents were visiting me at my house in Durham, North Carolina, from the apartment in Bensonhurst where they have lived since 1942: three small rooms, rent-controlled, floor clean enough to eat off, every corner and crevice known and organized. My parents' longevity in a single apartment is unusual even for Bensonhurst, but not that unusual; many people live for decades in the same place or move within a ten-block radius. When I lived in this apartment, there were four rooms; one has since been ceded to a demanding landlord, one of the various landlords who have haunted my parents' life and must always be appeased lest the ultimate threat — removal from the rent-controlled apartment — be brought into play. That summer, during their visit, on August 23 (my younger daughter's birthday) a shocking, disturbing, news report issued from the neighborhood: it had become another Howard Beach.

Three black men, walking casually through the streets at night, were attacked by a group of whites. One was shot dead, mistaken, as it turned out, for another black youth who was dating a white, although part-Hispanic, girl in the neighborhood. It all made sense: the crudely protective men, expecting to see a black arriving at the girl's house and overreacting; the rebellious girl dating the outsider boy; the black dead as a sacrifice to the feelings of the neighborhood.

I might have felt outrage, I might have felt guilt or shame, I might have despised the people among whom I grew up. In a way I felt all four emotions when I heard the news. I expect that there were many people in Bensonhurst who felt the same rush of emotions. But mostly I felt that, given the set-up, this was the only way things could have happened. I detested the racial killing, but I also understood it. Those streets, which should be public property available to all, belong to the neighborhood. All the people sitting on the stoops on August 23 knew that as well as they knew their own names. The black men walking through probably knew it too — though their casual walk sought to deny the fact that, for the neighbors, even the simple act of blacks walking through the neighborhood would be seen as invasion.

Italian Americans in Bensonhurst are notable for their cohesiveness and provinciality; the slightest pressure turns those qualities into prejudice and racism. Their cohesiveness is based on the stable economic and ethical level that links generation to generation, keeping Italian Americans in Bensonhurst and the Italian-American community alive as the Jewish-American community of my youth is no longer alive. (Its young people routinely moved to the suburbs or beyond and were never replaced, so that Jews in Bensonhurst today are almost all very old people.) Their provinciality results from the Italian Americans' devotion to jealous distinctions and discriminations. Jews are suspect, but (the old Italian women admit) "they make good husbands." The Irish are okay, fellow Catholics, but not really "like us"; they make bad husbands because they drink and gamble. Even Italians come in varieties, by region (Sicilian, Calabrian, Neapolitan, very rarely any region further north) and by history in this country (the newly arrived and ridiculed "gaffoon" versus the second or third generation).

Bensonhurst is a neighborhood dedicated to believing that its values are the only values; it tends toward certain forms of inertia. When my parents visit me in Durham, they routinely take chairs from the kitchen and sit out on the lawn in front of the house, not on the chairs on the back deck; then they complain that the streets are too quiet. When they walk around my neighborhood (these De Marcos who have friends named Travaglianti and Occhipinti), they look at the mailboxes and report that my neighbors have strange names. Prices at my local supermarket are compared, in unbelievable detail, with prices on Eighty-sixth Street. Any rearrangement of my kitchen since their last visit is registered and criticized. Difference is not only unwelcome, it is unacceptable. One of the most characteristic things my mother ever said was in response to my plans for renovating my house in Durham. When she heard my plans, she looked around, crossed her arms, and said, "If it was me, I wouldn't change nothing." My father once asked me to level with him about a Jewish boyfriend who lived in a different part of the neighborhood, reacting to his Jewishness, but even more to the fact that he often wore Bermuda shorts: "Tell me something, Marianna. Is he a Communist?" Such are the standards of normality and political thinking in Bensonhurst.

I often think that one important difference between Italian Americans in New York neighborhoods like Bensonhurst and Italian Americans elsewhere is that the others moved on — to upstate New York, to Pennsylvania, to the Midwest. Though they frequently settled in communities of fellow Italians, they did move on. Bensonhurst Italian Americans seem to have felt that one large move, over the ocean, was enough. Future moves could be only local: from the Lower East Side, for example, to Brooklyn, or from one part of Brooklyn to another. Bensonhurst was for many of these people the summa of expectations. If their America were to be drawn as a *New Yorker* cover, Manhattan itself would be tiny in proportion to Bensonhurst and to its satellites, Staten Island, New Jersey, and Long Island.

"Oh, no," my father says when he hears the news about the shooting. Though he still refers to blacks as "coloreds," he's not really a racist and is upset that this innocent youth was shot in his neighborhood. He has no trouble acknowledging the wrongness of the death. But then, like all the news accounts, he turns to the fact, repeated over and over, that the blacks had been on their way to look at a used car when they encountered the hostile mob of whites. The explanation is right before him but, "Yeah," he says, still shaking his head, "yeah, but what were they *doing* there? They didn't belong."

Over the next few days, the television news is even more disturbing. Rows of screaming Italians lining the streets, most of them looking like my relatives. I focus especially on one woman who

resembles almost completely my mother: stocky but not fat, mid-
seventies but well preserved, full face showing only minimal
wrinkles, ample steel-gray hair neatly if rigidly coiffed in a modified beehive hairdo left over from the sixties. She shakes her fist
at the camera, protesting the arrest of the Italian-American youths
in the neighborhood and the incursion of more blacks into the
neighborhood, protesting the shooting. I look a little nervously
at my mother (the parent I resemble), but she has not even noticed the woman and stares impassively at the television.

What has Bensonhurst to do with what I teach today and write?
Why did I need to write about this killing in Bensonhurst, but
not in the manner of a news account or a statistical sociological
analysis? Within days of hearing the news, I began to plan this
essay, to tell the world what I knew, even though I was aware that
I could publish the piece only someplace my parents or their
neighbors would never see or hear about it. I sometimes think
that I looked around from my baby carriage and decided that
someday, the sooner the better, I would get out of Bensonhurst.
Now, much to my surprise, Bensonhurst — the antipodes of the
intellectual life I sought, the least interesting of places — had become a respectable intellectual topic. People would be willing to
hear about Bensonhurst — and all by the dubious virtue of a racial killing in the streets.

The story as I would have to tell it would be to some extent a
class narrative: about the difference between working class and
upper middle class, dependence and a profession, Bensonhurst
and a posh suburb. But I need to make it clear that I do not imagine myself as writing from a position of enormous self-satis-
faction, or even enormous distance. You can take the girl out of
Bensonhurst (that much is clear), but you may not be able to take
Bensonhurst out of the girl. And upward mobility is not the essence of the story, though it is an important marker and symbol.

In Durham today, I live in a twelve-room house surrounded
by an acre of trees. When I sit on my back deck on summer evenings, no houses are visible through the trees. I have a guaran-
teed income, teaching English at an excellent university, removed by my years of education from the fundamental economic
and social conditions of Bensonhurst. The one time my mother
ever expressed pleasure at my work was when I got tenure, what

my father still calls, with no irony intended, "ten years." "What does that mean?" my mother asked when she heard the news. Then she reached back into her experience as a garment worker, subject to periodic layoffs. "Does it mean they can't fire you just for nothing and can't lay you off?" When I said that was exactly what it means, she said, "Very good. Congratulations. That's *wonderful.*" I was free from the *padrones,* from the network of petty anxieties that had formed, in large part, her very existence. Of course, I wasn't really free of petty anxieties: would my salary increase keep pace with my colleagues', how would my office compare, would this essay be accepted for publication, am I happy? The line between these worries and my mother's is the line between the working class and the upper middle class.

But getting out of Bensonhurst never meant to me a big house, or nice clothes, or a large income. And it never meant feeling good about looking down on what I left behind or hiding my background. Getting out of Bensonhurst meant freedom — to experiment, to grow, to change. It also meant knowledge in some grand, abstract way. All the material possessions I have acquired, I acquired simply along the way — and for the first twelve years after I left Bensonhurst, I chose to acquire almost nothing at all. Now, as I write about the neighborhood, I recognize that although I've come far in physical and material distance, the emotional distance is harder to gauge. Bensonhurst has everything to do with who I am and even with what I write. Occasionally I get reminded of my roots, of their simultaneously choking and nutritive power.

Scene one: It's after a lecture at Duke, given by a visiting professor from Princeton. The lecture was long and a little dull and — bad luck — I had agreed to be one of the people having dinner with the lecturer afterward. We settle into our table at the restaurant: this man, me, the head of the comparative literature program (also a professor of German), and a couple I like who teach French, the husband at my university, the wife at one nearby. The conversation is sluggish, as it often is when a stranger, like the visiting professor, has to be assimilated into a group, so I ask the visitor from Princeton a question to personalize things a bit. "How did you get interested in what you do? What made you become a professor of German?" The man gets going and begins talking about how it was really unlikely that he, a nice Jewish boy from Bensonhurst, would have chosen, in the mid-fifties, to study German. Unlikely indeed.

I remember seeing *Judgment at Nuremberg* in a local movie theater and having a woman in the row in back of me get hysterical when some clips of a concentration camp were shown. "My God," she screamed in a European accent, "look at what they did. Murderers, MURDERERS!" — and she had to be supported out by her family. I couldn't see, in the dark, whether her arm bore the neatly tattooed numbers that the arms of some of my classmates' parents did — and that always affected me with a thrill of horror. Ten years older than me, this man had lived more directly through those feelings, lived with and *among* those feelings. The first chance he got, he raced to study in Germany. I myself have twice chosen not to visit Germany, but I understand his impulse to identify with the Other as a way of getting out of the neighborhood.

At the dinner, the memory about the movie pops into my mind but I pick up instead on the Bensonhurst — I'm also from there, but Italian American. Like a flash, he asks something I haven't been asked in years: Where did I go to high school and (a more common question) what was my maiden name? I went to Lafayette High School, I say, and my name was De Marco. Everything changes: his facial expression, his posture, his accent, his voice. "Soo, Dee Maw-ko," he says, "dun anything wrong at school today — got enny pink slips? Wanna meet me later at the parrk or maybe bye the Baye?" When I laugh, recognizing the stereotype that Italians get pink slips for misconduct at school and the notorious chemistry between Italian women and Jewish men, he says, back in his Princetonian voice: "My God, for a minute I felt like I was turning into a werewolf."

It's odd that although I can remember almost nothing else about this man — his face, his body type, even his name — I remember this lapse into his "real self" with enormous vividness. I am especially struck by how easily he was able to slip into the old, generic Brooklyn accent. I myself have no memory of ever speaking in that accent, though I also have no memory of trying not to speak it, except for teaching myself, carefully, to say "oil" rather than "earl."

But the surprises aren't over. The female French professor,

whom I have known for at least five years, reveals for the first time that she is also from the neighborhood, though she lived across the other side of Kings Highway, went to a different, more elite high school, and was Irish American. Three of six professors, sitting at an eclectic vegetarian restaurant in Durham, all from Bensonhurst — a neighborhood where (I swear) you couldn't get the *New York Times* at any of the local stores.

Scene two: I still live in Bensonhurst. I'm waiting for my parents to return from a conference at my school, where they've been summoned to discuss my transition from elementary to junior high school. I am already a full year younger than any of my classmates, having skipped a grade, a not uncommon occurrence for "gifted" youngsters. Now the school is worried about putting me in an accelerated track through junior high, since that would make me two years younger. A compromise was reached: I would be put in a special program for gifted children, but one that took three, not two, years. It sounds okay.

Three years later, another wait. My parents have gone to school this time to make another decision. Lafayette High School has three tracks: academic, for potentially college-bound kids; secretarial, mostly for Italian-American girls or girls with low aptitude-test scores (the high school is de facto segregated, so none of the tracks is as yet racially coded, though they are coded by ethnic group and gender); and vocational, mostly for boys with the same attributes, ethnic or intellectual. Although my scores are superb, the guidance counselor has recommended the secretarial track; when I protested, the conference with my parents was arranged. My mother's preference is clear: the secretarial track — college is for boys; I will need to make a "good living" until I marry and have children. My father also prefers the secretarial track, but he wavers, half proud of my aberrantly high scores, half worried. I press the attack, saying that if I were Jewish I would have been placed, without question, in the academic track. I tell him I have sneaked a peek at my files and know that my IQ is at genius level. I am allowed to insist on the change into the academic track.

What I did, and I was ashamed of it even then, was to play upon my father's competitive feelings with Jews: his daughter could and should be as good as theirs. In the bank where he was a messenger, and at the insurance company where he worked in the mailroom, my father worked with Jews, who were almost always his immediate supervisors. Several times, my father was offered the supervisory job but turned it down after long conversations with my mother about the dangers of making a change, the difficulty of giving orders to friends. After her work in a local garment shop, after cooking dinner and washing the floor each night, my mother often did piecework making bows; sometimes I would help her for fun, but it *wasn't* fun, and I was free to stop while she continued for long, tedious hours to increase the family income. Once a week, her part-time boss, Dave, would come by to pick up the boxes of bows. Short, round, with his shirttails sloppily tucked into his pants and a cigar almost always dangling from his lips, Dave was a stereotyped Jew but also, my parents always said, a nice guy, a decent man.

Years later, similar choices come up, and I show the same assertiveness I showed with my father, the same ability to deal for survival, but tinged with Bensonhurst caution. Where will I go to college? Not to Brooklyn College, the flagship of the city system — I know that, but don't press the invitations I have received to apply to prestigious schools outside of New York. The choice comes down to two: Barnard, which gives me a full scholarship, minus five hundred dollars a year that all scholarship students are expected to contribute from summer earnings, or New York University, which offers me one thousand dollars above tuition as a bribe. I waver. My parents stand firm: they are already losing money by letting me go to college; I owe it to the family to contribute the extra thousand dollars plus my summer earnings. Besides, my mother adds, harping on a favorite theme, there are no boys at Barnard; at NYU I'm more likely to meet someone to marry. I go to NYU and do marry in my senior year, but he is someone I didn't meet at college. I was secretly relieved, I now think (though at the time I thought I was just placating my parents' conventionality), to be out of the marriage sweepstakes.

The first boy who ever asked me for a date was Robert Lubitz, in eighth grade: tall and skinny to my average height and teenage chubbiness. I turned him down, thinking we would make a ridiculous couple. Day after day, I cast my eyes at stylish Juliano, the class cutup; day after day, I captivated Robert Lubitz. Occasionally, one of my brother's Italian-American friends would ask me out, and I would go, often to ROTC dances. My specialty was making political remarks so shocking that the guys rarely asked me again. After a while I recognized destiny: the Jewish man was a passport out of Bensonhurst. I of course did marry a Jewish man, who gave me my freedom and, very important, helped remove me from the expectations of Bensonhurst. Though raised in a largely Jewish section of Brooklyn, he had gone to college in Ohio and knew how important it was, as he put it, "to get past the Brooklyn Bridge." We met on neutral ground, in Central Park, at a performance of Shakespeare. The Jewish-Italian marriage is a common enough catastrophe in Bensonhurst for my parents to have accepted, even welcomed, mine — though my parents continued to treat my husband like an outsider for the first twenty years ("Now Marianna. Here's what's going on with you brother. But don't tell-a you husband").

Along the way I make other choices, more fully marked by Bensonhurst cautiousness. I am attracted to journalism or the arts as careers, but the prospects for income seem iffy. I choose instead to imagine myself as a teacher. Only the availability of NDEA fellowships when I graduate, with their generous terms, propels me from high school teaching (a thought I never much relished) to college teaching (which seems like a brave new world). Within the college teaching profession, I choose offbeat specializations: the novel, interdisciplinary approaches (not something clear and clubby like Milton or the eighteenth century). Eventually I write the book I like best about primitive others as they figure within Western obsessions: my identification with "the Other," my sense of being "Other," surfaces at last. I avoid all mentoring structures for a long time but accept aid when it comes to me on the basis of what I perceive to be merit. I'm still, deep down, Italian-American Bensonhurst, though by this time I'm a lot of other things as well.

Scene three: In the summer of 1988, a little more than a year before the shooting in Bensonhurst, my father woke up trembling and in what appeared to be a fit. Hospitalization revealed that he had a pocket of blood on his brain, a frequent consequence of falls for older people. About a year earlier, I had stayed home, using my children as an excuse, when my aunt, my father's much loved sister, died, missing her funeral; only now does my mother tell me how much my father resented my taking his suggestion that I stay home. Now, confronted with what is described as brain surgery but turns out to be less dramatic than it sounds, I fly home immediately.

My brother drives three hours back and forth from New Jersey every day to chauffeur me and my mother to the hospital: he is being a fine Italian-American son. For the first time in years, we have long conversations alone. He is two years older than I am, a chemical engineer who has also left the neighborhood but has remained closer to its values, with a suburban, Republican inflection. He talks a lot about New York, saying that (except for neighborhoods like Bensonhurst) it's a "third-world city now." It's the summer of the Tawana Brawley incident, when Brawley accused white men of abducting her and smearing racial slurs on her body with her own excrement. My brother is filled with dislike for Al Sharpton and Brawley's other vocal supporters in the black community — not because they're black, he says, but because they're troublemakers, stirring things up. The city is drenched in racial hatred that makes itself felt in the halls of the hospital: Italians and Jews in the beds and as doctors; blacks as nurses and orderlies.

This is the first time since I left New York in 1975 that I have visited Brooklyn without once getting into Manhattan. It's the first time I have spent several days alone with my mother, living in her apartment in Bensonhurst. My every move is scrutinized and commented on. I feel like I am going to go crazy.

Finally, it's clear that my father is going to be fine, and I can go home. She insists on accompanying me to the travel agent to get my ticket for home, even though I really want to be alone. The agency (a Mafia front?) has no one who knows how to ticket me for the exotic destination of North Carolina and no computer for doing so. The one person who can perform this feat by hand is out. I have to kill time for an hour and suggest to my mother that she go home, to be there for my brother when he arrives from Jersey. We stop in a Pork Store, where I buy a stash of cheeses, sausages, and other delicacies unavailable in Durham. My mother walks home with the shopping bags, and I'm on my own.

More than anything I want a kind of *sorbetto* or ice I remember from my childhood, a *cremolata*, almond-vanilla-flavored with large chunks of nuts. I pop into the local bakery (at the unlikely hour of 11 A.M.) and ask for a *cremolata,* usually eaten after dinner. The woman — a younger version of my mother — refuses: they haven't made a fresh ice yet, and what's left from the day before is too icy, no good. I explain that I'm about to get on a plane for North Carolina and want that ice, good or not. But she has her standards and holds her ground, even though North Carolina has about the same status in her mind as Timbuktoo and she knows I will be banished, perhaps forever, from the land of *cremolata.*

Then, while I'm taking a walk, enjoying my solitude, I have another idea. On the block behind my parents' house, there's a club for men, for men from a particular town or region in Italy: six or seven tables, some on the sidewalk beneath a garish red, green, and white sign; no women allowed or welcome unless they're with men, and no women at all during the day when the real business of the club — a game of cards for old men — is in progress. Still, I know that inside the club would be coffee and a *cremolata* ice. I'm thirty-eight, well dressed, very respectable looking; I know what I want. I also know I'm not supposed to enter that club. I enter anyway, asking the teenage boy behind the counter firmly, in my most professional tones, for a *cremolata* ice. Dazzled, he complies immediately. The old men at the card table have been staring at this scene, unable to place me exactly, though my facial type is familiar. Finally, a few old men's hisses pierce the air. *"Strega,"* I hear as I leave, *"mala strega"* — "witch," or "brazen whore." I have been in Bensonhurst less than a week, but I have managed to reproduce, on my final day there for this visit, the conditions of my youth. Knowing the rules, I have broken them. I shake hands with my discreetly rebellious past, still an outsider walking through the neighborhood, marked and insulted — though unlikely to be shot.

MARIO VARGAS LLOSA

# Questions of Conquest

FROM HARPER'S MAGAZINE

IN MADRID not long ago, a shadowy group calling itself the Association of Indian Cultures held a press conference to announce that its members (it was not clear who these men and women might be) were preparing to undertake, in Spain and also throughout Latin America, a number of acts of "sabotage." It is, of course, a sad fact of life that in a number of Latin American countries — in Spain as well — the planting of bombs and the destruction of property continue to be perceived by some as a means of achieving justice, or self-determination, or, as in my country, Peru, the realization of a revolutionary utopia. But the Association of Indian Cultures did not seem interested in seizing the future. Their battle was with the past.

What are to be sabotaged by this group are the numerous quincentennial ceremonies and festivities scheduled for 1992 to commemorate the epochal voyage nearly five hundred years ago of Columbus's three small caravels. The Association of Indian Cultures believes that the momentous events of 1492 should in no way be celebrated; and although I have yet to hear of other persons willing to make the point through subversion, I do know that the group will not lack for sympathizers.

The question most crucial to these individuals is the oldest one: Was the discovery and conquest of America by Europeans the greatest feat of the Christian West or one of history's monumental crimes? It is a question they ask rhetorically and perhaps will answer with violence. This is not to say that to discuss what could have happened as opposed to what did happen is a useless undertaking; historians and thinkers have pondered the question since the seventeenth century, producing wonderful books and speculations. But to me the debate serves no practical purpose, and I intend to stay out of it. What would America be like in the 1990s if the dominant cultures were those of the Aztecs and Incas? The only answer, ultimately, is that there is no way to know.

I have two other questions, both having to do with the conquest, and I happen to think that an honest and thoughtful discussion of them is as timely and urgent as any others one could pose just now about Latin America. First: How was it possible that cultures as powerful and sophisticated as those of the ancient Mexicans and Peruvians — huge imperial cultures, as opposed to the scattered tribes of North America — so easily crumbled when encountered by infinitesimally small bands of Spanish adventurers? This question is itself centuries old, but not academic. In its answer may lie the basis for an understanding of the world the conquest engendered, a chronically "underdeveloped" world that has, for the most part, remained incapable of realizing its goals and visions.

The second question is this: Why have the postcolonial republics of the Americas — republics that might have been expected to have deeper and broader notions of liberty, equality, and fraternity — failed so miserably to improve the lives of their Indian citizens? Even as I write, not only the Amazonian rain forests but the small tribes who have managed for so long to survive there are being barbarously exterminated in the name of progress.

To begin to answer these questions, we must put down our newspapers and open the pages of the books that allow us to see close up the era when the Europeans dared to venture to sea in search of a new route to India and its spices, and happened instead on an unspoiled continent with its own peoples, customs, and civilizations. The chronicles of the conquest form an astonishingly rich literature — a literature at once fantastical and true. Through these books we can rediscover a period and a place, much as the readers of contemporary Latin American fiction discover the contemporary life of a continent. In their own way, the early chroniclers were the first Magical Realists.

*

The historian who mastered the subject of the discovery and conquest of Peru by the Spaniards better than anyone else had a tragic story. He died without having written the book for which he had prepared himself his whole life and whose theme he knew so well that he almost gave the impression of being omniscient. His name was Raúl Porras Barrenechea. He was a small, potbellied man with a large forehead and a pair of blue eyes that became impregnated with malice every time he mocked someone. He was the most brilliant teacher I have ever had.

In the big old house of San Marcos, the first university founded by the Spaniards in the New World, a place that had already begun to fall into an irreparable process of decay when I passed through it in the 1950s, Porras Barrenechea's lectures on historical sources attracted such a vast number of listeners that it was necessary to arrive well in advance so as not to be left outside the classroom listening together with dozens of students literally hanging from the doors and windows.

Whenever Porras Barrenechea spoke, history became anecdote, gesture, adventure, color, psychology. He depicted history as a series of mirrors that had the magnificence of a Renaissance painting and in which the determining factor of events was never the impersonal forces, the geographical imperative, the economic relations of divine providence, but a case of certain outstanding individuals whose audacity, genius, charisma, or contagious insanity had imposed on each era and society a certain orientation and shape. As well as this concept of history, which the scientific historians had already named as romantic in an effort to discredit it, Porras Barrenechea demanded knowledge and documentary precision, which none of his colleagues and critics at San Marcos had at that time been able to equal. Those historians who dismissed Porras Barrenechea because he was interested in simple, narrated history instead of a social or economic interpretation had been less effective than he was in explaining to us that crucial event in the destiny of Europe and America — the destruction of the Inca Empire and the linking of its vast territories and peoples to the Western world. This was because for Porras Barrenechea, although history had to have a dramatic quality, architectonic beauty, suspense, richness, and a wide range of human types and excellence in the style of a great fiction, everything in it also had to be scrupulously true, proven time after time.

In order to be able to narrate the discovery and conquest of Peru in this way, Porras Barrenechea first had to evaluate very carefully all the witnesses and documents so as to establish the degree of credibility of each one of them. And in the numerous cases of deceitful testimonies, Porras Barrenechea had to find out the reasons that led the authors to conceal, misrepresent, or overclaim the facts; knowing their peculiar limitations, those sources had a double meaning — what they revealed and what they distorted.

For forty years Porras Barrenechea dedicated all his powerful intellectual energy to this heroic hermeneutics. All the works he published while he was alive constitute the preliminary work for what should have been his magnum opus. When he was perfectly ready to embark upon it, pressing on with assurance through the labyrinthine jungle of chronicles, letters, testaments, rhymes, and ballads of the discovery and conquest that he had read, cleansed, confronted, and almost memorized, sudden death put an end to his encyclopedic information. As a result, all those interested in that era and in the men who lived in it have had to keep on reading the old but so far unsurpassed history of the conquest written by an American who never set foot in the country but who sketched it with extraordinary skill, William Prescott.

Dazzled by Porras Barrenechea's lectures, at one time I seriously considered the possibility of putting literature aside so as to dedicate myself to history. Porras Barrenechea had asked me to work with him as an assistant in an ambitious project on the general history of Peru under the auspices of the Lima bookseller and publisher Juan Mejía Baca. It was Porras Barrenechea's task to write the volumes devoted to the conquest and emancipation. For four years I spent three hours a day, five days a week, in that dusty house on Colina Street in Lima, where the books, the card indexes, and the notebooks had slowly invaded and devoured everything except Porras Barrenechea's bed and the dining table. My job was to read and take notes on the chronicles' various themes, but principally the myths and legends that preceded and followed the discovery and conquest of Peru. That experience has become an unforgettable memory for me. Whoever is familiar with the chronicles of the discovery and conquest of America will understand why. They represent for us Latin Americans what the novels of chivalry represent for Europe, the beginning of literary fiction as we understand it today. The tradition from which sprang books like *One Hundred Years of Solitude*, Julio Cortázar's short stories, and the works of the Paraguayan novelist Augusto Roa Bastos, books in which we are exposed to a world totally reconstructed and subverted by fantasy, started without doubt in those chronicles of the conquest and discovery that I read and annotated under the guidance of Porras Barrenechea.

The chronicle, a hermaphrodite genre, is distilling fiction into life all the time, as in Jorge Luis Borges's tale "Tlon, Uqbar, Orbis Tertius." Does this mean that its testimony must be challenged from a historical point of view and accepted only as literature? Not at all. Its exaggerations and fantasies often reveal more about the reality of the era than its truths. Astonishing miracles from time to time enliven the tedious pages of the *Crónica Moralizada*, the exemplary chronicle of Father Calancha; sulfurous outrages come from the male and female demons, fastidiously catechized in the Indian villages by the extirpators of idolatries like Father Arriaga, to justify the devastations of idols, amulets, ornaments, handicrafts, and tombs. This teaches more about the innocence, fanaticism, and stupidity of the time than the wisest of treatises.

As long as one knows how to read them, everything is contained in these pages written sometimes by men who hardly knew how to write and who were impelled by the unusual nature of contemporary events to try to communicate and register them for posterity, thanks to an intuition of the privilege they enjoyed, that of being the witnesses of and actors in events that were changing the history of the world. Because they narrated these events under the passion of recently lived experience, they often related things that to us seem like naïve or cynical fantasies. For the people of the time, this was not so; they were phantoms that credulity, surprise, fear, and hatred had endowed with a solidity and vitality often more powerful than beings made of flesh and blood.

*

The conquest of the Tawantinsuyu — the name given to the Inca Empire in its totality — by a handful of Spaniards is a fact of history that even now, after having digested and ruminated over all the explanations, we find hard to unravel. The first wave of conquistadores, Francisco Pizarro and his companions, was fewer than two hundred, not counting the black slaves and the collaborating Indians. When the reinforcements started to arrive, this first wave had already dealt a mortal blow and taken over an empire that had ruled over at least twenty million people. This was not a primitive society made up of barbaric tribes, like the ones the Spaniards had found in the Caribbean or in Darién, but a civilization that had reached a high level of social, military, agricultural, and handicraft development that in many ways Spain itself had not reached.

The most remarkable aspects of this civilization, however, were not the paths that crossed the four *suyus,* or regions, of the vast territory, the temples and fortresses, the irrigation systems, or the complex administrative organization, but something about which all the testimonies of the chronicles agree. This civilization managed to eradicate hunger in that immense region. It was able to distribute all that was produced in such a way that all its subjects had enough to eat. Only a very small number of empires throughout the whole world have succeeded in achieving this feat. Are the conquistadores' firearms, horses, and armor enough to explain the immediate collapse of this Inca civilization at the first clash with the Spaniards? It is true the gunpowder, the bullets, and the charging of beasts that were unknown to them paralyzed the Indians with a religious terror and provoked in them the feeling that they were fighting not against men but against gods who were invulnerable to the arrows and slings with which they fought. Even so, the numerical difference was such that the Quechua ocean would have had simply to shake in order to drown the invader.

What prevented this from happening? What is the profound explanation for that defeat from which the Inca population never recovered? The answer may perhaps lie hidden in the moving account that appears in the chronicles of what happened in the Cajamarca Square the day Pizarro captured the last ruler of the empire, Inca Atahualpa. We must, above all, read the accounts of those who were there, those who lived through the event or had direct testimony of it.

At the precise moment the Inca emperor is captured, before the battle begins, his armies give up the fight as if manacled by a magic force. The slaughter is indescribable, but only from one of the two sides. The Spaniards discharged their harquebuses, thrust their pikes and swords, and charged their horses against a bewildered mass, which, having witnessed the capture of their god and master, seemed unable to defend itself or even to run away. In the space of a few minutes, the army, which defeated Prince Huáscar, the emperor's half brother, in a battle for rule, and which dominated all the northern provinces of the empire, disintegrated like ice in warm water.

The vertical and totalitarian structure of the Tawantinsuyu was without doubt more harmful to its survival than all the conquistadores' firearms and iron weapons. As soon as the Inca, that figure who was the vortex toward which all the wills converged searching for inspiration and vitality, the axis around which the entire society was organized and upon which depended the life and death of every person, from the richest to the poorest, was captured, no one knew how to act. And so they did the only thing they could do with heroism, we must admit, but without breaking the 1,001 taboos and precepts that regulated their existence. They let themselves get killed. And that was the fate of dozens and perhaps hundreds of Indians stultified by the confusion and the loss of leadership they suffered when the Inca emperor, the life force of their universe, was captured right before their eyes. Those Indians who let themselves be knifed or blown up into pieces that somber afternoon in Cajamarca Square lacked the ability to make their own decisions either with the sanction of authority or indeed against it and were incapable of taking individual initiative, of acting with a certain degree of independence according to the changing circumstances.

Those 180 Spaniards who had placed the Indians in ambush and were now slaughtering them did possess this ability. It was this difference, more than the numerical one or the weapons, that created an immense inequality between those civilizations. The individual had no importance and virtually no existence in that pyramidal and theocratic society whose achievements had always been collective and anonymous — carrying the gigantic stones of the Machu Picchu citadel or of the Ollantay fortress up the steepest of peaks, directing water to all the slopes of the cordillera hills by building terraces that even today enable irrigation to take place in the most desolate places, and making paths to unite regions separated by infernal geographies.

A state religion that took away the individual's free will and crowned the authority's decision with the aura of a divine mandate turned the Tawantinsuyu into a beehive — laborious, efficient, stoic. But its immense power was, in fact, very fragile. It rested completely on the sovereign god's shoulders, the man whom the Indian had to serve and to whom he owed a total and selfless obedience. It was religion rather than force that preserved the people's metaphysical docility toward the Inca. It was an essentially political religion, which on the one hand turned the Indians into diligent servants and on the other was capable of receiving into its bosom as minor gods all the deities of the peoples that had been conquered, whose idols were moved to Cuzco and enthroned by the Inca himself. The Inca religion was less cruel than the Aztec one, for it performed human sacrifices with a certain degree of moderation, if this can be said, making use only of the necessary cruelty to ensure hypnosis and fear of the subjects toward the divine power incarnated in the temporary power of the Inca.

We cannot call into question the organizing genius of the Inca. The speed with which the empire, in the short period of a century, grew from its nucleus in Cuzco high in the Andes to become a civilization that embraced three quarters of South America is incredible. And this was the result not only of the Quechua's military efficiency but also of the Inca's ability to persuade the neighboring peoples and cultures to join the Tawantinsuyu. Once these other peoples and cultures became part of the empire, the bureaucratic mechanism was immediately set in motion, enrolling the new servants in that system that dissolves individual life into a series of tasks and gregarious duties carefully programmed and supervised by the gigantic network of administrators whom the Inca sent to the farthest borders. Either to prevent or to extinguish rebelliousness, there was a system called *mitimaes,* by which villages and people were removed en masse to faraway places where, feeling misplaced and lost, these exiles naturally assumed an attitude of passivity and absolute respect, which of course represented the Inca system's ideal citizen.

Such a civilization was capable of fighting against the natural elements and defeating them. It was capable of consuming rationally what it produced, heaping together reserves for future times of poverty or disaster. And it was also able to evolve slowly and with care in the field of knowledge, inventing only that which could support it and deterring all that which in some way or another could undermine its foundation — as, for example, writing or any other form of expression likely to develop individual pride or a rebellious imagination.

It was not capable, however, of facing the unexpected, that absolute novelty presented by the balance of armored men on horseback who assaulted the Incas with weapons transgressing all the war-and-peace patterns known to them. When, after the initial confusion, attempts to resist started breaking out here and there, it was too late. The complicated machinery regulating the empire had entered a process of decomposition. Leaderless with the murder of Inca Huayna Capac's two sons, Huáscar and Atahualpa, the Inca system seems to fall into a monumental state of confusion and cosmic deviation, similar to the chaos that, according to the Cuzcan sages, the Amautas, had prevailed in the world before the Tawantinsuyu was founded by the mythical Manco Capac and Mama Ocllo.

While on the one hand caravans of Indians loaded with gold and silver continued to offer treasures to the conquistadores to pay for the Inca's rescue, on the other hand a group of Quechua generals, attempting to organize a resistance, fired at the wrong target, for they were venting their fury on the Indian cultures that had begun to collaborate with the Spaniards because of all their grudges against their ancient masters. At any rate, Spain had already won the game. Rebellious outbreaks were always localized and counterchecked by the servile obedience that great sectors of the Inca system transferred automatically from the Incas to the new masters.

Those who destroyed the Inca Empire and created that country called Peru, a country that four and a half centuries later has not yet managed to heal the bleeding wounds of its birth, were men whom we can hardly admire. They were, it is true, uncommonly courageous, but, contrary to what the edifying stories teach us, most of them lacked any idealism or higher purpose. They possessed only greed, hunger, and in the best of cases a certain vocation for adventure. The cruelty in which the Spaniards took pride, and the chronicles depict to the point of making us shiver, was inscribed in the ferocious customs of the times and was without doubt equivalent to that of the people they subdued and almost extinguished. Three centuries later, the Inca population had been reduced from twenty million to only six.

But these semiliterate, implacable, and greedy swordsmen, who even before having completely conquered the Inca Empire were already savagely fighting among themselves or fighting the pacifiers sent against them by the faraway monarch to whom they had given a continent, represented a culture in which, we will never know whether for the benefit or the disgrace of mankind, something new and exotic had germinated in the history of man. In this culture, although injustice and abuse often favored by religion had proliferated, by the alliance of multiple factors — among them chance — a social space of human activities had evolved that was neither legislated nor controlled by those in power. This evolution would produce the most extraordinary economic, scientific, and technical development human civilization has ever known since the times of the cavemen with their clubs. Moreover, this new society would give way to the creation of the individual as the sovereign source of values by which society would be judged.

Those who, rightly, are shocked by the abuses and crimes of the conquest must bear in mind that the first men to condemn them and ask that they be brought to an end were men, like Father Bartolomé de Las Casas, who came to America with the conquistadores and abandoned the ranks in order to collaborate with the vanquished, whose suffering they divulged with an indignation and virulence that still move us today.

Father Las Cases was the most active, although not the only one, of those nonconformists who rebelled against the abuses inflicted upon the Indians. They fought against their fellow men and against the policies of their own country in the name of a moral principle that to them was higher than any principle of nation or state. This self-determination could not have been possible among the Incas or any other pre-Hispanic cultures. In these cultures, as in the other great civilizations of history foreign to the West, the individual could not morally question the social organism of which he was a part, because he existed only as an integral atom of that organism and because for him the dictates of the state could not be separated from morality. The first culture to interrogate and question itself, the first to break up the masses into individual beings who with time gradually gained the right to think and act for themselves, was to become, thanks to that unknown exercise, freedom, the most powerful civilization in our world.

It seems to me useless to ask oneself whether it was good that it happened in this manner or whether it would have been better for humanity if the individual had never been born and the tradition of the antlike societies had continued forever. The pages of the chronicles of the conquest and discovery depict that crucial, bloody moment, full of phantasmagoria, when — disguised as a handful of invading treasure hunters, killing and destroying — the Judeo-Christian tradition, the Spanish language, Greece, Rome, the Renaissance, the notion of individual sovereignty, and the chance of living in freedom reached the shores of the Empire of the Sun. So it was that we as Peruvians were born. And, of course, the Bolivians, Chileans, Ecuadoreans, Colombians, and others.

Almost five centuries later, this notion of individual sovereignty is still an unfinished business. We have not yet, properly speaking, seen the light. We in Latin America do not yet constitute real nations. Our contemporary reality is still impregnated with the violence and marvels that those first texts of our literature, those novels disguised as history or historical books corrupted by fiction, told us about.

At least one basic problem is the same. Two cultures, one Western and modern, the other aboriginal and archaic, hardly coexist, separated from each other because of the exploitation and discrimination that the former exercises over the latter. Our country, our countries, are in a deep sense more a fiction than a reality. In the eighteenth century, in France, the name of Peru rang with a golden echo. And an expression was then born: *Ce n'est pas le Pérou,* which is used when something is not as rich and extraordinary as its legendary name suggests. Well, *Le Pérou n'est pas le Pérou.* It never was, at least for the majority of its inhabitants, that fabulous country of legends and fictions but rather an artificial gathering of men from different languages, customs, and traditions whose only common denominator was having been condemned by history to live together without knowing or loving one another.

Immense opportunities brought by the civilization that discovered and conquered America have been beneficial only to a minority, sometimes a very small one; whereas the great majority managed to have only the negative share of the conquest — that is, contributing in their serfdom and sacrifice, in their misery and neglect, to the prosperity and refinement of the westernized elites. One of our worst defects, our best fictions, is to believe that our miseries have been imposed on us from abroad, that others, for example, the conquistadores, have always been responsible for our problems. There are countries in Latin America — Mexico is the best example — in which the Spaniards are even now severely indicted for what they did to the Indians. Did they really do it? We did it; we are the conquistadores.

They were our parents and grandparents who came to our shores and gave us the names we have and the language we speak. They also gave us the habit of passing to the devil the responsibility for any evil we do. Instead of making amends for what they did, by improving and correcting our relations with our indigenous compatriots, mixing with them and amalgamating ourselves to form a new culture that would have been a kind of synthesis of the best of both, we, the westernized Latin Americans, have persevered in the worst habits of our forebears, behaving toward the Indians during the nineteenth and twentieth centuries as the Spaniards behaved toward the Aztecs and the Incas, and sometimes even worse. We must remember that in countries like Chile and Argentina, it was during the republic (in the nineteenth century), not during the colony, that the native cultures were systematically exterminated. In the Amazon jungle, and in the mountains of Guatemala, the exterminating continues.

It is a fact that in many of our countries, as in Peru, we share, in spite of the pious and hypocritical indigenous rhetoric of our men of letters and our politicians, the mentality of the conquistadores. Only in countries where the native population was small or nonexistent, or where the aboriginals were practically liquidated, can we talk of integrated societies. In the others, discreet, sometimes unconscious, but very effective apartheid prevails. Important as integration is, the obstacle to achieving it lies in the huge economic gap between the two communities. Indian peasants live in such a primitive way that communication is practically impossible. It is only when they move to the cities that they have the opportunity to mingle with the other Peru. The price they must pay for integration is high — renunciation of their culture, their language, their beliefs, their traditions and customs, and the adoption of the culture of their ancient masters. After one generation they become mestizos. They are no longer Indians.

Perhaps there is no realistic way to integrate our societies other than by asking the Indians to pay that price. Perhaps the ideal — that is, the preservation of the primitive cultures of America — is a utopia incompatible with this other and more urgent goal: the establishment of societies in which social and economic inequalities among citizens be reduced to human, reasonable limits and where everybody can enjoy at least a decent and free life. In any case, we have been unable to reach any of those ideals and are still, as when we had just entered Western history, trying to find out what we are and what our future will be.

If forced to choose between the preservation of Indian cultures and their complete assimilation, with great sadness I would choose modernization of the Indian population, because there are priorities; and the first priority is, of course, to fight hunger and misery. My novel *The Storyteller* is about a very small tribe in the Amazon called the Machiguengas. Their culture is alive in spite of the fact that it has been repressed and persecuted since Inca times. It should be respected. The Machiguengas are still resisting change, but their world is now so fragile that they cannot resist much longer. They have been reduced to practically nothing. It is tragic to destroy what is still living, still a driving cultural possibility, even if it is archaic; but I am afraid we shall have to make a choice. For I know of no case in which it has been possible to have both things at the same time, except in those countries in which two different cultures have evolved more or less simultaneously. But where there is such an economic and social gap, modernization is possible only with the sacrifice of the Indian cultures.

One of the saddest aspects of the Latin American culture is that, in countries like Argentina, there were men of great intelligence, real idealists, who gave moral and philosophical reasons to continue the destruction of Indian cultures that began with the conquistadores. The case of Domingo F. Sarmiento is particularly sad to me, for I admire him very much. He was a great writer and also a great idealist. He was totally convinced that the only way in which Argentina could become modern was through westernization; that is, through the elimination of everything that was non-Western. He considered the Indian tradition, which was still present in the countryside of Argentina, a major obstacle for the progress and modernization of the country. He gave the moral and intellectual arguments in favor of what proved to be the decimation of the native population. That tragic mistake still looms in the Argentine psyche. In Argentine literature there is an emptiness that Argentine writers have been trying to fill by importing everything. The Argentines are the most curious and cosmopolitan people in Latin America, but they are still trying to fill the void caused by the destruction of their past.

This is why it is useful for us to review the literature that gives testimony to the discovery and the conquest. In the chronicles we not only dream about the time in which our fantasy and our realities seem to be incestuously confused. In them there is an extraordinary mixture of reality and fantasy, of reality and fiction in a united work. It is a literature that is totalizing, in the sense that it is a literature that embraces not only objective reality but also subjective reality in a new synthesis. The difference, of course, is that the chronicles accomplished that synthesis out of ignorance and naïveté and that modern writers have accomplished it through sophistication. But a link can be established. There are chronicles that are especially imaginative and even fantastic in the deeds they describe. For instance, the description of the first journey to the Amazon in the chronicle of Gaspar de Carvajal. It is exceptional, like a fantastic novel. And, of course, Gabriel García Márquez has used themes from the chronicles in his fiction.

In the chronicles we also learn about the roots of our problems and the challenges that are still there unanswered. And in these half-literary, half-historical pages we also perceive — formless, mysterious, fascinating — the promise of something new and formidable, something that if it ever turned into reality would enrich the world and improve civilization. Of this promise we have only had until now sporadic manifestations — in our literature and in our art, for example. But it is not only in our fiction that we must strive to achieve. We must not stop until our promise passes from our dreams and words into our daily lives and becomes objective reality. We must not permit our countries to disappear, as did my dear teacher, the historian Porras Barrenechea, without writing in real life the definite masterwork we have been preparing ourselves to accomplish since the three caravels stumbled onto our coast.

JOY WILLIAMS

# The Killing Game

FROM ESQUIRE

DEATH AND SUFFERING are a big part of hunting. A big part.
Not that you'd ever know it by hearing hunters talk. They tend
to downplay the killing part. To kill is to put to death, extinguish,
nullify, cancel, destroy. But from the hunter's point of view, it's
just a tiny part of the experience. *The kill is the least important part
of the hunt,* they often say, or, *Killing involves only a split second of
the innumerable hours we spend surrounded by and observing nature . . .*
For the animal, of course, the killing part is of considerably more
importance. José Ortega y Gasset, in *Meditations on Hunting,* wrote,
*Death is a sign of reality in hunting. One does not hunt in order to kill;
on the contrary, one kills in order to have hunted.* This is the sort of
intellectual blather that the "thinking" hunter holds dear. The
conservation editor of *Field & Stream,* George Reiger, recently
paraphrased this sentiment by saying, *We kill to hunt, and not the
other way around,* thereby making it truly fatuous. A hunter in West
Virginia, one Mr. Bill Neal, blazed through this philosophical fog
by explaining why he blows the toes off tree raccoons so that they
will fall down and be torn apart by his dogs. *That's the best part of
it. It's not any fun just shooting them.*

Instead of monitoring animals — many animals in managed
areas are tagged, tattooed, and wear radio transmitters — wildlife managers should start hanging telemetry gear around hunters' necks to study their attitudes and listen to their conversations. It would be grisly listening, but it would tune out for good
the *suffering as sacrament* and *spiritual experience* blather that some
hunting apologists employ. *The unease with which the good hunter*

*inflicts death is an unease not merely with his conscience but with affirm-*
*ing his animality in the midst of his struggles toward humanity and clar-*
*ity,* Holmes Rolston III drones on in his book *Environmental*
*Ethics.*

There is a formula to this in literature — someone the protag-
onist loves has just died, so he goes out and kills an animal. This
makes him feel better. But it's kind of a sad feeling-better. He
gets to relate to Death and Nature in this way. Somewhat. But
not really. Death is still a mystery. Well, it's hard to explain. It's
sort of a semireligious thing . . . Killing and affirming, affirming
and killing, it's just the cross the "good" hunter must bear. The
bad hunter just has to deal with postkill letdown.

Many are the hunter's specious arguments. Less semireligious
but a long-standing favorite with them is the vegetarian approach: you eat meat, don't you? If you say no, they feel they've
got you — you're just a vegetarian attempting to impose your
weird views on others. If you say yes, they accuse you of being
hypocritical, of allowing your genial A&P butcher to stand between you and reality. The fact is, the chief attraction of hunting
is the pursuit and murder of animals — the meat-eating aspect
of it is trivial. If the hunter chooses to be *ethical* about it, he might
cook his kill, but the meat of most animals is discarded. Dead bear
can even be dangerous! A bear's heavy hide must be skinned at
once to prevent meat spoilage. With effort, a hunter can make
okay chili, *something to keep in mind,* a sports rag says, *if you take two*
*skinny spring bears.*

As for subsistence hunting, please . . . Granted that there might
be one "good" hunter out there who conducts the kill as spiritual
exercise and two others who are atavistic enough to want to sup-
plement their Chicken McNuggets with venison, most hunters
hunt for the hell of it.

For hunters, hunting is fun. Recreation is play. Hunting is recreation. Hunters kill for play, for entertainment. They kill for
the thrill of it, to make an animal "theirs." (The Gandhian doctrine of nonpossession has never been a big hit with hunters.)
The animal becomes the property of the hunter by its death. Alive,
the beast belongs only to itself. This is unacceptable to the hunter.
*He's yours . . . He's mine . . . I decided to . . . I decided not to . . . I de-*
*bated shooting it, then I decided to let it live . . .* Hunters like beautiful

creatures. A "beautiful" deer, elk, bear, cougar, bighorn sheep.
A "beautiful" goose or mallard. Of course, they don't stay "beautiful" for long, particularly the birds. Many birds become rags in
the air, shredded, blown to bits. *Keep shooting till they drop!* Hunters get a thrill out of seeing a plummeting bird, out of seeing it
crumple and fall. *The big pheasant folded in classic fashion.* They get
a kick out of "collecting" new species. *Why not add a unique harlequin duck to your collection?* Swan hunting is satisfying. *I let loose a
three-inch Magnum. The large bird only flinched with my first shot and
began to gain altitude. I frantically ejected the round, chambered another, and dropped the swan with my second shot. After retrieving the bird
I was amazed by its size. The swan's six-foot wingspan, huge body, and
long neck made it an impressive trophy.* Hunters like big animals, trophy animals. A "trophy" usually means that the hunter doesn't
deign to eat it. Maybe he skins it or mounts it. Maybe he takes a
picture. *We took pictures, we took pictures.* Maybe he just looks at it
for a while. The disposition of the "experience" is up to the hunter.
He's entitled to do whatever he wishes with the damn thing. It's
dead.

Hunters like categories they can tailor to their needs. There
are the "good" animals — deer, elk, bear, moose — which are allowed to exist for the hunter's pleasure. Then there are the "bad"
animals, the vermin, varmints, and "nuisance" animals, the rabbits and raccoons and coyotes and beavers and badgers, which
are disencouraged to exist. The hunter can have fun killing them,
but the pleasure is diminished because the animals aren't "magnificent."

Then there are the predators. These can be killed any time,
because, hunters argue, they're predators, for godssakes.

Many people in South Dakota want to exterminate the red fox
because it preys upon some of the ducks and pheasant they want
to hunt and kill each year. They found that after they killed the
wolves and coyotes, they had more foxes than they wanted. The
ring-necked pheasant is South Dakota's state bird. No matter that
it was imported from Asia specifically to be "harvested" for sport,
it's South Dakota's state bird and they're proud of it. A group
called Pheasants Unlimited gave some tips on how to hunt foxes.
*Place a small amount of larvicide* [a grain fumigant] *on a rag and
chuck it down the hole . . . The first pup generally comes out in fifteen*

*minutes . . . Use a .22 to dispatch him . . . Remove each pup shot from the hole. Following gassing, set traps for the old fox who will return later in the evening . . .* Poisoning, shooting, trapping — they make up a sort of sportsman's triathlon.

In the hunting magazines, hunters freely admit the pleasure of killing to one another. *Undeniable pleasure radiated from her smile. The excitement of shooting the bear had Barb talking a mile a minute.* But in public, most hunters are becoming a little wary about raving on as to how much fun it is to kill things. Hunters have a tendency to call large animals by cute names — "bruins" and "muleys," "berry-fed blackies" and "handsome cusses" and "big guys," thereby implying a balanced jolly game of mutual satisfaction between the hunter and the hunted — *Bam, bam, bam, I get to shoot you and you get to be dead.* More often, though, when dealing with the nonhunting public, a drier, businesslike tone is employed. Animals become a "resource" that must be "utilized." Hunting becomes "a legitimate use of the resource." Animals become a product like wool or lumber or a crop like fruit or corn that must be "collected" or "taken" or "harvested." Hunters love to use the word *legitimate.* (Oddly, Tolstoy referred to hunting as "evil legitimized.") *A legitimate use, a legitimate form of recreation, a legitimate escape, a legitimate pursuit.* It's a word they trust will slam the door on discourse. Hunters are increasingly relying upon their spokesmen and supporters, state and federal game managers and wildlife officials, to employ the drone of a solemn bureaucratic language and toss around a lot of questionable statistics to assure the nonhunting public (93 percent!) that there's nothing to worry about. The pogrom is under control. The mass murder and manipulation of wild animals is just another business. Hunters are a tiny minority, and it's crucial to them that the millions of people who don't hunt not be awakened from their long sleep and become antihunting. Nonhunters are okay. Dweeby, probably, but okay. A hunter *can respect the rights* of a nonhunter. It's the "antis" he despises, those *misguided, emotional, not-in-possession-of-the-facts, uninformed zealots who don't understand nature . . . Those dime-store ecologists cloaked in ignorance and spurred by emotion . . . Those doggy-woggy types, who under the guise of being environmentalists and conservationists are working to deprive him of his precious right to kill.* (Some-

times it's just a *right;* sometimes it's a *God-given* right.) Antis can
be scorned, but nonhunters must be pacified, and this is where
the number crunching of wildlife biologists and the scripts of
*professional resource managers* come in. Leave it to the professionals. They know what numbers are the good numbers. Utah determined that there were six hundred sandhill cranes in the state,
so permits were issued to shoot one hundred of them. Don't want
to have too many sandhill cranes. California wildlife officials re-
ported "sufficient numbers" of mountain lions to "justify" re-
newed hunting, even though it doesn't take a rocket scientist to
know the animal is extremely rare. (It's always a dark day for
hunters when an animal is adjudged *rare.* How can its numbers
be "controlled" through hunting if it scarcely exists?) A recent
citizens' referendum prohibits the hunting of the mountain lion
in perpetuity — not that the lions aren't killed anyway, in California and all over the West, hundreds of them annually by the
government as part of the scandalous Animal Damage Control
Program. Oh, to be the lucky hunter who gets to be an official
government hunter and can legitimately kill animals his buddies
aren't supposed to! Montana officials, led by K. L. Cool, that state's
wildlife director, have definite ideas on the number of buffalo
they feel can be tolerated. Zero is the number. Yellowstone National Park is the only place in America where bison exist, having
been annihilated everywhere else. In the winter of 1988, nearly
six hundred buffalo wandered out of the north boundary of the
park and into Montana, where they were immediately shot at
point-blank range by lottery-winning hunters. It was easy. And it
was obvious from a video taken on one of the blow-away-the-bi-
son days that the hunters had a heck of a good time. The buffalo,
Cool says, threaten ranchers' livelihoods by doing damage to
property — by which he means, I guess, that they eat the grass.
Montana wants zero buffalo; it also wants zero wolves.

Large predators — including grizzlies, cougars, and wolves —
are often the most "beautiful," the smartest and wildest animals
of all. The gray wolf is both a supreme predator and an endangered species, and since the Supreme Court recently affirmed
that ranchers have no constitutional right to kill endangered
predators — apparently some God-given rights are not constitutional ones — this makes the wolf a more or less lucky dog. But

not for long. A small population of gray wolves has recently established itself in northwestern Montana, primarily in Glacier National Park, and there is a plan, long a dream of conservationists, to "reintroduce" the wolf to Yellowstone. But to please ranchers and hunters, part of the plan would involve immediately removing the wolf from the endangered-species list. Beyond the park's boundaries, he could be hunted as a "game animal" or exterminated as a "pest." (Hunters kill to hunt, remember, except when they're hunting to kill.) The area of Yellowstone where the wolf would be restored is the same mountain and high-plateau country that is abandoned in winter by most animals, including the aforementioned luckless bison. Part of the plan, too, is compensation to ranchers if any of their far-ranging livestock is killed by a wolf. It's a real industry out there, apparently, killing and controlling and getting compensated for losing something under the Big Sky.

Wolves gotta eat — a fact that disturbs hunters. Jack Atcheson, an outfitter in Butte, said, *Some wolves are fine if there is control. But there never will be control. The wolf-control plan provided by the Fish and Wildlife Service speaks only of protecting domestic livestock. There is no plan to protect wildlife . . . There are no surplus deer or elk in Montana . . . Their numbers are carefully managed. With uncontrolled wolf populations, a lot of people will have to give up hunting just to feed wolves. Will you give up your elk permit for a wolf?*

It won't be long before hunters start demanding compensation for animals they aren't able to shoot.

Hunters believe that wild animals exist only to satisfy their wish to kill them. And it's so easy to kill them! The weaponry available is staggering, and the equipment and gear limitless. *The demand for big boomers has never been greater than right now,* Outdoor Life *crows, and the makers of rifles and cartridges are responding to the craze with a variety of light artillery that is virtually unprecedented in the history of sporting arms . . .* Hunters use grossly overpowered shotguns and rifles and compound bows. They rely on four-wheel-drive vehicles and three-wheel ATVs and airplanes . . . *He was interesting, the only moving, living creature on that limitless white expanse. I slipped a cartridge into the barrel of my rifle and threw the safety off . . .* They use snowmobiles to run down elk, and dogs to run down and tree cougars. It's easy to shoot an animal out of a tree. It's virtually impossible to miss a moose, a conspicuous and placid animal of steady habits . . . *I took a deep breath and pulled the trigger. The bull dropped. I looked at my watch: 8:22. The big guy was early. Mike started whooping and hollering and I joined him. I never realized how big a moose was until this one was on the ground. We took pictures . . .* Hunters shoot animals when they're resting . . . *Mike selected a deer, settled down to a steady rest, and fired. The buck was his when he squeezed the trigger. John decided to take the other buck, which had jumped up to its feet. The deer hadn't seen us and was confused by the shot echoing about in the valley. John took careful aim, fired, and took the buck. The hunt was over . . .* And they shoot them when they're eating . . . *The bruin ambled up the stream, checking gravel bars and backwaters for fish. Finally he plopped down on the bank to eat. Quickly, I tiptoed into range . . .* They use decoys and calls . . . *The six point gave me a cold-eyed glare from ninety steps away. I hit him with a 130-grain Sierra boat-tail handload. The bull went down hard. Our hunt was over . . .* They use sex lures . . . *The big buck raised its nose to the air, curled back its lips, and tested the scent of the doe's urine. I held my breath, fought back the shivers, and jerked off a shot. The 180-grain spire-point bullet caught the buck high on the back behind the shoulder and put it down. It didn't get up . . .* They use walkie-talkies, binoculars, scopes . . . *With my 308 Browning BLR, I steadied the 9X cross hairs on the front of the bear's massive shoulders and squeezed. The bear cartwheeled backward for fifty yards . . . The second Federal Premium 165-grain bullet found its mark. Another shot anchored the bear for good . . .* They bait deer with corn. They spread popcorn on golf courses for Canada geese and they douse meat baits with fry grease and honey for bears . . . *Make the baiting site redolent of inner-city doughnut shops.* They use blinds and tree stands and mobile stands. They go out in groups, in gangs, and employ "pushes" and "drives." So many methods are effective. So few rules apply. It's fun! . . . *We kept on repelling the swarms of birds as they came in looking for shelter from that big ocean wind, emptying our shell belts . . .* A species can, in the vernacular, be *pressured by hunting* (which means that killing them has decimated them), but that just increases the fun, the *challenge.* There is practically no criticism of conduct within the ranks . . . *It's mostly a matter of opinion and how hunters have been brought up to hunt . . .* Although a recent editorial in *Ducks Unlimited* magazine did venture to primly suggest that one should *not fall victim to greed-induced stress through piggish competition with others.*

But hunters are piggy. They just can't seem to help it. They're overequipped . . . insatiable, malevolent, and vain. They maim and mutilate and despoil. And for the most part, they're inept. Grossly inept.

Camouflaged toilet paper is a must for the modern hunter, along with his Bronco and his beer. Too many hunters taking a dump in the woods with their roll of Charmin beside them were mistaken for white-tailed deer and shot. Hunters get excited. They'll shoot anything — the pallid ass of another sportsman or even themselves. A Long Island man died last year when his shotgun went off as he clubbed a wounded deer with the butt. Hunters get mad. They get restless and want to fire! They want to use those assault rifles and see foamy blood on the ferns. Wounded animals can travel for miles in fear and pain before they collapse. Countless gut-shot deer — *if you hear a sudden, squashy thump, the animal has probably been hit in the abdomen* — are "lost" each year. "Poorly placed shots" are frequent, and injured animals are seldom tracked, because most hunters never learned how to track. The majority of hunters will shoot at anything with four legs during deer season and anything with wings during duck season. Hunters try to nail running animals and distant birds. They become so overeager, so *aroused,* that they misidentify and misjudge, spraying their "game" with shots but failing to bring it down.

The fact is, hunters' lack of skill is a big, big problem. And nowhere is the problem worse than in the new glamour recreation, bow hunting. These guys are elitists. They doll themselves up in camouflage, paint their faces black, and climb up into tree stands from which they attempt the penetration of deer, elk, and turkeys with modern, multiblade, broadhead arrows shot from sophisticated, easy-to-draw compound bows. This "primitive" way of hunting appeals to many, and even the nonhunter may feel that it's a "fairer" method, requiring more strength and skill, but bow hunting is the cruelest, most wanton form of wildlife disposal of all. Studies conducted by state fish and wildlife departments repeatedly show that bow hunters wound and fail to retrieve as many animals as they kill. An animal that flees, wounded by an arrow, will most assuredly die of the wound, but it will be days before he does. Even with a "good" hit, the time elapsed between the strike and death is exceedingly long. *The rule of thumb has long been that we should wait thirty to forty-five minutes on heart and lung hits, an hour or more on a suspected liver hit, eight to twelve hours on paunch hits, and that we should follow immediately on hindquarter and other muscle-only hits, to keep the wound open and bleeding,* is the advice in the magazine *Fins and Feathers.* What the hunter does as he hangs around waiting for his animal to finish with its terrified running and dying hasn't been studied — maybe he puts on more makeup, maybe he has a highball.

Wildlife agencies promote and encourage bow hunting by permitting earlier and longer seasons, even though they are well aware that, in their words, *crippling is a by-product of the sport,* making archers pretty sloppy for elitists. The broadhead arrow is a very inefficient killing tool. Bow hunters are trying to deal with this problem with the suggestion that they use poison pods. These poisoned arrows are illegal in all states except Mississippi *(Ah'm gonna get ma deer even if ah just nick the little bastard),* but they're widely used anyway. You wouldn't want that deer to suffer, would you?

The mystique of the efficacy and decency of the bow hunter is as much an illusion as the perception that a waterfowler is a refined and thoughtful fellow, a *romantic aesthete,* as Vance Bourjaily put it, equipped with his faithful Labs and a love for solitude and wild places. More sentimental drivel has been written about bird shooting than any other type of hunting. It's a soul-wrenching pursuit, apparently, the execution of birds in flight. Ducks Unlimited — an organization that has managed to put a spin on the word *conservation* for years — works hard to project the idea that duck hunters are blue bloods and that duck stamps with their pretty pictures are responsible for saving all the saved puddles in North America. *Sportsman's conservation* is a contradiction in terms (We protect things now so that we can kill them later) and is broadly interpreted (Don't kill them all, just kill most of them). A hunter is a conservationist in the same way a farmer or a rancher is: he's not. Like the rancher who kills everything that's not stock on his (and the public's) land, and the farmer who scorns wildlife because "they don't pay their freight," the hunter uses nature by destroying its parts, mastering it by simplifying it through death.

George ("We kill to hunt and not the other way around") Reiger, the conservationist-hunter's spokesman (he's the best they've got, apparently), said that the "dedicated" waterfowler will shoot other game "of course," but *we do so much in the same spirit of the lyrics, that when we're not near the girl we love, we love the girl we're near.* (Duck hunters practice tough love.) The fact is, far from being a "romantic aesthete," the waterfowler is the most avaricious of all hunters . . . *That's when Scott suggested the friendly wager on who would take the most birds* . . . and the most resistant to minimum ecological decency. Millions of birds that managed to elude shotgun blasts were dying each year from ingesting the lead shot that rained down in the wetlands. Year after year, birds perished from feeding on spent lead, but hunters were "reluctant" to switch to steel. They worried that it would impair their shooting, and ammunition manufacturers said a changeover would be "expensive." State and federal officials had to weigh the poisoning against these considerations. It took forever, this weighing, but now steel-shot loads are required almost everywhere, having been judged "more than adequate" to bring down the birds. This is not to say, of course, that most duck hunters use steel shot almost everywhere. They're traditionalists and don't care for all the new, pesky rules. Oh, for the golden age of waterfowling, when a man could measure a good day's shooting by the pickup load. But those days are gone. Fall is a melancholy time, all right.

*Spectacular abuses occur wherever geese congregate, Shooting Sportsman* notes quietly, something that the more cultivated Ducks Unlimited would hesitate to admit. Waterfowl populations are plummeting and waterfowl hunters are out of control. "Supervised" hunts are hardly distinguished from unsupervised ones. A biologist with the Department of the Interior who observed a hunt at Sand Lake in South Dakota said, *Hunters repeatedly shot over the line at incoming flights where there was no possible chance of retrieving. Time and time again I was shocked at the behavior of hunters. I heard them laugh at the plight of dazed cripples that stumbled about. I saw them striking the heads of retrieved cripples against fence posts.* In the South, wood ducks return to their roosts after sunset when shooting hours are closed. Hunters find this an excellent time to shoot them. Dennis Anderson, an outdoors writer, said, *Roost shooters just fire at the birds as fast as they can, trying to drop as many as they can. Then they grab what birds they can find. The birds they can't find in the dark, they leave behind.*

Carnage and waste are the rules in bird hunting, even during legal seasons and open hours. Thousands of wounded ducks and geese are not retrieved, left to rot in the marshes and fields . . . *When I asked Wanda where hers had fallen, she wasn't sure.* Cripples, and there are many cripples made in this pastime, are still able to run and hide, eluding the hunter even if he's willing to spend time searching for them, which he usually isn't . . . *It's one thing to run down a cripple in a picked bean field or a pasture, and quite another to watch a wing-tipped bird drop into a huge block of switch grass.* Oh nasty, nasty switch grass. A downed bird becomes invisible on the ground and is practically unfindable without a good dog, and few "waterfowlers" have them these days. They're hard to train — usually a professional has to do it — and most hunters can't be bothered. Birds are easy to tumble . . . *Canada geese — blues and snows — can all take a good amount of shot. Brant are easily called and decoyed and come down easily. Ruffed grouse are hard to hit but easy to kill. Sharptails are harder to kill but easier to hit* . . . It's just a nuisance to recover them. But it's fun, fun, fun swatting them down . . . *There's distinct pleasure in watching a flock work to a good friend's gun.*

Teal, the smallest of common ducks, are really easy to kill. Hunters in the South used to *practice* on teal in September, prior to the "serious" waterfowl season. But the birds were so diminutive and the limit so low (four a day) that many hunters felt it hardly worth going out and getting bit by mosquitoes to kill them. Enough did, however, brave the bugs and manage to "harvest" 165,000 of the little migrating birds in Louisiana in 1987 alone. *Shooting is usually best on opening day. By the second day you can sometimes detect a decline in local teal numbers. Areas may deteriorate to virtually no action by the third day* . . . The area *deteriorates.* When a flock is wiped out, the skies are empty. *No action.*

Teal declined more sharply than any duck species except mallard last year; this baffles hunters. Hunters and their procurers — wildlife agencies — will *never* admit that hunting is responsible for the decimation of a species. John Turner, head of the federal Fish and Wildlife Service, delivers the familiar and litanic line. Hunting is not the problem. *Pollution* is the problem. *Pesticides, urbanization, deforestation, hazardous waste,* and *wetlands destruction* are the problem. And drought! There's been a big drought! Antis should devote their energies to solving these problems if they care about wildlife, and leave the hunters alone.

While the Fish and Wildlife Service is busily conducting experiments in cause and effect, like releasing mallard ducklings on a wetland sprayed with the insecticide ethyl parathion (they died — it was known they would, but you can never have enough studies that show guns aren't a duck's only problem), hunters are killing some 200 million birds and animals each year. But these deaths are incidental to the problem, according to Turner. A factor, perhaps, but a *minor* one. Ducks Unlimited says the problem isn't hunting, it's *low recruitment* on the part of the birds. To the hunter, *birth* in the animal kingdom is *recruitment*. They wouldn't want to use an emotional, sentimental word like *birth*. The black duck, a very "popular" duck in the Northeast, so "popular," in fact, that game agencies felt that hunters couldn't be asked to refrain from shooting it, is scarce and getting scarcer. Nevertheless, it's still being hunted. *A number of studies are currently under way in an attempt to discover why black ducks are disappearing, Sports Afield* reports. Black ducks are disappearing because they've been shot out, their elimination being a dreadful example of game management, and managers who are loath to "displease" hunters. The skies — *flyways* — of America have been divided into four administrative regions, and the states, advised by a federal government coordinator, have to agree on policies.

There's always a lot of squabbling that goes on in flyway meetings — lots of complaints about short-stopping, for example. Short-stopping is the deliberate holding of birds in a state, often by feeding them in wildlife refuges, so that their southern migration is slowed or stopped. Hunters in the North get to kill more than hunters in the South. This isn't fair. Hunters demand equity in opportunities to kill.

Wildlife managers hate closing the season on anything. Closing the season on a species would indicate a certain amount of *mis*management and misjudgment at the very least — a certain reliance on overly optimistic winter counts, a certain overappeasement of hunters who would be "upset" if they couldn't kill their favorite thing. And worse, closing a season would be considered victory for the antis. Bird-hunting "rules" are very complicated, but they all encourage killing. There are shortened seasons and split seasons and special seasons for "underutilized" birds. (Teal were very recently considered "underutilized.") The limit on coots is fifteen a day — shooting them, it's easy! They don't fly high — giving the hunter something to do while he waits in the blind. Some species are "protected," but bear in mind that hunters begin blasting away one half hour before sunrise and that most hunters can't identify a bird in the air even in broad daylight. Some of them can't identify birds in hand either, and even if they can (*#%\*! I got me a canvasback, that duck's frigging protected . . .*), they are likely to bury unpopular or "trash" ducks so that they can continue to hunt the ones they "love."

Game "professionals," in thrall to hunters' "needs," will not stop managing bird populations until they've doled out the final duck (*I didn't get my limit but I bagged the last one, by golly . . .*). The Fish and Wildlife Service services legal hunters as busily as any madam, but it is powerless in tempering the lusts of the illegal ones. Illegal kill is a monumental problem in the not-so-wonderful world of waterfowl. Excesses have always pervaded the "sport," and bird shooters have historically been the slobs and profligates of hunting. *Doing away with hunting would do away with a vital cultural and historical aspect of American life,* John Turner claims. So, do away with it. Do away with those who have already done away with so much. Do away with them before the birds they have pursued so relentlessly and for so long drop into extinction, sink, in the poet Wallace Stevens's words, "downward to darkness on extended wings."

"Quality" hunting is as rare as the Florida panther. What you've got is a bunch of guys driving over the plains, up the mountains, and through the woods with their stupid tag that cost them a couple of bucks and immense coolers full of beer and body parts. There's a price tag on the right to destroy living creatures for play, but it's not much. *A big-game hunting license is the greatest deal going since the Homestead Act,* Ted Kerasote writes in *Sports Afield. In many states residents can hunt big game for more than a month for about $20.* It's cheaper than taking the little woman out to lunch. It's cheap all right, and it's because killing animals is considered *recreation* and is underwritten by state and federal funds. In Florida, state moneys are routinely spent on "youth hunts," in which kids are guided to shoot deer from stands in wildlife-management areas. The organizers of these events say that these staged hunts *help youth to understand man's role in the ecosystem.* (Drop a doe and take your place in the ecological community, son . . .)

Hunters claim (they don't actually believe it but they've learned to say it) that they're doing nonhunters a favor, for if they didn't *use* wild animals, wild animals would be useless. They believe that they're just *helping Mother Nature control populations (you wouldn't want those deer to die of starvation, would you?).* They claim that their tiny fees provide *all* Americans with wild lands and animals. (People who don't hunt get to enjoy animals all year round while hunters get to enjoy them only during hunting season . . .) Ducks Unlimited feels that it, in particular, is a selfless provider and environmental champion. Although members spend most of their money lobbying for hunters and raising ducks in pens to release later over shooting fields, they do save some wetlands, mostly by persuading farmers not to fill them in. *See that little pothole there the ducks like? Well, I'm gonna plant more soybeans there if you don't pay me not to* . . . Hunters claim many nonsensical things, but the most nonsensical of all is that they *pay their own way.* They do not pay their own way. They *do* pay into a perverse wildlife-management system that manipulates "stocks" and "herds" and "flocks" for hunters' killing pleasure, but these fees in no way cover the cost of highly questionable ecological practices. For some spare change . . . *the greatest deal going* . . . hunters can hunt on public lands — national parks, state forests — preserves for hunters! — which the nonhunting and antihunting public pay for. (Access to private lands is becoming increasingly difficult for them, as experience has taught people that hunters are obnoxious.) Hunters kill on millions of acres of land all over America that are maintained with general taxpayer revenue, but the most shocking, really twisted subsidization takes place on national wildlife refuges. Nowhere is the arrogance and the insidiousness of this small, aggressive minority more clearly demonstrated. Nowhere is the murder of animals, the manipulation of language, and the distortion of public intent more flagrant. The public perceives national wildlife refuges as safe havens, as sanctuaries for animals. And why wouldn't they? The word *refuge* of course *means* shelter from danger and distress. But the dweeby nonhunting public — they tend to be so literal. The word has been reinterpreted by management over time and now hunters are invited into more than half of the country's more than 440 wildlife "sanctuaries" each year to bang them up and kill more than half a million animals. This is called *wildlife-oriented recreation.* Hunters think of this as being no less than their due, claiming that refuge lands were purchased with duck stamps (. . . *our duck stamps paid for it . . . our duck stamps paid for it . . .*). Hunters equate those stupid stamps with the mystic, multiplying power of the Lord's loaves and fishes, but of 90 million acres in the Wildlife Refuge System, only 3 million were bought with hunting-stamp revenue. Most wildlife "restoration" programs in the states are translated into clearing land to increase deer habitats (so that too many deer will require hunting . . . you wouldn't want them to die of starvation, would you?) and trapping animals for restocking and study (so hunters can shoot more of them). Fish and game agencies hustle hunting — instead of conserving wildlife, they're killing it. It's time for them to get in the business of protecting and preserving wildlife and creating balanced ecological systems instead of pimping for hunters who want their deer/duck/pheasant/turkey — animals stocked to be shot.

Hunters' self-serving arguments and lies are becoming more preposterous as nonhunters awake from their long, albeit troubled, sleep. Sport hunting is immoral; it should be made illegal. Hunters are persecutors of nature who should be prosecuted. They wield a disruptive power out of all proportion to their numbers, and pandering to their interests — the special interests of a group that just wants to kill things --- is mad. It's preposterous that every year less than 7 percent of the population turns the skies into shooting galleries and the woods and fields into abattoirs. It's time to stop actively supporting and passively allowing hunting, and time to stigmatize it. It's time to stop being conned and cowed by hunters, time to stop pampering and coddling them, time to get them off the government's duck-and-deer dole, time to stop thinking of wild animals as "resources" and "game," and start thinking of them as sentient beings that deserve our wonder and respect, time to stop allowing hunting to be creditable by calling it "sport" and "recreation." Hunters make wildlife *dead, dead, dead.* It's time to wake up to this indisputable fact. As for the hunters, it's long past check-out time.

*Biographical Notes*
*Notable Essays of 1990*

# Biographical Notes

Woody Allen is a writer, actor, and film director. His books include *Without Feathers, Getting Even,* and *Side Effects.*

Margaret Atwood's most recent publication is *Wilderness Tips,* a book of short stories. She resides in Toronto, and is currently at work on a novel.

Judith Ortiz Cofer is the author of the first original novel published by the University of Georgia Press, *The Line of the Sun* (1989); two poetry collections, *Terms of Survival* (1987) and *Reaching for the Mainland* (1987); and *Peregrina,* a chapbook that won the 1985 Riverstone Press International Poetry Competition. Her prose and poetry have appeared in *Glamour, The Georgia Review, Prairie Schooner, The Kenyon Review, Antioch Review, The Southern Review, New Letters,* and other magazines. She has received fellowships from the National Endowment for the Arts, the Witter Bynner Foundation for Poetry, the Florida and the Georgia Councils for the Arts, and the Bread Loaf Writers' Conference. The essay in this volume also appears in *Silent Dancing,* a collection of personal essays and poems published by Arte Publico Press in 1990.

Frank Conroy, director of the Iowa Writers' Workshop, is the author of *Stop-Time* and *Midair.* His stories and essays have appeared in *The New Yorker, Esquire, Harper's Magazine, GQ,* and many other publications. He has worked as a jazz pianist and has often written about American music. He is currently working on a long novel called *Body and Soul.*

Gerald Early is the author of *Tuxedo Junction: Essays on American Culture* (Ecco Press) and the editor of *My Soul's High Song: The Collected Writings of Countee Cullen* (Anchor Books). He is the editor of *Speech and Power: The African-American Essay, from Polemic to Pulpit,* which will be published by Ecco Press in the fall of 1991, and the author of *The Culture of Bruising: Prizefighting, Literature, and Modern American Culture,* which Ecco will publish in February 1992. He teaches at Washington University in St. Louis.

GRETEL EHRLICH is the author of *The Solace of Open Spaces* and *Wyoming Stories.* Her essays have appeared in *Harper's Magazine, The Atlantic Monthly, Time,* the *New York Times, Outside, Traveler,* and *Antaeus.* Her novel, *Heart Mountain,* and a new collection of essays, *Islands, the Universe, Home,* are forthcoming from Viking Penguin in October 1991. She lives on a ranch in northern Wyoming.

DIANA HUME GEORGE is a professor of English and women's studies at Pennsylvania State University, Behrend College. In addition to essays, poetry, and reviews in *The Missouri Review, The Georgia Review, The Ontario Review,* and *Spoon River Quarterly,* she writes literary criticism (*Blake and Freud,* which was nominated for the Pulitzer Prize, *Oedipus Anne: The Poetry of Anne Sexton,* and numerous essays on poetry and psychoanalytic feminism). Her second volume of poetry, *The Resurrection of the Body,* was published in 1989.

STEPHEN JAY GOULD teaches biology, geology, and the history of science at Harvard University. He is the author of *Ontogeny and Phylogeny, The Mismeasure of Man, Wonderful Life,* and six collections of essays: *Ever Since Darwin, The Panda's Thumb, Hens' Teeth and Horses' Toes, The Flamingo's Smile, An Urchin in the Storm,* and *Bully for Brontosaurus.* A MacArthur Prize Fellow, he writes a monthly scientific essay for *Natural History* magazine.

ELIZABETH HARDWICK is the author of three novels, the last of which is *Sleepless Nights.* Her three volumes of essays include, most recently, *Bartleby in Manhattan.* Stories and essays have appeared in all the leading magazines and especially in *The New York Review of Books,* of which she was a founder and is at present the advisory editor. "New York City: Crash Course" has been translated into several European languages.

GARRETT HONGO is a poet who returns regularly to his home village in Hawaii, where he is writing a memoir entitled *Volcano Journal.* His honors include the Lamont Poetry Prize and a Discovery/*The Nation* Award. Twice awarded fellowships from the National Endowment for the Arts, he is currently a Fellow of the John Simon Guggenheim Foundation. His books are *Yellow Light* (Wesleyan, 1982) and *The River of Heaven* (Knopf, 1988), which was a finalist for the 1989 Pulitzer Prize in poetry. When not in Hawaii, he is associate professor of English and director of creative writing at the University of Oregon.

NAOMI SHIHAB NYE is the author of three collections of poems, *Different Ways to Pray, Hugging the Jukebox,* which was part of the National Poetry Series, and *Yellow Glove.* She has received the I. B. Lavan Award for Younger Poets from the Academy of American Poets and the Charity Randall Prize for Spoken Poetry from the International Poetry Forum, and is currently at work on a book of stories. In fall 1991 she will be visiting writer at the University of Hawaii.

RICHARD RODRIGUEZ, a journalist and writer, is the author of *Hunger and Memory,* an intellectual autobiography. His second book, which is about the memory of Mexico in California, will be published in 1992. He contributes regularly to the *Los Angeles Times* and to *Harper's Magazine,* and he works as an associate editor for the Pacific News Service in San Francisco. An earlier version of "Late Victorians" was commissioned by the San Francisco Museum of Modern Art as part of an architectural exhibit called "Visionary San Francisco."

DORIEN ROSS is a writer and poet. She has completed one novel, *Falsetas,* and is working on a second novel, *A Train Going North.* She is currently writing *The Impossible Home: Jewish Activism in Central Europe.* Her essays have appeared in *Tikkun.* She is also a psychotherapist and teaches at New College of California.

MARK RUDMAN is an adjunct professor in the writing programs at New York University and Columbia. His books of poetry include *By Contraries* and *The Nowhere Steps.* His poems and essays have appeared in *The American Poetry Review, Best American Poetry, The New Yorker, Ploughshares,* and many other publications. He has translated (with Bohdan Boychuk) Boris Pasternak's *My Sister Life* and published a critical study, *Robert Lowell: An Introduction to the Poetry.* A collection of essays, *Diverse Voices,* will be published by Story Line Press in the spring of 1992. He is at work on a group of "mosaics" and a new book of poems tentatively titled *West of Here, East of There.*

REG SANER teaches at the University of Colorado in Boulder. He is the author of four volumes of poetry, three of which have won major awards, and of a forthcoming collection of essays on American space and the natural world, *The Magpie Scapular.*

AMY TAN is the author of *The Joy Luck Club,* which was a finalist for a National Book Award and a National Book Critics Circle Award. Her second book, *The Kitchen God's Wife,* was published in June 1991. She lives in San Francisco, where she is at work on a children's book, a screenplay, essays on her most recent trip to China, and a new novel.

JANE TOMPKINS teaches at Duke University — American literature, popular culture, women's writing, and pedagogy. She is the author of *Sensational Designs: The Cultural Work of American Fiction, 1790–1860* and has just published *West of Everything*, a study of westerns in American life. She lives in Chapel Hill, North Carolina, and is currently writing an autobiographical book on teaching called *A Life in School*.

MARIANNA DE MARCO TORGOVNICK is the author of three books on literature, society, and the arts, the most recent of which is *Gone Primitive: Savage Intellects, Modern Lives*. She is currently working on a sequel to this book and also on *Crossing Ocean Parkway*, a collection of essays that combine autobiography and cultural criticism. She has written for general-interest periodicals such as *South Atlantic Quarterly, Partisan Review,* and *Art Forum,* and is interested in doing more of this kind of writing.

JOHN UPDIKE was born in 1932, in Shillington, Pennsylvania. After graduation from Harvard in 1954 and a year at an English art school, he worked two years for *The New Yorker*'s "Talk of the Town" department. Since 1957 he has lived in Massachusetts as a free-lance writer. His last novel was *Rabbit at Rest,* and out this fall will be *Odd Jobs,* a collection of his criticism and essays, including this one.

MARIO VARGAS LLOSA is the author of *The War at the End of the World, In Praise of the Stepmother,* and other novels. He has also published several collections of essays. "Questions of Conquest" was originally a lecture delivered at Syracuse University, and it appears in a slightly different version in *A Writer's Reality* (Syracuse University Press, 1991).

JOY WILLIAMS is the author of three novels and two collections of stories, *Taking Care* and *Escapes,* as well as a history and guide to the Florida Keys. Her nonfiction includes articles on sharks, James Dean, and the electric chair, and her essay on the environment, "Save the Whales, Screw the Shrimp," was included in the 1990 *Best American Essays.* Her short stories have frequently appeared in "best" story collections. She lives in Arizona and Key West.

# Notable Essays of 1990

SELECTED BY ROBERT ATWAN

ROBERT M. ADAMS
Montaigne and the Ladies. *Hudson Review,* Summer.

A. ALVAREZ
Romance. *Lear's,* November.

TED ANTON
Too Many Moms. *Chicago,* November.

MICHAEL ARLEN
Invisible People. *The New Yorker,* April 16.

NICHOLSON BAKER
War and Pieces. *Esquire,* March.

HELEN BAROLINI
Shutting the Door on Someone. *Southwest Review,* Autumn.

JOCELYN BARTKEVICIUS
Animus. *Iowa Woman,* Spring/Summer.

RICK BASS
The Afterlife. *Witness,* Vol. 3, No. 4.

MARTHA BAYLES
Feminism and Abortion. *The Atlantic Monthly,* April.

SUSAN BERGMAN
Anonymity. *North American Review,* Spring.

WENDEL L. BERRY
An Argument for Diversity. *Hudson Review,* Winter.

SVEN BIRKERTS
Reflections of a Non-Political Man. *Agni Review,* No. 1 29/30.

MICHELLE BOBIER
The Great Pretender: A Memoir of My Father. *The American Scholar,* Winter.

EAVAN BOLAND
The Woman, The Place, The Poet. *Georgia Review,* Spring/Summer.

CHARLES BOWDEN
Turtle Made the World. *Buzzworm,* September/October.

NICHOLAS BROMELL
ManHunt. *Boston Review,* December.

E. M. BRONER
Ghost Stories. *Tikkun,* November/December.

FRANKLIN BURROUGHS, JR.
Dawn's Early Light. *Georgia Review,*
  Winter.

HAYDEN CARRUTH
Suicide. *Southern Review,* Winter.

KELLY CHERRY
An Underground Hotel in Lenin-
  grad. *Witness,* Vol. 4, No. 1.
Love. *Southern Review,* Spring.

JAN CLAUSEN
My Interesting Condition. *Out/Look,*
  Winter.

TED COHEN
There Are No Ties at First Base. *Yale
  Review,* Winter.

BERNARD COOPER
Dreaming Aloud. *Kenyon Review,*
  Spring.

GEORGE CORE
Life's Bright Parenthesis: The Ex-
  ample of Robert Penn Warren.
  *Hudson Review,* Summer.

ARTHUR C. DANTO
Masterpieces and the Museum. *Grand
  Street,* Winter.

CONRAD E. DAVIDSON
Listening for the Father's Voice.
  *North Dakota Quarterly,* Spring.

LORE DICKSTEIN
Southern Discomfort. *Tikkun,* Novem-
  ber/December.

JOAN DIDION
Letter from Los Angeles. *The New
  Yorker,* February 26.

BRUCE DUFFY
Feeling Something. *Harper's Magazine,*
  June.

GERALD EARLY
The Unquiet Kingdom of Provi-
  dence: The Patterson-Liston Fight,
  *Antioch Review,* Winter.

STANLEY ELKIN
Pieces of Soap. *Art & Antiques,* November.

DANIEL MARK EPSTEIN
Lust and Eros. *GQ,* January.

HELEN EPSTEIN
Lost Lives: Portraits from the Velvet
  Revolution. *Boston Review,* October.

JOSEPH EPSTEIN
Money Is Funny. *The American
  Scholar,* Summer.
Dancing in the Darts. *The American
  Scholar,* Spring.

REBECCA BLEVINS FAERY
On the Possibilities of the Essay: A
  Meditation. *Iowa Review,* Spring/
  Summer.

ROBERT FINCH
Nature in the Nuclear Age. *New Eng-
  land Review and Bread Loaf Quarterly,*
  Summer.

JOHN HOPE FRANKLIN
W.E.B. Dubois: A Personal Memoir.
  *Massachusetts Review,* Autumn.

IAN FRAZIER
Canal Street. *The New Yorker,*
  April 30.

MIKE GADDIS
Taking a Life. *Audubon,* November.

ERNEST J. GAINES
A Very Big Order: Reconstructing
  Identity. *Southern Review,* Spring.

DAVID GAMBLE
Thinking of Something Else. *High Plains Literary Review*, Fall.

GEORGE GARRETT
Uncles and Others. *Missouri Review*, Vol. 13, No. 1.

PHILIP GARRISON
Borders. *Northwest Review*, Vol. 28, No. 1.
Monument. *High Plains Literary Review*, Winter.

ROBERT F. GISH
Bridges. *North Dakota Quarterly*, Spring.

JOHN A. GLUSMAN
Heroes and Sons: Coming to Terms. *Virginia Quarterly Review*, Autumn.

MARY GORDON
A Moral Choice. *The Atlantic Monthly*, April.

VIVIAN GORNICK
Who Says We Haven't Made a Revolution? *The New York Times Magazine*, April 15.

MARGARET MORGANROTH GULLETTE
A Good Girl. *North American Review*, Fall.

ADAM GUSSOW
The Color of Blues. *Boston Review*, June.

RACHEL HADAS
Mornings in Ormos. *Yale Review*, Spring.

PHILIP P. HALLIE
A Choice of Weapons. *Commonweal*, October 26.

DAVID HAMILTON
In an Innertube, On the Amazon. *Michigan Quarterly Review*, Summer.

DANIEL HARRIS
Life and Death: Some Meditations. *Antioch Review*, Fall.

MARK HARRIS
Tragedy as Pleasure: Giamatti and Rose. *Michigan Quarterly Review*, Summer.

BARBARA GRIZZUTI HARRISON
Women and Blacks and Bensonhurst. *Harper's Magazine*, March.

LINDA HASSELSTROM
The Land Circle: Lessons. *North American Review*, December.

DEWITT HENRY
On My Racism: Notes by a WASP. *Ploughshares*, Fall.

GEORGE V. HIGGINS
Fields of Broken Dreams. *The American Scholar*, Spring.

JOANNA HIGGINS
New Myths. *MSS*, Vol. 1, No. 1.

DANIEL HILL
The Enigma of Sitting Bull's Remains. *High Plains Literary Review*, Spring.

ROALD HOFFMANN
Natural/Unnatural. *New England Review and Bread Loaf Quarterly*, Summer.

LINDA HOGAN
Medicine Tree. *Northern Lights*, Spring.

WILLIAM HOLTZ
A Gathering of Family: A Memoir. *The American Scholar*, Autumn.

LARRY JOSEPHS
The Harrowing Plunge. *The New York Times Magazine*, November 11.

ALFRED KAZIN
Wellfleet. *Lear's*, June.

JAMES KILGO
Open House. *New England Review and Bread Loaf Quarterly*, Summer.

LISA KNOPP
Pheasant Country. *Northwest Review*, Vol. 28, No. 2.

LEONARD KRIEGEL
La Belle Américaine (A Modern Love Story). *The American Scholar*, Summer.
In Kafka's House. *Partisan Review*, No. 4.

MARILYN KRYSL
Dirt. *High Plains Literary Review*, Winter.

NATALIE KUSZ
Taking the Waters. *Anna's House*, Spring/Summer.

LEWIS LAPHAM
Democracy in America? *Harper's Magazine*, November.

DAVID LAZAR
Calling for His Past. *Southwest Review*, Summer.

SYDNEY LEA
Presences. *Prairie Schooner*, Spring.

MICHAEL LERNER
After the Cold War: Possibilities for Human Liberation, *Tikkun*, January/February.

SETH LLOYD
The Calculus of Intricacy. *The Sciences*, September/October.

PHILLIP LOPATE
Misunderstood Men. *New York Woman*, April.

BARRY LOPEZ
Apologia. *Witness*, Winter.

NANCY MAIRS
Where I Never Dreamed I'd Go, and What I Did There. *The American Voice*, Summer.

MICHAEL MARTONE
Living Downtown. *North American Review*, Spring.

WILLIAM MATTHEWS
Shortages. *New England Review and Bread Loaf Quarterly*, Spring.

KRISTINA MCGRATH
My Father's Room. *The American Voice*, Fall.

JAY MCINERNEY
Big Fish. *Esquire*, December.

LARRY MCMURTRY
How the West Was Won or Lost. *The New Republic*, October 22.

JOHN MCPHEE
Travels of the Rock. *The New Yorker*, February 26.

JAMES ALAN MCPHERSON
The *Done* Thing. *Ploughshares*, Fall.

DAPHNE MERKIN
Secrets of a Pregnant Woman. *New York Woman*, March.

JANE MILLER
Sea Level. *Ohio Review*, No. 45.

SUSAN MITCHELL
Notes Toward a History of Scaffolding. *Provincetown Arts/90.*

JUDITH MOORE
On Reading to Children. *Express*, February 9.

WILLIE MORRIS
Here Lies My Heart. *Esquire*, June.

CULLEN MURPHY
The 40th Parallel. *The Atlantic Monthly*, May.

ROBERT NEWTON
How to Help the Dead. *Grand Street*, Spring.

KATHLEEN NORRIS
The Rule of St. Benedict. *North Dakota Quarterly*, Fall.

ROBERT PHILLIPS
Visiting the Gregorys. *The New Criterion*, September.

DAVID PLANTE
Tales of Chatwin. *Esquire*, October.

RICHARD POIRIER
Hum 6, or Reading Before Theory. *Raritan*, Spring.

MICHAEL POLLAN
Putting Down Roots. *The New York Times Magazine*, May 6.

TERRENCE RAFFERTY
The Essence of the Landscape. *The New Yorker*, June 25.

DIANE RAVITCH
Multiculturalism: E Pluribus Plures. *The American Scholar*, Summer.

DAVID RIEFF
The Case Against Sensitivity. *Esquire*, November.
Homelands. *Salmagundi*, Winter/ Spring.

BILL ROORBACH
Mola Mola. *Iowa Review*, Winter.

ROY ROWAN
Homeless Bound. *People*, February.

SALMAN RUSHDIE
Is Nothing Sacred? *Granta*, Spring.

SHARMAN APT RUSSELL
Homebirth. *Missouri Review*, Vol. 13, No. 1.

JAMES SALTER
Europe. *Esquire*, December.

SCOTT RUSSELL SANDERS
Reasons of the Body. *Georgia Review*, Winter.
Grub. *Wigwag*, March.

REG SANER
The Mind of a Forest. *Gettysburg Review*, Summer.

WILLIAM J. SCHAFER
Air Trails. *Gettysburg Review*, Spring.

PETER SCHNEIDER
Concrete and Irony. *Harper's Magazine*, April.

MIMI SCHWARTZ
Living with Loss, Dreaming of Lace. *Lear's*, October.

RICHARD SELZER
Crematorium. *Missouri Review*, Vol. 13, No. 2.

RICHARD SENNETT
New York Reflections. *Raritan*, Summer.

DAVID SHAPIRO
Repose and Light. *Art & Antiques,*
   March.

WILFRID SHEED
One Man Out . . . Too Long. *GQ,*
   August.

RANDY SHILTS
Naming Names. *GQ,* August.

CHARLES SIEBERT
The Rehumanization of the Heart.
   *Harper's Magazine,* February.

JOHN P. SISK
The Guiana Connection. *Hudson Review,* Spring.

GARY SNYDER
The Woman Who Married a Bear.
   *Witness,* Vol. 3, No. 4.

TED SOLOTAROFF
Massaging My Father. *Salmagundi,*
   Winter/Spring.

GARY SOTO
The Buddha. *Threepenny Review,*
   Winter.

BERT O. STATES
Dreaming and Storytelling. *Hudson
   Review,* Spring.

SHELBY STEELE
White Guilt. *The American Scholar,* Autumn.

HARRY STEINHAUER
Holy Headgear. *Antioch Review,*
   Winter.

ROBERT STONE
Fighting the Wrong War. *Playboy,*
   July.

MARK STRAND
Fantasia on the Relations Between
   Poetry and Photography. *Grand
   Street,* Winter.

LEWIS THOMAS
The World at a Glance. *Grand Street,*
   No. 36.

SALLIE TISDALE
Bound upon a Wheel of Fire. *Harper's
   Magazine,* January.

GUY TREBAY
Dunes. *Grand Street,* No. 36.

CALVIN TRILLIN
The Italian Thing. *The New Yorker,*
   November 19.

GEORGE W. S. TROW
Devastation. *The New Yorker,* October 22.

GORE VIDAL
Notes on Our Patriarchal State. *The
   Nation,* August 27/September 3.

ANDREW WARD
Haunted Home. *American Heritage,*
   July/August.

GERALD WEISSMANN
To the Nobska Lighthouse. *Hospital
   Practice,* January.

STEPHEN J. WHITFIELD
The Stunt Man: Abbie Hoffman
   (1936–1989). *Virginia Quarterly Review,* Autumn.

TERRY TEMPEST WILLIAMS
The Clan of One-Breasted Women.
   *Northern Lights,* Winter.

S. L. WISENBERG
Loss of Property. *Wigwag,* April.

SAL WOELFEL
The Duckling Essays. *Virginia Quarterly Review,* Spring.

GEOFFREY WOLFF
Writers and Booze. *Lear's,* March.
The Great Santa. *Granta,* Autumn.

ROBERT WRIGHT
Are Animals People Too? *The New Republic,* March 12.

ERIC ZENCEY
The Hand That Wounds. *North American Review,* Summer.